DATE DUE

JE - 5 '00			

DEMCO 38-296

Joey Adams'
Speaker's Bible
of Humor

BOOKS BY JOEY ADAMS

GAGS TO RICHES

THE CURTAIN NEVER FALLS

JOEY ADAMS' JOKE BOOK

STRICTLY FOR LAUGHS

IT TAKES ONE TO KNOW ONE

JOEY ADAMS' JOKE DICTIONARY

CINDY AND I

ON THE ROAD FOR UNCLE SAM

JOEY ADAMS' ROUND THE WORLD JOKE BOOK

LBJ'S TEXAS LAUGHS

HOW TO MAKE AND TELL JOKES FOR ALL OCCASIONS

THE BORSCHT BELT

YOU COULD DIE LAUGHING

THE SWINGERS

JOEY ADAMS' ENCYCLOPEDIA OF HUMOR

SON OF ENCYCLOPEDIA OF HUMOR

LAUGH YOUR CALORIES AWAY

Joey Adams'
Speaker's Bible
of Humor

BY JOEY ADAMS

DOUBLEDAY & COMPANY, INC. · 1972
Garden City, New York

Library of Congress Catalog Card Number 72–79431
Copyright © 1972 by Joey Adams
All Rights Reserved
Printed in the United States of America

Dedicated to Maria Ouspenskaya, Sessue Hayakawa, Akim Tamiroff, and Arthur Murray, without whom this book was written . . .

Also, mainly for the fact that nobody else ever dedicated a book to them before.

Contents

Forewarned

Anybody can make a speech if he is prepared for battle. To attack a roomful of rich men, poor men, beggar men or even friends, Romans or countrymen—you've got to be ready. And in this arena your weapons are words.

That's the idea of this book—to arm you with words, jokes, gags, anecdotes, stories, insults and roasts; for when you meet the butcher, the baker, the candlestick maker or a family gathering, a dais of murderers, or an audience of fans.

The important thing is that the word fits—and fits you. Once when Will Rogers was criticized for using the word "ain't," he said: "Maybe ain't ain't correct—but I notice a lot of folks who ain't usin' ain't—ain't eatin'."

I'll give you the gems to fit every occasion and I'll pick out the right setting. I'll tell you how and where to tell that joke and how to switch it to your particular needs. At a Catholic gathering for Paul Cardinal Yu Pin I said: "I never refuse to do a Catholic benefit—I did once—and it snowed in my living room for five days." And, conversely, when I was master of ceremonies at Greenhaven State Prison, I opened my routine by saying to the inmates: "I really don't care if I'm a hit here—If I do good—you'll want to hold me over."

I'll tell you how to accept the cheers: "I'm not really as good as you said—but I'm much better than you're thinking." And I'll set you up with savers when you feel the flop sweat: "Did you ever have the feeling you were walking up a long gangplank and there was no ship at the other end of it?" I'll even give you your own portable gag file.

In other words, when you're called on to "say a few words" at the roast for the governor, the stag for the star, the lodge meeting, the convention or the dinner in your honor, I'll have you ready for anything but failure.

These notes do not distinguish between amateur or professional. When you are on your feet and the spotlight is on your face—*you* are the star whether you're Bob Hope or Irving Schwartz. It doesn't matter if the audience is twenty million on TV or two Jews in a kibbutz. To be the life of the party—for fun or profit—you've got to be prepared for battle.

A plumber can't work without his tools. Liberace could never light up without his neon jackets. "The only thing that looks good in a brown jacket," says Liberace, "is a baked potato." Sophia Loren never shows without her props—she doesn't need words. And what would Guy Lombardo do with that stick if his band didn't show up? Now take Engelbert Humperdinck—please. His trousers are so tight they wear out from the inside, but if he wore loose ones it would hide his talent. Even old Hump is ready with words when he faces those female piranhas. One old broad actually threw her bra on stage. "If you'll fill that, lady," he said, "I'll take it home."

When a pro says he is speaking off the cuff—it only means he's got his notes written on his shirt sleeve. Bob Hope uses idiot cards and reads every line prepared for him by his army of writers. Me, I use index cards. I used to write my notes on my cuff but I cut it out when I heard my laundryman on the "David Frost Show"—and he was getting laughs, too.

Hope told me he is prepared with gags even if he is just going to dinner with friends or on a golf date with the President. Bob's writers work overtime when he is golfing with Richard M. He got his biggest laugh during one game when he told the President, "You should send Agnew into Vietnam with a number three wood." Hope's audience of one howled when he noted that Palm Springs, California, where Agnew hit three tournament fans with wild drives, is now known as Agnew's Fault. He told Nixon that on one of the Vice-President's drives, Agnew got a birdie, an elk, a moose, and a mason, adding, "It's hard to concentrate when the entire gallery is saying the Lord's Prayer."

Of course, Hope was prepared with his studied ad libs—even though he acted like he was talking without a cuff.

That was George M. Cohan's trick. He could tell a story that he had told a thousand times and make it sound like he was rattling it off for the first time. Georgie Jessel told me: "I learned that shtik from Cohan. He taught me how to pause while talking to an audience, so as to make them believe that I was thinking of something important, or some new line that had just come to mind—when it was actually something tried and true that I knew would get a laugh."

Every speaker has his own way of pausing before the punch line. Sam Levinson laughs before he drops his funny. Groucho Marx flicks his cigar. The wit glares before he fires his shot—the humorist scratches his head.

Everybody needs practice. Thomas Edison wasn't born with a light bulb in his mouth. I'm sure Genghis Khan and his bunch didn't win every battle when they started. Even Milton Berle didn't have a great delivery when he was born, no matter what his mother told us. My wife, Cindy, is the exception that proves the rule. She was a great cook when we first got married. She made me toast every morning—until she lost the recipe.

I'll supply the material and the examples but you'll have to practice by yourself. Choose the joke that fits and fits you and then repeat it to any friend that will listen—and if you don't have a friend, buy a dog. Most men use their wives to try out their material. In some cases that's helped them win an audience—but lose a wife—which could have been their idea in the first place.

George Bernard Shaw was admittedly one of the great storytellers of all time—and he was the first to admit it. Mr. Shaw always used his wife to rehearse his ad libs. One friend who was visiting the famous wit noticed Mrs. Shaw knitting while her famous husband kept spinning his yarns. The visitor asked her: "What are you knitting?" Mrs. Shaw replied: "Nothing in particular—it's just that I've heard these stories of his a thousand times—and if I didn't do something with my hands—I'd choke him."

I'm not saying it's easy to be a good storyteller. A comedian's job is the toughest of all. His option comes up after every joke. But if you practice over and over again with the taxi driver, the doorman, or your friendly bookie, your option is bound to be picked up—at least for the next gag.

Naturally, you can't be a Joey Adams the first time out—but then neither am I. I try all my gags on Cindy and you know something? Now she tells them better than I and I have to fight *her* for the spotlight.

The human brain is a wonderful machine. It starts working the moment you are born and never stops until you stand up to speak in public. That's why you need the notes to tell you where to go—or the audience will.

Of course, you've got to make sure that the material fits the occasion, but more importantly, it must be tailored to fit you. I remember one big-shot manufacturer who had to make a speech at his organization dinner. He bought the best writers to get him ready. When he was introduced that night he pulled his prepared speech from his pocket and put it on the lectern. "Now before I start my speech," he said, "I would like to say something."

I recall one candidate who was called on to make a speech. "I was so surprised in getting the nomination," he blurted out, "I almost dropped my acceptance speech."

Speeches are like babies—easy to conceive—but hard to deliver—unless you've done your homework.

Joey Adams'
Speaker's Bible
of Humor

Keep it short

The guy that drives me up a dais is the one who always rises to the occasion but never knows when to sit down. The first thing a good speaker should learn is that the Constitution guarantees free speech —but it doesn't guarantee listeners. I remember sitting in the audience once listening to some poor soul drone on until there was nobody left but me. "This is terrible," he said looking out at the seats. "I really don't know what to say—" "You could say good-by," I shouted up. "Anyway," he continued, "it is nice of you to stay." "What nice?" I growled. "I'm the next speaker."

Just remember that the mind cannot accept what the seat cannot endure. A good speech should have a good beginning—a good ending—and keep them close together. I keep remembering Winston Churchill's advice to speakers on a dais: "Say what you have to say and the first time you come to a sentence with a grammatical ending—*sit down!*"

I would rather people say "Why has he stopped speaking?" than "Why doesn't he?" A good speech should be like a woman's skirt— short enough to retain the interest—but long enough to cover the essentials.

To prove this point, Mark Twain often told of his experience in attending church services one Sunday. He was captivated by the minister's appeal for funds. So much so that he decided to give at least a couple of hundred dollars. Unfortunately, the revered gentleman kept talking on and on and Twain kept mentally reducing the original sum. By the time the collection plate reached him, he said, "Not only did I put in nothing—I took out a dollar."

If you don't know what to talk about—talk about three minutes and when you are halfway through your speech—*sit down!* Jessel warns all speakers: "Public speaking is like drilling for oil—if you don't strike oil in three minutes—stop boring!"

Will Rogers was a great toastmaster who never stayed on too long and resented those who did. One speaker whom he introduced bored on for over an hour and finally said: "I am sorry, Mr. Toastmaster, that I stayed on longer than the allotted time, but I left my watch at home."

Said our Will: "Don't you even have a pocket calendar?"

"Friends," said another speaker, "I know I have been on a long time—but I am speaking for the benefit of posterity—" "And if you don't hurry," shouted a heckler, "they'll hear you!"

If a thing goes without saying—let it. The best after-dinner speakers have learned that they must stand up to be seen, speak up to be heard, and shut up to be appreciated.

Fred Allen found himself in great discomfort listening to a long-playing bore at a banquet. After an eternity of saying nothing, the speaker said: "Well, to make a long story short—"

"It's too late now," Allen barked.

You can't fool the people all the time. There's this politician who was explaining to the lady that he didn't go in for sports. "I got this tan making speeches—outdoors—in Florida."

"Well," the woman heckled, "if you got so brown—you talked too long."

Another time, William Collier, Sr., one of the silver-tongued talkers of his time, had to follow a dozen long-winded orators. When the toastmaster said: "Mr. Collier will now give his address," Collier got up and announced: "My address is the Lambs Club, 128 West Forty-fourth Street!" and sat down.

Have you had enough? Are you convinced? Maybe I have been on too long telling you to keep it short but I only did it to make sure that you leave your audience before they leave you. Timing is so important—when you see your audience looking at their watches—get the hell off.

Make your speech as short as your prayers and you'll never be on too long.

Don't believe it

You don't have to thank me for reminding you that you can't take your introduction too seriously. It's the duty of a toastmaster to alibi for the last speaker and exaggerate the next one. You can never live up to what he said so you must find a way to live down what he's thinking.

I recall the story of the minister who was delivering an extravagant eulogy of some notorious character who had just died. The church was filled to overflowing but mostly because they wanted to make sure he was gone. As some wag put it: "Give the public what they want and you're sure to get a packed house." Even his widow and son sitting in the front row knew him as a bum. Only the minister shouted his praises. As he reached his climax, describing the deceased as a fine husband, father, and citizen, the widow turned to her son and said, "Charlie, you better sneak up to the coffin and see if that's your father they're burying."

Georgie Jessel has often delivered two or more eulogies in one day. He is proud that he is known as the greatest orator at these funerals. At a particularly tender moment during an impassioned eulogy, he accidentally glanced down on the deceased in the coffin. "My God," Jessel gasped, "I *know* this man."

Jack Benny tells of Georgie delivering the eulogy for James Mason's cat. "When Jessel finished eulogizing the cat, there wasn't a dry eye —I never knew that cats did so much for Israel and the Democrats."

You're never helping the speaker when you give him too big a buildup. In fact, you're not doing yourself any good either. I was sitting on the dais at some dinner listening to the toastmaster introduce his boss. He spent twenty minutes telling us how great he was. According to him, the saints came to his boss for help. "No wonder that guy has bad breath," the man next to me said. "And it's not from kissing the boss's *ring*."

If you're stuck with a grandiose introduction, you can always use it to help you by doing the humble bit. Jack Benny always says after one of those embarrassing buildups, "I don't deserve this—but I have arthritis and I don't deserve that either."

Georgie Jessel usually cracks: "That was a beautiful introduction— and for a moment I thought I was dead."

Almost every big star has stolen—I mean switched that line to fit the crime.

Harry Hershfield's line is: "If I had any class, I'd lie down right now."

Will Rogers invariably scratched his head in disbelief when he copped one of those intros: "Thanks—you couldn't have been nicer to me if I died—or maybe you're anticipating my act."

Harry Truman remarked after a hefty welcome: "I am really over-come—you don't know how difficult it is to be present at your own funeral—and still be able to walk around."

When I feel my intro is too sweet-'n'-low, even for me, I will say: "Thank you—you said it exactly as I wrote it out for you."

I remember introducing Lyndon Baines Johnson at a Madison Square Garden rally. I really put it on this time. I called him the greatest President of our time. Twenty thousand people stood up and cheered him. "Thank you," said LBJ. "This is a moment that I deeply wish my parents could have lived to share. My father would have enjoyed what you so generously said of me—and my mother would have believed it—It's one of the best introductions I ever re-ceived—if not *the* best—except once down in the hills of Tennessee and the governor was supposed to introduce me. He didn't show up—and I had to introduce myself."

Wildly received at a fund-raising dinner in New York, John F. Kennedy quipped, "I'm deeply touched, but not as deeply touched as you have been by coming to this dinner."

Again, in Columbus, Ohio, he received a tremendous welcome and when the cheers finally subsided he said: "There isn't a town in America where I get a bigger hand and a smaller vote than Colum-bus, Ohio."

"I appreciate your welcome," JFK said to a group of farmers who greeted him as his train stopped in the Midwest one early morning. The mayor's speech was endless and the applause tumultuous. "As the cow said to the Maine farmer," he smiled, "thank you for a warm hand on a cold morning."

President Theodore Roosevelt introduced as "the greatest man in the world," added: "Well—I have nothing to add to that!"

Steve Allen has his own way of loosening a tight halo: "It is always gratifying for a television entertainer to stand up in front of so many people who can't turn him off."

Robert Montgomery said it: "If you get applause, enjoy it—but never quite believe it."

I keep thinking of Adlai Stevenson's tough spot when he was introduced as a substitute speaker for Vice-President Nixon. The toastmaster figured he had to double the praise. When Stevenson finally got to the microphone, he said: "This reminds me of the vicar in a remote corner of England. He wired his bishop, 'MY WIFE JUST PASSED AWAY—PLEASE DISPATCH A SUBSTITUTE FOR THE WEEKEND.'"

Adlai Stevenson was one of the great public speakers of our time. His wit could always get him out of any situation. He followed me on one of my great nights—and would I lie to you?—I was hilarious. After twenty minutes of howls, Stevenson was introduced. "I met Joey Adams in the lobby right before we sat down," he said. "Poor Joey—he was distraught—he's a comic—that's his trade—and he wanted to make good for you because you are a show business audience—and he didn't have a speech—so I gave him mine—you just heard it—so good night."

When Gary Moore received a television award for his spontaneity and it was his turn, he humbly paid tribute to "the four guys responsible for my spontaneity—my writers."

The next to receive the award was Bishop Fulton J. Sheen who gave it this: "I also want to pay tribute to my four writers—Matthew, Mark, Luke, and John!"

It was Bishop Sheen who said in response to a big introduction and a big hand: "Applause before a speaker begins his talk is an act of faith—applause during the speech is an act of hope—applause after is an act of charity."

Four ways to throw the bull

If you want to flavor your speech with humor—you must be aware that dinners come in four different varieties. If it's laughter you're after—plan your diet of jokes accordingly:

1. THE ROAST

In this era of masochistic comedy, our most famous personalities have accepted testimonials just to be carved to pieces by their "friends." To be part of this new school of dais assassins, you must adhere to the motto: "If you can't say anything nice about the guy— let's hear it."

Ed Sullivan loved it when I jabbed: "Everybody is always picking on Sullivan—and with good reason." I always enjoy flattening Dean Martin: "Dean is the most relaxed performer on TV—he never spills a word." Bob Hope was toastmaster at a dinner for some astronauts and one of them had the nerve to make a funny. Bob cracked: "If there is one thing I can't stand it's a smart astronaut." I don't remember who said it—I think it was me: "Everybody says David Merrick has a dull personality—that's not true—he has no personality at all." Georgie Jessel said: "Don Rickles has become a household word—garbage is also a household word." Jack Carter addressed Johnny Carson: "I was going to bring you a present but what do you give a man who has nothing?"

Some of the nicest murderers I know pride themselves on the massacre of their honored guests and you better have a sense of humor, especially if you're the guest of honor. A sense of humor is what makes you laugh at something that would make you mad if it happened to you—So, when you are on the firing line—laugh—laugh and the world laughs with you—cry and it means you can't take a joke; or even worse—you can't dish it out.

There is no such thing as gentle humor. If you want to be funny —somebody must be hurt—even if it's only yourself. Good taste and humor are a contradiction in terms—like a chaste whore. The important thing to remember is that you've got to do it with conviction. Comedy in order to be effective must be devastating, and consequently you must deliver that line as though you mean it. When you insert the scalpel, you can't dull the edge by saying, "I'm only joking" or "He's really a great friend." You can't say: "Phyllis Diller has turned many a head in her day—and a few stomachs, too" and then add, "but she's a nice girl." You've got to stick with your incisions. Pat Henry, at a dinner for Cardinal Cooke, said: "Talking about the Pill, Your Eminence, if you don't play the game—don't make the rules." But he said it like he meant it—and that's what you must do—say it like you mean it.

Of course, we play it strictly for laughs. We don't want to leave any scars. Don Rickles claims only one person ever objected to his needling: "I made fun of a ringsider's beard and almost got belted— that broad had no sense of humor."

Calvin Coolidge said it: "Whenever I indulge my sense of humor, I get in trouble." But you don't have to if you play it cool. I like to hit like a heavyweight, but I always watch the eyes of my target or his family—if they're happy, I continue the operation. If not, I switch to somebody else, something else, or me. Of course, if you want to avoid criticism, say nothing, do nothing, be nothing. My job is to give you the ammunition to say something, do something, and be somebody.

2. THE SITUATION

If you're not the kind of guy that can trigger the slaughter of a poor suspecting guest, or if you're too chicken to face your victim, or if you can't pick on your superiors or your inferiors—hit the situation—and hit it hard. If it's a dinner for a banking group, pick your strongest ammunition! "The same guy that writes the advertising for the bank is not the same guy that gives you the loan." If it's a church affair: "My wife is so Catholic we can't get fire insurance—too many candles in the house." Suppose it's a charity. You've got to hit the jackpot if you welcome them with your definition of a philanthropist: "That's a guy who gives away publicly what he stole personally." Everybody will scream because he thinks you mean the next guy— right? You can't miss at a labor rally if you start by saying: "I have always found that a good labor leader is the kind of guy who believes that a kind word and a kick in the ass is always better than just a kind word." Is it a parents and teachers meeting? Open with my favorite line: "Slap your child at least once a day—if you don't know why—he does."

This book is filled with gags, jokes, stories, and anecdotes to fit any category. All you do is look them up in the Index and you will have enough material to cover any situation.

If you can't pick on the guest of honor, it doesn't mean you must avoid all targets. Don Rickles walks in a room and starts shooting from the mouth at anybody in sight. To Mayor Lindsay he barked: "Congratulations on being such a nice guy while the city is being destroyed." Even though Don wasn't the guest of honor, I hit him with: "Folks, you know Don Rickles—the original Rat Patrol. Don is the man about whom Hitler once said, 'From him I could learn!'" Jack E. Leonard is another marksman that doesn't wait to slaughter the honored guest—he uses a machine gun and hits everybody. Jack said to Steve Allen: "Some day you'll go too far and I hope you stay there." To Henny Youngman he said: "I think the world of you —and you know what I think of the world!" To Frank Sinatra: "You got a great voice—too bad it hasn't reached your throat." To Milton Berle: "You got a nice personality—but not for a human being."

Notice that the killers only pick on the giants who are trained to take it and are big enough to defend themselves.

I hope you've also noticed that they never pick on anybody's physical handicaps—like his glasses or his size or bald head. This must turn the audience and the laughs off. In fact, you can use it for good instead of evil and then he's an easy target. For instance, you must win a bald heart if you say: "God made a lot of heads—those he was ashamed of, he put a lot of hair on," or if the man is wearing glasses: "He is so rich—he even has a prescription windshield," or if he's a little guy: "He's so cute—he sits down and stands up and he's the same size."

It's easy after that: "I've been asked to say something nice about my friend who God wasn't ashamed of—and I will—he's got more talent in his little finger than he's got in his big finger"—"About my friend who sees the world through rose-colored glasses I must say— he's got more talent than Ed Sullivan"—"About little David I must say—he knows a lot—he just can't think of it."

Another target to fit the situation is your audience. You can't show that you're afraid of them. You must be the boss. Jack E. Leonard starts by saying, "Good evening—opponents." Milton Berle looked out at a half-filled theater and barked: "Well, you're not a vast audience—in fact, you look half-vast." Joe Frisco faced a handful of patrons in his club and groaned: "I left more people in my bed at home." Jerry Lewis told one dull gathering: "Come back and see me sometime—but not as a group." My favorite line when I have nobody to heckle but my audience: "This is a night I'll remember—until about ten o'clock."

A lot of us have had to follow some long, dull speeches. You got a fighting chance if you tell the audience you're hep. "I was a young man when I got here before the speeches," or "I wouldn't give a spot like this to a dry cleaner," or "I don't care if you walk out on me—it's when you walk towards me that I worry."

And you must be ready with the savers. You can win back your opponents if you let them know you're not afraid of them: "You people look at me like I invented income tax," or "This is a live show —I wish I had an audience to match," or "I don't see how all you people can sleep out there with the lights on." If it looks like a staring contest and you can't break them down or up, try the all-time saver: "I hope you are enjoying yourself—don't give me a thought— you don't have to laugh or applaud just because I'm the sole support of eight children and a sick wife. So I served my country in the fox-holes of Vietnam—if you feel you don't want to laugh it's okay with me—Thank you anyway—."

3. KID YOURSELF

When everything else fails—shoot yourself—full of gags. If comedy must be devastating, better you than he: "My mother told me I'd come out on top some day—she was right—I'm getting bald."

If there is nobody to pick on, there is always yourself: "I'm sorry I'm not prepared—I didn't know I was going to be here till six weeks ago." Harry Hershfield gets them right from the start when he talks about his age: "I'm at the stage now when I go with a girl, I can't take yes for an answer." Jack E. Leonard says: "I won't tell you how much I weigh—but don't ever get in the elevator with me unless you're going down." Georgie Jessel admits he has just reached middle age for the third time: "There are three ways you can tell when you're getting old. The first is loss of memory—the other two I forget."

Gene Baylos opens by telling how he became a comedian: "I walked around with a mouthful of marbles and every day I dropped one marble—when they discovered I lost all my marbles—I became a comedian."

My switch is just as effective: "When I was a kid my father gave me a rocking chair. I loved that rocking chair. I used to rock in it day and night. One day it broke. And when they discovered I was off my rocker—I became a comedian."

Milton Berle always had a sure-fire opening: "I'm here by request —request hell—I begged them." Phyllis Diller loves to destroy herself: "This dress hides the eighth wonder of the world—I'm the only human being in the world who wears prescription underwear." Totie Fields brags: "I got an eighteen-inch waist—through the center." Totie claims she has the same measurements as Raquel Welch—"Her living room is eighteen by twenty-five and so is mine."

Phyllis Diller is a gorgeous gal on the inside. "Leave it to me," says Phyllis, "to be born inside out." Phyllis' trick is to pick on the person she knows best—herself: "I'm the only woman who can walk Central Park at night and reduce the crime rate"—"I went to a topless party —my upper plate fell out"—"Most people get a reservation at a beauty parlor—I was committed."—"I've been robbed four times— I just can't get raped."

Wrecking yourself brings out the sympathy and the laughs: "This is a return engagement for me—I was here twenty years ago."

"Did you notice the sign in front of the theater saying WELCOME JOEY ADAMS—THE WORLD'S GREATEST COMEDIAN?—It really embarrassed me—they caught me putting up the sign."

Henny Youngman sometimes opens by reading a letter aloud: "Dear Henny—I've been watching you for over thirty years and I want to tell you—I don't like you any more as a man than I did as a boy."

Milton Berle: "Thank you for the wonderful hand of indifference."

Morey Amsterdam: "Before I start the show, I have something to say to all the fans who have written to me—*the same to you!*"

Jack Carter: "This could be worse—I could be here in person."

Georgie Jessel: "I am not a rich man—but whatever I have is profit. I began with nothing—not only that—after I was a few days old—they took yet something away from me."

Rodney Dangerfield admits right off he gets no respect: "The other day a doorman asked me to get him a cab—I called up for the right time and the record hung up on me—When I was a kid and I played hide and seek—they didn't even look for me."

How could he lose with that humble bit. And he's got a lot to be humble about. "I don't get no respect at all," he says. "I have no luck with women—The other day I asked a girl to see her apartment —so she drew me a sketch."

Milton Berle: "I lost my TV show. I knew I was in trouble when I found 50 per cent of the studio audience wasn't listening."

4. TOPICS OF THE DAY

The safest kind of target practice is to aim at what's happening: "I don't want to scare you about our ecology problems—but if that poet were around today he would put it this way—'I shot an arrow into the air—it stuck!'—But don't worry—Mayor Lindsay is doing something about the air pollution—he's put the street signs up in braille—Now the tourist can feel the sights and go home."

The idea is to take any subject that's bugging you and build a routine around it. The pan is mightier than the sword. Oh, maybe it won't get you any results at City Hall or the Halls of Congress— but it will get you the laughs you want. For instance, you can't miss when your target is taxes—it's every tax-payers favorite pastime:

"Have you seen the new income tax forms? They're printing them on Kleenex. That's to keep you comfortable while you pay through the nose. . . ."

"The tax forms are down to only two lines now—HOW MUCH DID YOU MAKE IN 1972?—SEND IT. . . ."

"I have no trouble filling out my tax forms—I have trouble paying it. . . ."

"Maybe our President can't cure poverty—but the way taxes are going—they're sure gonna cure wealth. . . ."

"There are only two things you can be sure of—death and taxes— too bad they can't come in that order."

"The income tax has made more liars out of the American people than golf has. . . ."

"I know one honest man who wrote a letter to the income tax bureau—He said, 'I haven't been able to sleep since I cheated on last year's income tax. Enclosed please find $1,000—If I find I still can't sleep—I'll send you the rest of the money. . . .'"

"I wrote to the income tax bureau to have a *heart* . . . and they wrote back and said, '*We'll take it!*'"

"Those government boys are pretty clever—they figured a way— *with that withholding tax*—to get my salary before my wife does. . . ."

"I feel wonderful, though, I went down to the Internal Revenue

Bureau and gave them all the cash I had—now I'm paid up to 1932. . . ."

"Tax collectors and psychiatrists are giving out the same advice—it's not good for a man to *keep too much to himself*."

"I know one thing, I'm putting all my money in taxes—it's the only thing sure to go up."

Another good subject is inflation. You start with a line like: "With the value of the dollar today—it's just as well money doesn't grow on trees—it would cheapen the neighborhood." Then you add a line that Jack Carter used on television: "There is only one consolation in inflation—The money you haven't got isn't worth as much as it used to be." Look up the Index in this book under "Inflation" and search your own files of jokes and gags you have recorded with your very witty ears—and you have the makings of a good routine:

"People say the dollar doesn't go far these days—now I don't know —it goes to Vietnam—India—Pakistan—the Philippines. . . ."

"Americans are getting stronger—twenty years ago it took two people to carry ten dollars worth of groceries—today my child could do it!—I bought eighty dollars worth of groceries the other day—it all fit in the glove compartment of my car."

"What used to cost five dollars to buy—now costs twenty-five dollars to fix—Today if you spend five dollars they ring up NO SALE."

"They say dollar bills carry germs—that's ridiculous—even a germ couldn't live on a dollar these days."

"Oh, there are still things you can get for a dollar—nickels—dimes and quarters."

"There is only one answer to inflation—production—that's why a rabbit coat is cheaper than mink."

"Now take the case of Hildegarde—she picked out a pair of pajamas for her uncle—the clerk said the price was $200. 'For that money,' Hildegarde snapped, 'they should come with a *man* in them.'"

"There are things money can't buy—like, for instance, the same things it bought last week."

"Inflation is when it's easier to earn money—than to earn a living —at today's prices, you're lucky if you can make *one* end meet."

"I'm not trying to scare you—anyone who sits around the house worrying about inflation is crazy. He should be out there—frantically *buying* things before prices go up again."

Another popular sport is hunting for new diets. Americans have more food to eat than people of any other nation on earth—and more diets to keep us from eating it—Just when you get to the point where menu prices don't matter—calories do.

Show me a family on a diet and I'll show you a very hungry family. Give a woman an inch and immediately the entire family is on a diet. Families that diet together—starve together. So you might as well laugh at it. After all, what is comedy but tragedy that has lost it's dignity:

"My wife is on a diet—coconuts and bananas—she hasn't lost weight but can she climb a tree!"

"Have you tried the vodka and carrot juice diet? You get drunk just as fast but your eyesight is better!"

"Jackie Gleason went on a three-week diet and lost twenty-one days."

"Dean Martin advocates the drinking man's diet—I don't know about the rest of your body but it sure makes your head lighter."

"My doctor warned me: 'No rich food—no meat—no drinks—that should save you enough money to pay my bill.'"

"A woman charged her husband with mental cruelty so severe that she lost thirty pounds. 'Divorce granted,' said the judge. 'Not yet,' the woman pleaded. 'First I want to lose another ten pounds.'"

"Marty Allen says: 'I've been losing weight and losing weight and I just found out why. My wife got a new rubber mattress, and at night I toss and turn and that's what's doing it. I'm erasing myself.'"

"Last month my wife went to a reducing farm—She lost $2,000."

"More diets begin in dress shops than in doctors' offices."

"Either she goes on a diet or we'll have to let out the couch."

You have noticed, I hope, that all these routines have a formula and a theme—they stick to the subject—one joke segues into the other. The master is Harry Hershfield. Every joke must fit into the package. He starts by taking a big slice out of his victim: "A juvenile delinquent is a kid who has been given a free hand—but not in the right place." And he never stops cutting until his object is completely destroyed: "I read in the papers that the government is making plans for forestry camps to combat juvenile delinquency—Sounds like a good idea—but how long can we grown-ups hide out there?"

A juvenile delinquent sometimes tries to do right—but only when he thinks it's wrong—I actually heard one mother shout after her son as he was driving away in the family car, "Have a good time." The kid shouted back, "Don't tell me what to do!"

On the other hand, there is Henny Youngman. He has no formula at all. There are some who say he has no act—but who listens to Milton Berle? Henny bills himself as the King of the One-Liners and since Moses is not around to dispute him, he is stuck with the title. There are some who say his jokes go back to Moses—but who listens to Henny Youngman?

Henny is free with his advice and jokes—no matter whose they are. He feels that each joke must be funny on its own and not necessarily in sequence. The gag is the thing, according to Youngman. His jokes don't have to match—only his laughs.

He could be at a dinner for President Nixon and start his routine with: "Show me a Jewish boy who doesn't go to medical school—and I'll show you a lawyer." Then for no other reason, except to get the laugh, he'll say: "Paying alimony is like having the TV set on after you've fallen asleep." His follow-up: "That reminds me—Do you know what it means to come home at night to a woman who will give you a little love—a little affection—a little tenderness?—It means you're in the wrong house!"

Each joke must stand on its own, according to the leader of non sequiturs. He throws them at you—and you pick out the ones you like: "I own a hundred and fifty books—but I have no bookcase—Nobody will loan me a bookcase."—"You know there is a new material you can wear in the rain—It gets wet but you can wear it in the rain"—"Which reminds me—My uncle is going through his second childhood—he just put braces on his plates."

It could be the hottest day of the year and he will segue into: "Cold weather is always a problem—how to get my car started in the morning—and my wife at night." And then for no apparent reason, except that he thinks it's a good joke, he will say: "And to top it all —with these new jet planes, my timing is off—I go to bed at night, I'm hungry—I sit down to eat, I'm sexy."

They pan everything but gold

1. THE ROASTMASTER

A good Roastmaster is a hangman who has vowed to dishonor the guest. This killer doesn't get the chair—unless it's the center one on some dais—to light the bomb under some poor suspecting guest.

It's up to the Roastmaster to set the pace for the rest of the firing squad that are waiting to find out if they can shoot to kill.

Old Will was right when he said: "They never give you a dinner until you don't need one." Why a guy that doesn't need it would want to be the toast of the town, I don't know. He must be aware that toast is always burnt a little—it's got to have some fire on it—and the Roastmaster is there to see that it's well done, just as the honored guest is sworn to take it. There are those who come to roast him and some even to electrocute—but it's laugh and the audience laughs with you—cry and you're a poor sport.

2. THE ROAST

The busiest at these dinners is the toastmaster—better known as the assassin—he doesn't even have time to eat his grapefruit—he's too busy shoving it in the face of the guest of honor.

I always let my fellow sharpshooters know where I'm aiming with my introduction of our honored guest. At the March of Dimes roast for Jerry Lewis, I drew first blood: "We have toasted the who's who of show business at our annual dinners—but this year we looked to top it. We wanted to honor the most beloved of all entertainers—but Bob Hope didn't want it—and Dean Martin said shove it and Milton Berle said stick it—so—we got *him*—Jerry Lewis."

I introduced Johnny Carson at a show business tribute at the Americana this way: "Every once in a while Broadway comes to its senses and honors a man that deserves it. A man of talent, integrity, sincerity—Unfortunately, this isn't the time—instead we honor *him* —Johnny Carson."

Georgie Jessel, who has been dubbed by a dozen presidents from McKinley to Nixon as the Toastmaster General of the United States, has a switch of his own when he starts his assault. At a Friars dinner for Joey Bishop, he started: "The poet Robert Burns in a melancholy mood, once wrote: 'The best laid plans of mice and men gang aft aglee.' For the non-Scotch it means: The plans of all living things, no matter how great or small, do not end the way they are planned—Our fall from grace is self-explanatory on this occasion tonight. This evening had been planned as a dinner for Richard M. Nixon, the President of the United States—*and look what we got*—Joey Bishop."

Henny Youngman introduced Phil Silvers this way: "For years the Frairs have always roasted the ones they love—today we break that tradition in honoring—Phil Silvers."

Steve Allen was the first to "honor" Ed Sullivan: "I remember that many years ago, when I was learning to read, I picked up a copy of a local paper one day—the Yonkers *Shopping News*—and I read a column written by a young newspaperman. Right away I realized that this fellow *had something!* I knew that some day he would do big things. You all know who I'm talking about—Walter Winchell—But we are here tonight to honor Ed Sullivan."

I started the massacre of Jack Benny with a sentimental pitch: "We honor tonight one of the great men of the world—a man of understanding, principle, love, a man of dignity and human decency—but enough about the Pope—Now we get to Jack Benny—It's appropriate that we give him a dinner—everybody does—when he picks up his own check—he's treating."

Bob Hope pointed out how much Benny has done for charity: "Why, he's raised millions with his violin—just by threatening to play."

3. INTRODUCTION

Everything and everybody comes under the sharp tongue of the Roastmaster: "I'm not going to stand up here and tell you a lot of old jokes—but I'll introduce speakers here who will."

Harry Hershfield says a toastmaster is a man who eats a meal he doesn't want, so he can get up and tell a lot of stories he doesn't remember, to people who've already heard them. Maybe that's why toastmasters are mad. I heard Jack E. Leonard put down an audience in Boston: "If I were Paul Revere, I never would have called you!"

Here are some wild lines that you can use at will or any other target:

"If they can make penicillin out of moldy bread—they can make something out of you."

"This man went from complete obscurity—to utter oblivion."

"He really is a kind and gentle man with a very warm heart. He never ran over a dog or a child—the fact that he can't drive a car has nothing to do with it."

"He made his mark in the world—and now wants to learn to write his full name."

Jackie Mason saluted Pat Henry: "Pat, you're very likable, and sometimes being likable will get you further than talent."

Jack Carter said: "Alan King is a truly great comedian—if you don't believe me, ask him."

There are many switches to this line:

"I think he's the greatest—that's not only my opinion—it's his as well."

"He's a very humble man—and he's got a lot to be humble about."

"It is said that Jack Carter is the greatest comedian in the business —and tonight we honor the man who said it—Jack Carter."

"Success hasn't changed him—he's still the same arrogant bastard he always was."

"He's lazy, stubborn, has a terrible temper, steals a little, undependable, would never help a friend in need, and is unreliable. But then no man is perfect."

"Here is the man about whom President Nixon once said: 'Who's he?'"

"I never saw this man before tonight—if he's good—let's hear him —if he's not—let's get it over with."

"Now here's a great man—star—producer—genius—the most beloved man of our time—and the man who wrote this introduction— John Finekuchen."

"This man was in the dress business and failed—then he went into the shoe business and failed—and then he went into show business. And tonight he makes his farewell appearance—before he goes back into the dress business."

It is a good idea to use an introduction that fits your pigeon:

Fighter: "He never knew the meaning of the word defeat—besides thousands of other words he didn't know the meaning of—perhaps you don't recognize him in a vertical position."

Bookmaker: "What do I know from Howard Samuels or horses?—To me the daily double is a way of making my wife happy."

Actor: "He's changing his faith—he no longer believes he's God—Always knew nothing could stop him—not even his talent."

Congressman: "They elected him—just to get him out of town."

Inventor: "They said Marconi was crazy—they said our next speaker Tom Schwartz was crazy—about *him* they were right."

Playboy: "I first met him at a singles weekend at the Concord. He's the kind of guy who invites you to dinner—then joins you."

Lawyer: "You can talk to him about anything—he doesn't understand but you can talk to him—He thinks he's a great lawyer because he tried to break some girl's will."

Doctor: "I'd like to introduce one of the finest doctors in the country—but right now he's operating at Mt. Sinai Hospital.—There is one advantage to being poor—a doctor will cure you faster—Actually our guest is a specialist—that's a doctor who feels your purse."

Politician:

1) "He used to be the Speaker of the House—until somebody listened to him."

2) "He knows a lot—he just can't think of it."

3) "There are two sides to every question—and this guy takes both."

4) "I like the straightforward way he has dodged the issues."

5) "He stands for what he thinks people will fall for."

Musician: "One of the finest artists in the country—in the city he's not too good."

Conservative:

1) "He's not really a conservative—the word is retarded."

2) "He is right of Genghis Khan."

3) "His life story is going to be done by Eighteenth Century-Fox."

Writer: "He once drove a cab—He must have—he's a hack writer."

Newspaperman: "He's an old newspaperman—but he found out there's no money in old newspapers."

Producer: "He discovered Richard Burton and Elizabeth Taylor—he discovered them in the back seat of a car."

Sex-pot: "They wrote about her in the Bible—Psalm 23, verse 5: Her cup runneth over. . . ."

Success: "He's one guy that never forgets his friends and his early days. Once a year he goes back to those lousy, dirty, filthy old slums where he came from in Chicago—just to visit his family."

TV Comic: "To date he's responsible for the sale of more TV

sets than any performer on television—I know I sold mine—and my neighbors sold theirs. . . ."

Businessman: "Do you know when he came to this country he was completely broke—and now after only ten years working like a dog—he owes over $500,000."

Banker:

1) "A banker is a man who lends you an umbrella when the sun is shining—and wants it back when the rains come."

2) "He's a good banker—he started the drive-in banks so that cars can see their real owners."

Drinker: "If I'm ever reincarnated, I want to come back with Einstein's mind, the Pope's heart, and Dean Martin's liver."

Teacher: "When he wants your opinion—he gives it to you."

Singer: "I always said he would make it someday—and I still say he'll make it."

Here are some good build-downs you can use on "friends":

"We have two disappointments tonight—Bob Hope couldn't make it—and Johnny Carson could."

"I'd love to say something nice about our next speaker—but I just can't think of it."

"He's hard to describe—like trying to explain a cigar butt in an old maid's bedroom."

"He hasn't an enemy in the world—but all his friends hate him."

"The secret of his success—still is."

"And now—a man who has been acclaimed by millions—his bookie has a claim—his wife has a claim—his tailor has a claim. . . ."

"And now I bring you the number one writer in the business—and the man who wrote this introduction—Joey Adams."

The roast of the town

The Friars, Actors Youth Fund, Saints and Sinners, Fall Guys, and other organizations pride themselves on the massacre of their dishonored guests.

Remarks that are uncalled for are usually delivered by the victim's best friends—often in the name of some charity. The truth is that all these caustic remarks are done with great affection—and if you buy that, I also have some swamp land for sale in New Jersey I would like to unload.

To show you what I mean, I'd like to take you to a typical roast dinner for Jerry Lewis. To make my point, I am combining several dinners run for Jerry Lewis in the past couple of years by the Actors Youth Fund, the Friars, the March of Dimes, and others. It so happens I was Roastmaster at most of these dinners.

I always fire first—

"We looked all over the world to bring you the greatest personality of all time for our guest of honor this year—but we couldn't find him—so instead we have Jerry Lewis." That was my opening line. After that the fireworks started. "I have been Roastmaster on many occasions to great comedians and tonight it is for Jerry Lewis—this is known as the law of diminishing returns."

When it was announced that Jerry was getting the Man-of-the-Year award, everybody in show business as one hollered: "Why?"

"A lot of people fought to be on this dais for Jerry tonight—those who won aren't here.

"It is said that Jerry Lewis is the most versatile producer, director, actor, and comedian in show business—and tonight we honor the man who said it—Jerry Lewis.

"Jerry was born in show business—and after his last picture he died in it.

"I go back a long way with Jerry. It was I who first sent Jerry to Hollywood—I remember my exact words—I said, 'Jerry—you got about as much chance in Hollywood as I have.'

"I remember his first picture with Dean Martin. Barney Balaban of Paramount saw the first rushes and hollered: 'Get that Italian organ grinder out of my studio—and tell him to take that skinny monkey with him.'

"Dean and Jerry—the greatest team since Leopold and Loeb—proves democracy—where else but in America can an Italian boy and a Jewish boy get together and the Italian boy gets the nose job.

"When you talk about Jerry there are two things you must mention—humility and modesty—because those are the two things he doesn't have.

"Jerry is an inspiration to the kids of America—they figure if he can make it—anybody can."

Now I introduced the rest of the killers.

Johnny Carson said: "Jerry is a unique individual. He was the only man in the world belted in the mouth by Mahatma Gandhi.

"Chaplin's career was ruined when sound came in—Jerry's was ruined when quality came in.

"No one is seated at a Jerry Lewis movie until after fifteen minutes of it. That's because most of them are on the way out to the parking lot by then.

"Behind every clown there is a sad man—in Jerry's case it's the president of ABC."

Jack Carter was the next pallbearer: "May I say that up to now it's been a repulsive evening—

"Jerry Lewis is a charitable man—last year an old-age home came to see him and he gave them a tremendous donation—his mother and father.

"Jerry has done more for my career than anyone else—he made forty-three movies and kept me out of all of them."

Jan Murray stormed on angry: "Jerry Lewis the 'Man of the Year'? I wouldn't vote him 'Jew of the Block.' When was the voting?—I demand a recount!"

Milton Berle: "Henny Youngman wants to be remembered—by anybody.

"It is indeed an honor to be here tonight to praise this Jewish Huntz Hall—the only man to get a 'Dear John' letter from Typhoid Mary.

"They caught him selling Portnoy coloring books on Sesame Street.

"Jerry came from a very poor family—they only had one room and Jerry always slept with his father and mother and never knew what it was like to sleep alone until he was married.

"Jerry has never forgotten. He goes down to the slums where he was born many times to see a reminder of his youth—his father and mother.

"Seriously, Jerry, I kid around, but there is only one great clown in our business—Emmett Kelly—that's all—"

"You haven't lost your touch, Milton," Johnny Carson said to Uncle Miltie, when he sat down, "only your memory."

"And now," I continued, "I'd like to introduce Bob Hope—but I'm stuck with Alan King—Alan King, a truly great comedian—If you don't believe me—ask him, he'll tell you.

"But he's a humble man—he has a humble home, a humble chauffeur, a humble tennis court, and only four staff photographers—"

Alan King: "Jerry has been described as a twentieth-century phenomenon—Well, like the moon landings—nobody talks about that anymore—like the atomic energy—it's the biggest bomb we ever had—and like a heart transplant—he is always being rejected. Now let's examine Jerry Lewis the man—and this man should have been examined years ago—In 1946 Dean Martin and Jerry Lewis were born. There was nothing they wouldn't do for a laugh. They would throw pies at each other, squirt seltzer at each other, hurl ice cubes at the audience, and at one time they covered the piano with shaving cream. They carried on like this for ten years. Then in 1956 they parted and the reason given was artistic differences.—Jerry has probably done much better than Dean. After all, in the last five years Jerry has had four television shows and Dean has only had one."

Charlie Callas: "In France he is hailed as a genius—that's the same country that burned Joan of Arc."

Jerry Lewis accepted the sneers with great humility. "Why is it," he asked, "that at such important moments, your throat dries up?" Johnny Carson called out: "Not when you're getting laughs."

"I want to thank all my friends for being here," Jerry continued. "It's appropriate they should be my pallbearers.

"On the dais tonight are some really extraordinary people—*and I'm going to get every one of them.*

"I must say that to follow great comedy like that I would be a fool to try and top them. A lot of you might think I'm saying that because it's easier to go the other way. I would not attempt to top them. I know I couldn't if I tried and with that kind of humility I must get off to a big hand.

"In summing up, I'm honored to be here tonight. I didn't realize the spritzes would be like they were, but these are the people I have grown up with in the business. They are beautiful people and if you were to sit here you would feel the loving side of their ambivalence and be terribly humble—like I am—Thank you all and good night."

ED SULLIVAN

At an annual March of Dimes dinner, Ed Sullivan was the Roast of the Town. A couple of thousand pounds of comedians showed up to make sure the roast was well done. The only reason Smiley graciously submitted to this vivisection was to raise $100,000 or more for the March of Dimes.

As roastmaster, I naturally take the first cut:

"You can sum up Ed Sullivan's career in one word—lucky.

"There is a new Ed Sullivan doll on the market—you wind it up and for one hour it does nothing.

"Ed is a great showman. After all, he's been on television for twenty-two years—and I finally figured out the reason for his success —he never improved.

"Everybody is always picking on poor Ed—and he deserves it.

"The truth is Ed cares about giving new people a chance on his television show. It was Ed who first started the one and only Bella Magdowitz. It was Ed and Ed alone who gave the first opportunity to Sylvia Cocktepple—and the Fiji Island Drum and Fife Corps.

"Ed has taken some of the biggest stars and made unknowns of them.

"It was Vincent Lopez who first predicted Ed would be our biggest TV personality in the twentieth century—but he also predicted Zsa Zsa Gabor would become a nun.

"This man has been on the same network—CBS—for over twenty years—You know why?—No other network wanted him.

"A lot of people say he has a lousy personality—that's not true— he has no personality at all—He has that unusual something that brightens a room—when he leaves it.

"Where else could Ed go from here? He's been a sports writer, columnist, TV star, movie actor—some people say he should do what George Murphy and Ronald Reagan did—get the hell out of show business.

"Personally—I love the man—I have no taste—but I love him— Ladies and gentlemen—Ed Sullivan."

Jack Carter: "Ed Sullivan looks great. I just spoke to his widow Sylvia. He should be President—he belongs up there on Mount Rushmore next to Jefferson and Washington and Lincoln. Don't even have to chisel him out of stone—He's ready now—Really, I have great respect and admiration for Ed Sullivan—it's more than that—it's FEAR."

Joan Rivers: "I was on the Ed Sullivan show and had to follow an elephant—and had to share a dressing room with the elephant. Ed came to the dressing room and apologized for putting us together. 'Oh, that's all right,' I said humbly—'I wasn't talking to you,' Ed snapped."

Peter Lind Hayes: "He's the only golfer who falls asleep in his own backswing."

Jan Murray: "Ed knows what the public likes—and one of these days he's going to give it to them."

Paul Ford: "I first met Ed Sullivan at the Actors Studio. He was their first drop-out—Later on he learned how to mumble by himself."

Georgie Jessel: "I wouldn't say Ed has no personality—but his TV show is in color and he comes out in black and white.

"I have never known anyone who was the recipient of a dinner who didn't have something that was pretty good. No one ever gave a dinner to Willie Sutton, Leftie Louie, or Sitting Bull.

"One thing you can be sure—there's never a dull moment when Ed is on the air—it lasts the entire show.

"The secret of his success—still is."

I introduced Milton Berle to present his protégé and pal Henny Youngman. "Henny," said Miltie, "is one of the great comedians of our generation. This is not only my opinion—it's Henny's.

"I've known Henny Youngman, man and joke file, for over forty years. Unlike myself, Henny did not steal jokes from the top comedians of that era. Henny stole from the unknowns—a word which later became synonymous with his career.

"The greatest form of flattery is imitation—and one of Henny's unusual traits is that he is flattered by the fact that for many years he has been an imitation of a comedian.

"Actually, I kid a lot about Henny—but the truth is he is the fastest comedian around. He has to be with *his* act.

"Ladies and gentlemen—I give you Henny Youngman—and you can have him—"

Henny Youngman: "I just finished filling out my income tax form. —Who said you can't get wounded by a blank?—Which reminds me— a drunk walked up to a parking meter and put in a dime. The dial went to 60. He said, 'How about that—I lost 100 pounds.'

"Want to drive somebody crazy? Send him a wire saying, IGNORE FIRST WIRE.

"Which reminds me. My wife went to the beauty show and got a mud pack. For two days she looked nice—then the mud fell off.

"That reminds me. I just solved the parking problem—I bought a parked car.

"Before I go, I have a message for all you parents out there. Is your teen-age son or daughter out for the evening? If so, take advantage of the opportunity. Pack your furniture, call a moving van, and don't leave a forwarding address—Good night folks."

"Henny," I said, "that was the most touching tribute to Ed Sullivan I ever heard in my life."

WILLIAM F. BUCKLEY, JR.

A good Roastmaster never unintentionally insults anybody. I was completely prepared when I was asked to dishonor Bill Buckley at the Fall Guy luncheon on Long Island:

"They say you should have a little respect for the guest of honor —and I have as little respect for him as possible.

"Bill Buckley took smiling lessons from Arthur Goldberg.

"Remember when he ran for mayor?—He could have gotten more votes at the cemetery.

"He made a lot of speeches—but who the hell could understand him? He uses such words—you put them where you think they belong.

"One thing about him—he's sweet and loving—a bee flew in his mouth and he stung *it*. Lots of people owe a lot to him—ulcers— nausea—diarrhea.

"As a Catholic he is often compared to St. Paul—one of the dullest towns in America—as a wit he is second only to Boris Karloff.

"As far as his politics are concerned—he's right of King Lear. To him the Birch Society are a bunch of communist bastards—His life story is being done by Eighteenth Century-Fox.

"This guy isn't conservative—the word is retarded."

JACK BENNY

It's true that a sense of humor is what makes you laugh at something that would make you mad if it happened to you. But given the choice, show people would rather be rapped than ignored. You can always pick out actors by the glazed look that comes into their eyes when the conversation wanders away from themselves.

At one party for Jack Benny, the dais was loaded with stars waiting to explode. I started the fireworks: "Any man who needs so many character witnesses shouldn't be a guest of honor.

"We wanted to make this a great party for Jack. We thought about digging up some of his old friends—and we'd have to—like Aaron Burr—Attila the Hun—Douglas Fairbanks, Sr.'s father—and the ever popular Mae Busch.

"I wouldn't say he's old—but his Social Security number is 2.

"He brought his violin with him tonight—and he may play for us —but I'm sorry his original piano player couldn't be with us—Ludwig van Beethoven—or his older brother Isaiah—

"I think Jack is one of the funniest violin players in the world— he has the only Stradivarius made in Japan.

"All I can tell you is Henny Youngman ain't got to worry— In fact, Venus de Milo could play better."

George Burns: "It's appropriate that we give Jack Benny a dinner —everybody does—he hasn't picked up a check in thirty years.

"You can always recognize Jack—sitting with his back towards the check.

"Benny is a friend—I'd give him the shirt off my back—He'd wash it—iron it—and charge me a dollar.

"Jack is the only guy who'll get off at Albuquerque and sell blankets to the Indians.

"Here's a guy who came to California for arthritis forty years ago —and he's finally got it."

Jack Carter: "Jack Benny is lucky to be here tonight. He was locked in a pay toilet at Kennedy Airport. Also, he has shingles—Mary caught him with a broad and the roof caved in."

Bob Hope: "I don't want to say Benny is cheap—but the only time he'll pick up a check is when it's made out to him.

"During the war Jack was a dollar-a-year man. That's not what he got—that's what he spent.

"Remember the total eclipse of the sun? Jack ran over to the Western Union office to send a night letter."

Georgie Jessel: "I've known Jack ever since I was a little boy. He used to hold me on his knee and tell me about his old friends William McKinley and Chester Arthur and Aaron Burr—Do you know what he did before he came here to get this honor?—He went to visit his son in the old-age home—Now isn't that nice?

"I don't know if you realize that Mr. Benny was also a producer. He produced one film—*The Lucky Stiff*—which, while it never played in any of the first-run theaters or second- or third-run theaters —or even the drive-ins—was very often used in penitentiaries and comfort stations. However, he was an astute enough producer to sell this project along with some other planned disasters to the Columbia Broadcasting System for some two million dollars.

"He is known and beloved from Waukegan to Wimpole Street— from Kishniff to Korea—from Pennsylvania to Polly Adler—Jack Benny."

Jack played the game when he was finally introduced: "I was so excited about this dinner—I almost paid for my ticket—of course, I did call to find out if the tips were included in the price of admission and if I could deduct my cab fare. . . .

"I really can't understand why everybody talks about my being cheap—just because I have a slight impediment of the reach—

"And about my violin playing—I remember Fred Allen once said— 'When Jack plays the violin it sounds like the strings are back in the cat'—Now that's not fair—Years ago in my home town of Waukegan, Illinois, they planted a tree in the courthouse square and called it the Jack Benny Tree. In a short time the tree died. The only one who could figure out what happened was Fred Allen. He said: 'How can a tree live in Waukegan with the sap in Hollywood.'

"Now to prove I can really play the violin—I brought my own Stradivarius with me—it was made in 1727—

"Did you buy it new?" George Burns yelled up.

GOVERNOR NELSON ROCKEFELLER

I have roasted Governor Rockefeller many times and he loves it. Here are some of my best lines:

"Here is a true story of success—he worked hard all his life—and before he was three years old he was a millionaire.

"I can't understand why he's bothering with politics—What's the worry about winning? If he loses New York, he can always buy New Jersey.

"He is so rich he sends CARE packages to Howard Hughes.

"He has a ranch in Venezuela—In fact, his ranch *is* Venezuela.

"Just from the popcorn stand at Radio City Music Hall alone he could retire.

"But one thing—In spite of his millions, he treats his kids normally. He has a six-year-old son but he doesn't spoil him. For Christmas he treated him like any normal parent and gave the kid a set of blocks—Fifty-first Street—Fifty-second Street—Fifty-third Street. . . .

"And, Mr. Governor, if the election is so important to you—take out a few bucks and pay for your opponent, Arthur Goldberg, to appear on TV—If he makes one more speech—you will carry Canada.

"I knew Goldberg was in trouble when he came on TV looking green—and we don't have a color set.

"There is talk about Rockefeller running for President—I don't see why he would want it—he'd have to move into a smaller house—Then he'd have to put the White House in his wife's name.

"Do you know this man has a solid gold bathtub in each room of his house?—When he leaves the bath, he leaves fourteen-carat rings.

"Everybody wants to run against Rocky—they don't have a chance. Goldberg is a nice man—My Uncle Morris is also a nice man.—My Uncle Morris shouldn't be governor—neither should Goldberg.

"Howard Samuels, the bookie, also wants to be governor. Now what the hell does he know about New York? He thinks Rockefeller Center is the governor's navel.

"John Lindsay? After his record in New York, even if he runs unopposed, he'll lose.—Lindsay would rather switch than fight.—That's his big problem—the waiters don't know how to serve him—from the right or left—Lindsay is the only man without a friend at Chase Manhattan.

"You gotta admit Rocky has done a big job with the Long Island Rail Road, like he promised. The commuters owe everything to him —ulcers, nausea, diarrhea.—Now I know what happened to Judge Crater—he took the 5:11 to Babylon—You can get to the moon faster than Jamaica Station.

"When our Governor makes up his mind—He's full of indecision —I asked him how he felt about the abortion bill—he said he would pay it himself—Now that's class.

"Don't worry about a thing, Mr. Governor—I predict a landslide even though you only paid for a simple victory—Of course, I also predicted *you* would be President."

PAUL CARDINAL YU PIN

Paul Cardinal Yu Pin is the only Chinese cardinal in the world and the head of Fu-Jen Catholic University in Taiwan. He had honored me by opening the Joey Adams American Library in Taipei and conferring a Doctor of Laws degree on me. Naturally, I was reluctant to make jokes or throw barbs at a dinner in his honor. His Eminence insisted that we pull no punch lines.

"I knew this was a Catholic benefit," I started. "I left my car in front of the hotel—and they raffled it off.

"One thing, Your Eminence, I will never refuse to do a Catholic benefit—I did once—and it snowed in my living room for four days—in Miami—during the Summer.

"Not being a Catholic, I know very little about your religion—In fact, the only two words I know in Latin are—rhythm and bingo.

"I am very glad that the Ecumenical Council cleared the Jews of all wrongdoing. And to show you our appreciation—we will lower the rent on the Vatican."

Pat Henry: "I am Catholic, Your Eminence, and I want to talk to you about the Pill—If you don't play the game—don't make the rules."

Bob Hope: "I came here to apologize to His Eminence. The last time I was on the dais with Cardinal Yu Pin I neglected to introduce him—He told me he forgave me—but I've noticed that ever since then I haven't won a single bingo game.

"I am the first to tell you that my wife is so Catholic we can't get insurance—too many candles in the house—Do you know our grocery bills are astronomical?—$3,000 a week—fifty dollars for food—the rest for candles.

"I know that religion is coming back—Dial-A-Prayer just ordered three more numbers."

GEORGIE JESSEL

Georgie Jessel, the Toastmaster General of the United States, has presided at almost every important dinner since anybody can remember. In fact, if you take a close-up of the "Last Supper"—he's third from the right.

That's why I'm honored that he calls me his favorite toastmaster. Georgie insists that I never pull my punch lines when I'm roasting him. I thought you might enjoy a combination of some of the dinners where Jessel sat still for the March of Dimes, the City of Hope, the State of Israel, and others, while his friends and colleagues used him for target practice for the sake of charity.

"Georgie Jessel," I started, "this year alone personally supported 1,250,000 Jews in Israel—and 325 chorus girls in the United States.

"In his honor we are going to plant an Arab in the lobby of the Actors' Temple.

"Georgie is the only American who has the distinction of being in Who's Who and the Kinsey Report at the same time.

"I'm sorry that Jessel's latest girl friend couldn't be here tonight —but her mother won't let her cross the streets by herself.—His fiancée is now a counselor at camp—and he's so proud of her—he just got a letter from her—she just made Eagle Scout."

Jack Carter: "Georgie is an unhappy man. He just got his first anti-Semitic letter—and it was in Yiddish."

George Burns: "Jessel is so sentimental he cries at card tricks."

Burns told this story when I called on him: "Years ago Georgie Jessel was starring in *The Jazz Singer* on Broadway, and he was a sensation. But when Jack Warner made the picture of *The Jazz Singer*, who do you think starred in it—Al Jolson. Well, naturally this upset Jessel, and Georgie took an oath that he'd break Jack Warner if it cost him his last cent. Jack Warner doesn't know this, but he's only got about two weeks to go because Jessel's down to his last $120. . . . If Jessel happens to meet a girl tonight, Warner will be broke tomorrow. . . .

"While I'm on the subject of *The Jazz Singer*, I saw Jessel do it on Broadway, and you remember the story. The father is a cantor, and the son wouldn't follow in his footsteps. And at the finish of the play the father dies and the son gives up show business and comes into the synagogue and sings "Kol Nidre." Well, this affected me very much. I felt like it was my life, because my father was a cantor. He wasn't exactly a full-time cantor, he was sort of like a disappointment act. . . . In case a real cantor got sick, my father would take his place. . . . I remember once during the high holidays a cantor got sick and they sent for my father. They said, 'Let's hear you sing something,' so my father sang. You know, that year the synagogue was closed on Rosh Hoshanah. . . .

"Well anyway, Jessel's performance in *The Jazz Singer* just took me apart, I cried like a baby. And when he finished 'Kol Nidre' I ran backstage with the tears streaming down my face to congratulate him. But Jessel's publicity man, Bennett, was standing outside his dressing room and wouldn't let me in. He said, 'You can't go in, Jessel has all his clothes off.' I said, 'What's that got to do with it, I've seen a naked Jew before. I want to tell him how great he was.'

Bennett said, 'Not now, he's got a girl in there who he's putting into show business.' . . . And I thought nothing could follow 'Kol Nidre.' . . ."

Bob Hope: "Georgie used to work as a producer for Darryl Zanuck at Twentieth Century. He was really the key man out there. Every time Zanuck went to the washroom—Jessel handed him the key.

"From the start of Georgie's career, you knew that he was destined for greatness. It was obvious nothing could stop him—not even his talent.

"Georgie is a sentimentalist. He cried like a baby when the President made that speech about the draft—he thought they were taking *girls* from eighteen to twenty-five.

"And I know him pretty well—I know he doesn't give a second thought to women—his first thought covers everything.

"And I'm happy to report tonight that he doesn't chase women as much as he used to—he had his desk sawed in half so he can take a short cut—

"Jessel is a loyal fellow. I remember he was crazy about his boss, Zanuck. I can just see the scene that night at the Academy Awards when Darryl bent over to kiss the Oscar, Jessel bent over to kiss Zanuck. It was a pretty sight. I can't tell you what he does to keep his job—but it is banned in Boston—"

DON RICKLES

Don Rickles is a very gentle man until he faces an audience and then he makes Mao Tse-tung sound like a Boy Scout. But as soon as the battle is over, he takes the wounded to his mother's house for chicken soup to get them well again.

Recently his victims turned the tide of battle and ran a dinner in his honor—and the boys exploded their biggest bombs:

Jessel: "Rickles has become a household word—Garbage is also a household word."

Morey Amsterdam: "Don is the original Rat Patrol."

Jan Murray: "Rickles, our guest of honor, what little he has left— is the man about whom Hitler said—'From him I could learn!'"

Jack Carter: "It was Don who taught the Arabs how to fight dirty."

Jack E. Leonard: "Don has a great comedy style—mine. He's one of America's greatest unknowns—he's gonna go a long way—and I hope he stays there—Rickles has a nice personality—but not for a human being."

Johnny Carson: "There is really nothing so bad about Rickles—except one thing—he despises the old and the lame."

Ed Sullivan: "Don likes everybody—he just doesn't show it. He was a good boy—Jesse James's mother said *he* was a good boy, too."

Red Buttons: "Don married a good girl—a sentimental girl—She saw a sign HELP THE HANDICAPPED—so she married him."

Charlie Callas: "Rickles made his first movie—and in tribute, every movie-goer is today eating black popcorn."

Bob Hope: "I think Vice-President Agnew's golf pro is writing Rickles' material."

As soon as Don was introduced, he started shooting from the lip:

To Joey Adams: "I hope you jump on a bicycle and discover it has no seat."

To Ed Sullivan: "What's your name? If you don't know—look inside your coat."

To Orson Welles: "Who makes those tents you wear?"

To Phil Harris: "He taught Dean Martin every drink he knows."

To Dean Martin: "You're not relaxed—you're just limp from being boozed up—You could build a skating rink with the ice cubes you use in your drinks each week."

The astronauts: "You dummies are making fools of yourself. You want to go to the moon? There are plenty of places to go right here. Smoke some funny cigarettes and imagine you're on the moon and you won't be so ridiculous."

To Jack E. Leonard: "Why don't you pull up six cots and lie down?"

To Bob Hope: "What the hell are you doing here? The government has no troops stationed here."

To Georgie Jessel: "Oh my God, look at you. Anybody else hurt in the accident?"

To the audience: "If anybody tells you you're a good audience —slug 'em—Thanks for the applause—my maid gets a bigger hand when she runs a rag over the piano keys."

BOBBY KENNEDY

When JFK was President, Bobby Kennedy had no sense of humor about himself. He insisted on being called Robert.—He wanted no jokes about his age—or his position or his family. JFK, who had the greatest sense of humor, was the first to break that down. When he appointed Robert Attorney General only a short time after he graduated law school, there was some criticism in the press. The President answered it simply: "I had to give him *some* experience before he opened his law office."

When JFK passed on, Robert became Bobby and he decided he was now big enough to take it—and like it. I became his favorite Roastmaster because, as he put it, I was his equalizer. At one Fall Guy luncheon I hit him with everything and he loved it:

"Robert Kennedy wants to be President. And he's got lots of experience. His first major job out of school was counselor at camp —his second job was Attorney General.—When he ran for senator his father told him—'Don't worry, son—I'll buy you a landslide'—

"Let's look at Bobby Kennedy the man—He's five feet eight inches tall—he takes a haircut and he's five feet two. He doesn't just get a haircut—first he gets an estimate—then he takes gas—

"Bobby Kennedy has a vigorous image—he has ten children— Everybody thinks that's because he's a devout Catholic—not so— he's a sex maniac.

"When he comes home he doesn't ask 'What's new?'—He asks 'Who's new?'

"George Washington may have been called the father of our country—but Bobby Kennedy *is*.

"When he married Ethel he promised her the world—and he damn near gave it to her.

"I just found out he is going to India to teach birth control. It was President Johnson's suggestion—he said 'Let's give Bobby back to the Indians.'

"They call him a carpetbagger—They said he doesn't know New York and has no right to run for senator—all lies—so what if he thought Rockefeller Center was the governor's navel?

"I happen to know that Bobby Kennedy does not want to be President—he wants to be king.

"Everybody loves Bobby—Cardinal Cooke was going to be here today—but he didn't want to kiss Bobby's ring again.

"And, now, gentlemen, here he is—the next President—of the men's club—Robert F. Kennedy."

PEARL BAILEY AND VIRGINIA GRAHAM

It's not easy to roast a gal—I told that to Pearl Bailey when I was asked to be her hangman when the March of Dimes put her up for slaughter. "If you spare the rod," she cracked, "I'll never figure you— If I can dish it out—I can take it—"

It was tough but how can you refuse such an invitation? "We are honoring Pearl Bailey," I started, "because she's a great star—the First Lady of Broadway—and the NAACP insisted.

"She was always a regular at the White House. When Lady Bird left, Pearl told her not to worry—she could always come in and work for her Tuesdays and Thursdays.

"If she becomes Jewish—I'll really make her a star—then she and Sammy Davis can open their own synagogue.

"She had it tough in the old days, when she was a little girl in Shanghai—Shanghai?—Pardon me—That's a line left over from an old Pearl *Buck* dinner.

"This is a classy girl—this Pearl Bailey—when she didn't get the picture for *Hello, Dolly!* she made no fuss—Ginger Rogers whimpered—Carol Channing cried—but not a word from Pearl—she did have the boys from the NAACP do a little picketing."

Virginia Graham is an old pal who throws punch lines like a heavyweight.—She, too, encouraged me to treat her like one of the boys —although she really couldn't fit into their clothes too good—:

"Virginia Graham is billed as the Peter Pan of the Lydia Pinkham set—or the menopausal Coty girl.

"She has just written a new book dedicated to her husband Harry Guttenberg—*Sex Without Laughter.*

"Virginia Graham—better known as the Madam of 'Girl Talk'—has just had her mouth declared a lethal weapon.

"They are now testing her at M-G-M to play the old Mae West parts—the only trouble is her old parts don't work as good as Mae West's did."

I adore Pearl and Virginia—two of the great talents and distinguished ladies of the theater—but if I didn't take my best shots they would think I didn't love them. I remember giving an especially nice introduction to Hildegarde one Dais night—after the dinner she asked Cindy, "What's the matter—is Joey angry at me?"

HAROLD GIBBONS

Harold Gibbons is the big teamster boss who is beloved by show people—he's always there with a helping hand or truck to help a friend in need—Naturally, the boys returned the compliment when the Actors Youth Fund put him up for target practice. I started the show:

"I came here tonight to pay tribute to a great human being—and after I do I'll say a few words about Harold Gibbons.

"Harold is a great labor leader—and has put more girls in labor than any other man in the movement.

"Even as a kid he was working for the people. When his son asked him to tell him a bedtime story—Harold started, 'Once upon a time-and-a-half—'

"Harold Gibbons believes you can get more with a kind word and a punch in the mouth—than just a kind word.

"When Harold makes a deal for labor—it's a deal—His last contract took only six days to negotiate—the minimum basic pay was tripled—guaranteed annual bonus—six coffee breaks—before lunch—pension plan—hospitalization for second cousins—birthday off—anniversary off—the butcher's birthday off—guaranteed vacation with pay—

"The owner said, 'Okay—okay—*now* what do you want?'

"Harold said: 'Now I want a guarantee you won't go broke.' "

In all the years Harold has been a labor leader he has never had trouble with one union member—That is—only one guy refused to sign—for six months nobody could get him to sign—Finally, Harold went to see him and said: "If you don't sign, we will break every bone in your body—we'll rip you to pieces—we'll send you to the hospital for a year"—The guy said, "Give me the pen—I'll sign." Harold said, "Tell me—why did you wait so long to sign up?"—The man said, "Nobody ever explained it before!"

Now that you saw the stars at war and at play, you must have noted that they only attack their equals. They pick their friends—to pieces—but ignore their enemies.

I can put the jokes in your mouth—as well as the studied ad libs, but you must fit them in the right place and do it with authority—that's the key—You must know your target—and you must prepare the roast well—and then serve it like you are proud of it.

Of course, I have tried to give you the laugh lines—the straight lines you will have to play with yourself.—If you mean them and if you have done your homework about the guest of honor—it will stand out like a beacon light—but the words must be yours—in your language—in your style—Nobody ever put it better than Champ Joe Louis when he faced a wartime audience at Madison Square Garden and said simply: "We can't lose—God is on our side."

If you have something to say and you say it in your own language —thought out—and to the point—and talk to them like you would to a group of friends at home—you can't lose. The punch lines are an added spice to your speech. You can do both—as long as you do both with authority and sincerity. Like the kid who was carrying the sign that said: MAKE LOVE—NOT WAR—and the man said, "I'm married—I do both."

The dearest speech I ever heard was delivered by a pal of mine at a dinner in my honor. It was the first time he had ever been called on to speak publicly—but his sincerity made him the hit of the evening: "Joey and I have cried together and laughed together—we have gotten drunk together and now I'm so proud that we can share his joy together—"

Everybody has his own way of kissing you in public—some do it with a smile—some with a sword. I'm sure Bob Hope loves Phyllis Diller—but that didn't stop him from saying: "The last guy Phyllis stirred up was Batman—he took one look and flew away."

Phyllis is a comedy masochist, but she could be a stinging sadist when the laughs are coming:

"Bob Hope can't resist a man in uniform—I saw him do twenty minutes for the bell captain—"

"Martha Mitchell is Spiro Agnew in pantyhose."

"Jackie Onassis is having a terrible operation. They're going to remove her navel—she's putting in a wall safe."

"When Nixon was campaigning, he said he had a secret way to end the war. And he sure knows how to keep a secret."

"Do you know what Twiggy has printed on her chest? IN CASE OF RAPE—THIS SIDE UP."

"You all know Doris Day—the last of the red hot virgins."

Of course, Phyllis the masochist hits herself the hardest:

"I am the Elizabeth Taylor of the 'Twilight Zone.'"

"I'm the Twiggy of the crab-grass set."

"I look like someone who went to the electric chair and lived."

"This dress I'm wearing hides the eighth wonder of the world. I'm the only living female who wears prescription underwear."

Wild lines

Here are some of my favorite lines—delivered by some of my favorite people about some of my favorite friends—

PHIL SILVERS

Pat Henry at a Friars roast for Phil Silvers said: "Phil's show is closing this week. The reviews were good—but the word-of-mouth killed it."

JACKIE MASON

Eli Basse: "I can't understand why Jackie Mason talks with an accent when his father James speaks so beautifully."

GEORGIE JESSEL

Jack Carter: "Jessel is the world's youngest dirty old man. Look at those medals on his rented USO soldier suit. The only thing he ever attacked was Sophie Tucker in her dressing room at Loew's State."

MAYOR JOHN V. LINDSAY

Milt Moss: "I asked one lady if she was voting for Lindsay. She said he's her second choice. When I asked who was her first choice, she said: 'Anybody that runs against him.'"

Joey Adams: "He'd rather switch than fight—the poor waiters don't know whether to serve him on the right or left.

"Lindsay would rather be in show business—he asked Mike Nichols to direct his next campaign.

"He called his office and his secretary reminded him he had an eleven o'clock appointment at City Hall. 'Why?' he asked. 'What's playing there?'

"Personally, I'd like to see him run for President—Anything to get him out of New York City."

HOWARD SAMUELS

Joey Adams: "Howard stands for progress. He came up the hard way. In a few short years he went from congressman to bookmaker.

"Howard Samuels has given up a career in politics to follow the horses. Now you know what his career is built on—and it goes with his initials—H.S.

"People have worried that some may get addicted to off-track betting and lose their shirts, but Howard Samuels has provided for that. He started up an organization called Off-Track Betting Anonymous. It works under the principle of exchanging one set of habits for another. Thus, if you call and say you're in trouble . . . you got a big hangup . . . you're addicted to gambling . . . no problem!! They'll just send over a hooker to sit with you.

"And he intends to run for governor on the same principles that Herbert Hoover had. You remember Hoover's famous slogan, 'a chicken in every pot?' Well, with Samuels it's going to be a hooker in every bed.

"They used to say the city's going to the dogs. Not any more. Now with Howard Samuels it's going to the horses.

"People point to Howard Samuels with pride. They say he's a success story. They say Howard Samuels has $5,000,000. And they say he did it all himself. That's true. He did wind up with $5,000,000. His father had left him ten!"

DANNY THOMAS

Jan Murray: "Can't you tell how thrilled I am to be here tonight to honor my good friend Danny Thomas? Because there are a lot of jokes tonight on all these Jews honoring an Arab, it's interesting to note that Danny kind of denies he's an Arab. . . . He always says, 'I am Lebanese'—as if it's a soft drink or something.

"And Danny always gives me that humble bit . . . 'Where else but this grand country like ours could a plain, little Lebanese like me be the biggest star on TV for twelve years?' . . . Well, Danny, there is a very good reason for this . . . there happen to be over ninety million Lebanese in this country . . . very few people know this because every night they move. . . . You show me an Arab who pays rent and I'll show you a Jewish landlord.

"But being an Arab actually has helped Danny's career immeasurably . . . you see, he has that one great talent that sets him apart from everyone else . . . he can go longer without water than anyone else in show business."

GEORGIE JESSEL

Jan Murray: "What could I possibly say about our great guest of honor. . . . There have been a lot of jokes tonight about Georgie and Israel but we all know that most of Georgie's adult life, his energies and affections have always been divided in two places . . . his heart is always in Israel and his body is in a little love nest on Fifty-eighth Street.

"But it's common knowledge what Georgie has done for the glorious State of Israel. As you all know, one time it was just a desert . . . but he helped to plant trees . . . homes . . . hospitals . . . schools . . . and an airport. . . . Can you imagine what he could have done if he didn't have a hernia?

"Look what this man has contributed to show business. Do you realize Georgie Jessel was the first comedian to do jazz songs on Broadway? . . . he was the first comedian to use a telephone in a monologue . . . but most important he was the first comedian to be tried under the Mann Act. . . . That was the time he carried Sophie Tucker over the state line. . . . How do you think he got the hernia?

"That's right, my friends, this great human being has never changed. . . . Even as a youngster he was what he is today . . . a dirty old man."

MILTON BERLE

Jan Murray: "Imagine me being here tonight honoring the great Milton Berle. . . . I have looked forward to this dinner tonight with the anticipation of a Buster Crabbe movie . . . but we are here to pay homage to Milton Berle . . . a man of rare gifts . . . I know, because I never got one from him.

"They have often said Milton is another Charlie Chaplin. . . . In fact, they have already taken steps to deport him. . . . But Milton, your talent has never been questioned . . . or even mentioned . . . come to think of it.

"Milton, all I can say to you . . . as a man, you're the greatest . . . as a relative, you're the greatest . . . as a friend, you're the greatest . . . and as a comedian . . . well, three out of four ain't bad, Milton."

PHIL HARRIS

George Burns: "Phil taught Dean Martin every drink he knows. His family didn't know he was a drunk until one day he showed up sober."

Jack E. Leonard: "He's the only man with an honorary drinking license."

BING CROSBY

Morey Amsterdam: "With his great song 'Love Thy Neighbor' he did so much good—he started more wife-swapping than any time in our history."

PRESIDENT HARRY TRUMAN

Bob Hope: "He runs the country with an iron hand—and plays the piano the same way."

MUHAMMAD ALI (CASSIUS CLAY)

Bob Hope: "When Cassius was born—he was a six-pound mouth."

JOEY ADAMS

Bob Hope: "Joey Adams received an honorary law degree at a Chinese university. I am told that a horse once graduated with an honorary degree from this institution—it was the first time in history a college gave an honorary degree to an *entire* horse."

OTTO PREMINGER

Joey Adams: "He is giving up show business to teach at Columbia University—broken English.

"He has been in this country forty years—and he still sounds like he's arriving Thursday."

DAVID MERRICK

Phyllis Diller: "If I ever have a heart transplant, I want David Merrick's—it's never been used."

Joey Adams: "He's got the personality of the back wall of a handball court."

VICE-PRESIDENT SPIRO AGNEW

Bob Hope: "Why is everybody picking on Agnew—he hasn't done anything."

ZSA ZSA GABOR

Oscar Levant: "She does social work among the rich."

Joey Adams: "She only marries for love—and she keeps on getting married till she finds it."

Mike Douglas: "She was married to Conrad Hilton—and has the towels to prove it."

Pat Henry: "Baseball is our national pastime—now go convince Zsa Zsa Gabor."

FRANK SINATRA

Jack E. Leonard: "He has a nice voice—one of these days it will reach his throat."

JACKIE GLEASON

Jack E. Leonard: "Gleason is so fat—when he walks down the street—he *is* the street."

JACK E. LEONARD

Joey Adams: "When Jack E. walks down Park Avenue, it becomes a one-way street."

Jack E.: "I won't tell you how much I weigh—but don't ever get in an elevator with me unless you're going down."

JOE KIPNESS

Joey Adams: "Joe Kipness is a famous producer and restaurateur —but he likes to fancy himself as a great lover. When he was in the dress business he was known as the Seventh Avenue continental. But he still brags about his sex life. Like his wife Janie says, 'What *was—was.*' Janie says his idea of an exciting night is to turn up his electric blanket."

BERT BACHARACH

Joey Adams: "He's a great newspaperman. You know him for his fearless reporting—his hard-hitting—thought-provoking—incisive— think pieces, like—*Kitchen Snooping*—'How to stuff a tomato up your meat loaf—' or 'How to suck a pickle for fun and profit.'"

BURT BACHARACH

Joey Adams: "It was obvious from the beginning—nothing could stop him—not even his talent.

"Bert's contemporaries are O. O. McIntyre—Karl K. Kitchen, and Ed Sullivan's father's father—Burt's contemporaries are Tiny Tim, the Animals, Sonny and Cher, and the Constipated Four."

EARL WILSON

Joey Adams: "He is one of the greatest writers since Shelley, Keats, and Browning—Shelley Berman—B. F. Keats—and Peaches Browning."

Henny Youngman: "Earl once drove a cab—he must have—he's a hack writer."

Milton Berle: "Earl is a familiar figure at all night-club openings —sleeping soundly at a ringside table. He is a great audience for comedians, because, compared to him, Ed Sullivan is a laughing hyena."

Bob Hope: "I've known Earl since he came to this town from Rockford, Ohio, and he hasn't changed one bit in spite of his great success—he's still shy, modest—retiring—backward—and a sex maniac."

RED BUTTONS

Jan Murray: "I always said Red Buttons would make it in pictures—and I still say he's gonna make it."

DISTRICT ATTORNEY WILLIAM CAHN

Joey Adams: "He's been campaigning against pornography and he doesn't even have a pornograph—He sees every dirty show three times before he makes an arrest—it takes him that long to catch on—Either that, or he's getting rid of his pimples."

HERMAN BADILLO

Don Rickles: "This great Puerto Rican leader did a lot for this country—The only trouble is he did it in my neighborhood."

DR. ALLYN ROBINSON, PRESIDENT OF DOWLING COLLEGE

Ray Heatherton: "Do you know how he avoids sex on his campus?—He steps, carefully."

Paul Townsend: "It's not easy to get into his college—you have to have A in pot."

PERLE MESTA

Joey Adams: "Mrs. Mesta—the hostess with the mostess—has been giving parties for every famous politician from Eisenhower to Woodrow Wilson to Aaron Burr, Chester Arthur, Eugene Victor Debs, and Kaiser Wilhelm—In fact, it was our Perle who was responsible for the Boston Tea Party."

JOEY ADAMS

The roast is the highest tribute you could give a guest of honor these days. It's not necessary to give him a hand—a finger will do—In fact, I preferred it when the boys got together at the Waldorf recently to squeeze a grapefruit and me.

If you were to take a bunch of comedians of different sizes, styles, and shapes and shove them into one room, you'd probably go nuts, which is what happened when the March of Dimes voted me the Man of the Year and gave me a roastimonial dinner at the Waldorf-Astoria.

Earl Wilson was the toastmaster and started lovingly: "It's about time we turned the tables and gave *you* a dinner—I think you're the funniest of all—not your comedy—the way you dress."

Jack Carter: "Joey claims he's a self-made man—next time I hope he calls in somebody else."

Henny Youngman: "Joey would be more popular if he were as well known as his jokes."

Jack E. Leonard: "Adams is living proof of reincarnation—nobody could be this dumb in just one lifetime."

Bob Hope: "Joey is the good-will ambassador for the President in Southeast Asia—I saw him recently in Vietnam. He is so popular there—they were shooting at him from *both* sides."

Don Rickles: "The things he does for his friends can be counted on his little finger."

Harry Hershfield: "When Joey was a boy, he dated a beautiful girl whose father objected because he was an actor. After seeing him work, the old man said: 'That's okay—you can marry my daughter —you're not an actor.'"

Myron Cohen: "Joey is one of the most sought-after people in the country today—for income tax evasion."

Governor Nelson Rockefeller: "From the moment I picked up Joey's book until I laid it down, I was convulsed with laughter—Someday I intend to read it."

Mayor John Lindsay: "Joey is a very humble man—and he's got a lot to be humble about."

Soupy Sales: "I'm glad to be here tonight because there is only one Joey Adams—I found that out by looking in the telephone directory—This boy has a lot of talent, but it's in his wife's name."

Milton Berle: "Joey has a great sense of humor. He doesn't care who's it is."

Henry Morgan: "I don't know what I'm doing here—I'm pretty unique—Nobody even invited me to this thing."

Steve Allen: "Maybe nobody invited Henry—I'm even more unique—Henry invited me—Joey always felt he could write. One day, in one of those cheap magazines, he spied an ad that said, 'How do you know you can't write?' Seeing that ad fired Joey to send his jokes, anecdotes, and other masterpieces. One month later he received a telegram which said, NOW YOU KNOW YOU CAN'T WRITE!"

Horace McMahon: "Everybody knows that the late Mayor Fiorello La Guardia raised Joey—But what they don't know is that La Guardia was a parole officer at the time."

Red Buttons: "Fooling around with charity has made Joey a very rich man—Joey works for every charity committee—The other day he joined an organization so small, they didn't have a disease yet."

Jan Murray came on furious: "I don't understand this whole bit. Who the hell elected him Man of the Year? We started together. I'm better looking than him. I have my own TV show—I work the finest clubs in the country. He's made Man of the Year and I can't even get chosen Jew of the block!

"Don't you think it's a little incongruous? They give this little jerk a big dinner at the Waldorf-Astoria—and Bernard Baruch sat on a park bench by himself. Don't you think it's blasphemous when Joey gets a plaque and Albert Schweitzer's trophy room was empty? Don't you people notice anything wrong? Here Joey is being honored by the March of Dimes and Dr. Jonas Salk can't get an interview on a local radio show."

Cindy Adams (I knew my darling wife would save me—for the knockout): "We've been wed for a long time and I think married life is wonderful—it's just Joey I can't stand—I find it hard to forget that Joey Adams is the world's foremost authority on humor today—and so would you if you had to write it on the blackboard five hundred times before you got your first mink coat."

To me, those were the sweetest sounds I ever heard. Roasting is a comic's way of kissing—and it meant they all loved me.

How do you thank a lifetime of friends who showed up with their money and their talent to help the March of Dimes and embrace a fellow minstrel? Some did it with a song—others with a gag. I could only think of one little poem that said it all for me:

> True friendship is like an old oak tree,
> When bending to the blast.
> It sinks its roots in safety
> And holds on to the last.
> And so it is with old-time friends,
> We'll never let them go.
> Until our earthly trouble ends,
> Because we love them so.

I can hardly wait to hear what I got to say

You can tell a pro by the way he walks to the microphone. You know from the very beginning that he's the boss. That's because he's ready. He knows where the laughs are because they all passed the test a thousand times.

I introduced Bob Hope grandly at a Boy Scout luncheon. In accepting the accolades, he grinned: "After that intro—I can hardly wait to hear what I got to say." That's because he saw the jokes his writers had written for him and he couldn't wait to try them out—and you better laugh or he'll never show up at any of your wars.

Another tip from Bob—he never uses any extra words. He cuts the joke right down to the funny bone.

The trouble with most speakers or storytellers is their inability to get to the point. They have a two-minute idea with a two-hour vocabulary. That's why they say talk is cheap—there's more supply than demand. Don't ad-lib; write your story, joke, gag, or toast down to the punch lines and you got to come out the winner.

The greatest after-dinner speech I ever heard was: "Waiter—bring me the check!"

A speech is like a love affair—any fool can start it—but to end it requires considerable skill. That's why you have to plan your talk, rehearse it and try it out on anybody who will listen, and then deliver it like you know where the laughs are.

There is only one sure way to stay awake during an after-dinner speech—*deliver it*—And if you deliver it with confidence and to the point—your audience will stay awake, too.

I don't guarantee to make you a great comic or a silver-tongued orator just by giving you my gag file. You couldn't expect to become a famous painter just because Picasso handed you his paint brush—even a house painter needs experience. You're not going to become a Hemingway or even a Joey Adams just because you borrowed Mickey Spillane's typewriter. Even a sexpot needs experience. I'm sure Elizabeth Taylor wasn't as great with her first few husbands. Even sex gets better as you grow older. As Dr. David Rubin says: "Use it or lose it."

The more time you put in—the more you are bound to succeed—
That goes for painting, writing, sex, or telling jokes.

When you're up there at the microphone—you are Picasso, Hemingway, Elizabeth Taylor, or Bob Hope—if you believe it. Remember
that if anybody in that audience could do it—they'd be up there
instead of you—so don't be nervous. . . .

I remember opening at the Steinway Theater in Astoria with the
five-times world champ Tony Canzoneri. It was his debut as an
actor and we were getting fifty dollars for the four days to break in
our act. After three weeks of rehearsing, Tony showed up five minutes before the curtain that first morning. I was furious—or as furious as you can get with a five-times champ. "Where the hell were
you?" I screamed. "We go on in a few minutes—aren't you nervous?"

"Nervous?" he asked quietly. "Why should I be nervous? I'm rehearsed—I know the act.—Anyway, I fought a guy called Barney Ross
that could knock your head off with a right or a left. There were
twenty thousand people at Madison Square Garden who paid to
come in—I got $250,000 for that fight. Here I'm getting a dollar and
a quarter a show—there are eleven people in the audience and I can
lick any one of them.—What the hell do you want me to be nervous
about?"

If you know the jokes—and you're rehearsed—and you got the
mike—you can lick anybody in that audience—so what is there to be
nervous about?

Some speakers write it all down and then record it—and play it
back—then if it sounds good to you—it will sound good to the audience.

And tell the story like it's your own. I am not a believer in quoting
others unless it suits my purpose for the switch bit. For instance, I
will quote a Will Rogers line only to turn it around: "Will Rogers
once said, 'I never met a man I didn't like'—Well, conversely, I never
met a man that doesn't like our guest of honor, Earl Wilson," or to
switch it another way: "Will Rogers once said I never met a man I
didn't like—I had a girl once that felt the same way."

Don't misunderstand, I think Oscar Wilde, George Bernard Shaw,
Shakespeare, and that bunch said some very clever things—but if the
people running the dinner wanted *their* opinion, *they* would be invited to speak at the dinner—although I admit it would be tough to
dig them up just for one banquet.

It's *your* words they want to hear—*your* opinions—*your* cracks—

your insults—*your* love—that's why *you* are up there and not the man or woman you're quoting.

The main thing is to believe what you say and say only what *you* believe.

If you must quote somebody to bring out your point—put your own tag on it so that now it becomes *your* story:

"Never put off for tomorrow what you can do today—There may be a tax on it tomorrow—"

"This is a great country where anybody can get to be President—that's one of the risks he has to take."

Another trick is to start a quote and finish it with your own punch line to suit your purpose:

"It is better to have loved and lost—much better."

"A friend in need—is a pest."

"A fool and his money—are some party."

"He who hesitates—loses his seat on the bus."

"As Adam said to Eve in the Garden of Eden—'Who's going to know?' "

"People who live in glass houses—should use their neighbor's bathroom."

"A house divided—brings in more rent."

"I'm writing a new book called *Everything You Always Wanted to Know About Sex—But Were Afraid to Ask Your Children.*"

"You only live once—but if you do it right—once is enough."

"She comes from a long line—that her mother listened to—"

The gag file, a to Z

Here comes the jokes. Study well before using. Then cut them down to your size and try them out—even if your audience is only a mirror—Then when you're called on—hit the line hard!

There is no such thing as an old joke. If you never heard it before—it's new. You'll never live to be as old as the jokes you hear at banquets—but if they fit or if you tell them well—go ahead. You can't change your act every day—it's easier to get a new audience. In England, the audience often holler up for you to repeat an old joke they heard you tell before.

It reminds me of the old gag about the comics sitting around the table at Lindy's. They were all throwing numbers at each other from the joke files. "Twenty-three," said Berle and everybody laughed. "Sixteen," said Hope and the others screamed. "Thirty-four," said Gleason and they banged the table. I said, "Sixty-five," and nobody even smiled. "That's a good joke," I yelled. "Why didn't you laugh?" Berle said, "I don't like the way you tell it."

A good joke or story or gag will never die if it's told right and if it fits. After all, where would Beethoven and Bach be if you only played their music once? Burt Bacharach and Hal David would starve if you turned off the TV or radio every time one of their tunes came on—just because you heard it before.

But just like Beethoven, Bach, or Bacharach, you got to be rehearsed to make them sound good.

It's a good idea to have stories or lines ready on all subjects in case you run into an audience or a situation—and it's funnier if it fits. It's not so good if you say, "I got a friend who is so cheap—he won't pick up a check unless it's made out to him." But if you use the same line on Jack Benny or a specific friend who is known to sit with his back towards the check—then it's more effective.

Likewise, it's stronger to use a line like "Never put off until tomorrow—what you can do at overtime rates today" at a union convention than at a religious meeting. Conversely, a better line at the church social would be: "I know a man who wrote a book on atheism—and then prayed it would be a best seller."

The only category you have to be careful about are political jokes

—some of them could get elected—We got enough comedians in Washington right now.

Here is your personal gag file—with jokes, stories, gags, and anecdotes looking for a home. All you have to do is lift them out and claim them as your own—and then fit them into your routine.

These are all the tools you need for any emergency. All you have to do is play the index for the joke, story, line, or insult from A for Age to Z for Zsa Zsa.

If you're looking to do a routine on ecology—look up P for Pollution or P for Politicians or M for Mother-in-Law.

If you are on a political kick—look up D for Democrats, R for Republicans, or C for Crooks. If you want to talk about an honest politician look up P for Psychiatrist or C for Cemetery.

If you're talking about a conservative—look up R for Retarded. If it's the left you are interested in—look up C for Communist or C for China or M for Mao or R for Russia.

If you come home late for dinner, you can pick your excuse from many categories; O for Office or C for Cheating or T for Traffic or D for Drinking.

We have ethnic jokes and religious stories—from the Bible to the Borscht Belt. Look under I for Italy or J for Jewish—C for Church or B for Bible or C for Christian Science. You'll find Black humor and Irish humor—Polish, Puerto Rican, and Scotch humor—all looking to be adopted by some nice family.

If you want lines about Texas, look up M for Money or B for Big or E for Exaggerate. If it's rich jokes you're after—you'll find them under R for Rockefeller, M for Money, T for Texas, I for Inflation, or T for Taxes.

There are stories from Sex to Boy Scouts to Sexy Boy Scouts—from Booze to Broads to Boozed-up Broads.

If you need happy jokes—look in the index under B for Bachelor or P for Prostitution. You will find Berle, Hope, and Youngman—old friends, with jokes to match. We also have the wit of George Bernard Shaw, Will Rogers, and Fred Allen—which Berle, Hope, and Youngman are still using.

Agnew is here, as well as Nixon, with lines to love them or leave them. There are heckle lines (look under I for Insults or S for Squelch) for your friends or foes.

Here is a lifetime of research that I give to you free. Use them with my blessing—they belong to you now. If you steal one joke, it's plagiarism—if you steal a lot of jokes—it's research—I did all the research for you—so be my guest.

If you do all these gags—from A to Z—I do not promise you'll be the greatest thing since Will Rogers or even Henny Youngman—but you will know the alphabet better. On the other hand, if you are a big hit—let me know and I'll try them myself—

a

Abortion

Doctor: This is the fourth time you have been here for an abortion —Is it the same man?
Patient: Yes, Doctor, why do you ask?
Doctor: Well, I know it's none of my business, but why don't you marry him?
Patient: He don't appeal to me!

"What do you think of the Abortion Bill?"
"I think we ought to pay it."

She: How many times have you had to worry about raising money for an abortion?
He: Many more times than you, madame.

Absent-minded

"What's Dick's last name?"
"Dick who?"

The professor mislaid his umbrella and went from store to store to find it. When he finally traced it he was jubilant. "You are the only honest shopkeeper in town," he told the owner. "All the others denied having it."

I was taking a course to improve my memory—but I've forgotten where the school is.

He was so absent-minded, he parked his car in front of the loan company.

This executive was so absent-minded, he took his wife to dinner instead of his secretary.

Secretary: "Your husband is so absent-minded that last night I had to keep reminding him that he's married to you and not to me."

How absent-minded can you get? The waitress kissed her boyfriend good-night and then said, "Is that all, sir?"

An elephant never forgets—but then what has he got to remember?

He threw his cigar out the window and forgot to let go.

He cut his finger and forgot to bleed.

The man was lying in the gutter in his pajamas. He explained to the cop, "As far as I can remember it, my wife and I were sleeping in bed when there was a knock on the door. My wife said, 'Good heavens—It's my husband' and the first thing you know—I jumped out the window."

The absent-minded auto mechanic was out in a motorboat when the engine stalled and he got out to get under and fix it.

Accidents

They say that 97 per cent of accidents are in the kitchen—I figure my wife cooked quite a few of them.

Pat Cooper says his wife worries about accidents—The other day she put a safety mat in the birdbath.

The Seventh Avenue manufacturer was hit by a car while crossing the street. As he lay there in pain a little old lady put his head in her lap and asked, "Are you comfortable?" He answered through his agony, "I make a living."

My father had a slight accident but he won't be back at work for a long time—compensation set in.

My brother-in-law was in a bad accident. He threw a cigarette in a manhole—and then stepped on it.

"It's a lucky thing for you this accident happened in front of a doctor's house."
"Yeah, but I'm the doctor."

The Scotsman was in a bad accident. He lit a bomb and hated to throw it away.

Actors

Lionel Barrymore was asked by a reporter if he still found acting as much fun as it used to be. "Look, son," said Barrymore, "I'm seventy-five years old—nothing is as much fun as it used to be."

Two old-time actors met at the Lambs in the early days of TV. "What do you think of the new medium?" one asked. "Great," the other responded, "just great—I can see a whole new field of unemployment opening up."

Michael Wilding: You can pick out actors by the glazed look that comes into their eyes when the conversation wanders away from themselves.

Sir Ralph Richardson: The art of acting consists of keeping people from coughing.

George Bernard Shaw: His trouble is that he is in love with his wife—and an actor can only afford to be in love with himself.

Somebody asked a famous actress what it had been like acting with her latest leading man. She answered, "Like acting with a ton of condemned veal."

Actor Lou Jacobi happened into a broken-down restaurant and spotted a fellow-actor sweeping the floor. "I can't understand," Lou cried. "Someone with your talent working in a joint like this?"
    "At least," snapped the other, "I don't *eat* here!"

Groucho: I have no advice to young struggling actors. To young struggling actresses, my advice is to keep struggling. If you struggle long enough you will never get in trouble and if you never get in trouble, you will never be much of an actress.

The difference between an actor and a civilian: When the civilian's house burns down he calls his insurance agent; when an actor's house burns down he calls his press agent.

"How could you stand up in court and say you're the greatest living actor of all time?" the agent asked his client. The ham pulled himself up to his full five-foot-two. "I was under oath—I didn't want to commit perjury."

The famous Jewish star entertained many young ladies in his dressing room. After one matinee—and there was no show on stage that day—the matinee idol handed the girl a pass for his performance that night. "But," she pleaded, "I'm hungry—I need bread!" "If you want bread," he emoted, "make love to a baker. I'm an actor—I give passes."

The first film made by Alfred Lunt and Lynn Fontanne, entitled *The Guardsman,* was good, but they, perfectionists that they are, were unsatisfied. Miss Fontanne was the first to view the film's rushes, and she sped back to their suite where her husband was waiting and burst into tears.

"Alfred, Alfred!" she cried. "We're ruined! I've seen the rushes. You photograph without lips and I come out old and haggard and ugly and my tongue is thick and I lisp and I stumble around ungracefully. I look like I forgot my lines and my feet are big and my clothes look like a sack on me!" Just then her tears overcame her voice and she faltered. In the silence that ensued, Lunt muttered, "No lips, eh?"

An actor has three salaries: the one he thinks he ought to get; the one he really gets; and the one he tells the income tax collector he gets.

Emil Cohen swears a lady came up to him at the end of a performance and asked if she could get a script of his act. "Is it printed anywhere, can I buy a copy?" He said, "I'm not that well known. Mine will probably be published posthumously." She said, "Oh, that's wonderful. I hope it'll be soon."

Stanley Myron Handelman says, "I once did a magic act and one night there was only one guy in the audience, and I needed a volunteer. He wouldn't come up because he wanted to see the show."

Alfred Hitchcock: I never said actors are cattle—I said they should be treated like cattle."

Somebody said about the big-headed star, "I hear he's changing his faith." "You mean," asked the other, "he no longer believes he's God?"

An actress explained her bit part in an off-Broadway play, "I have even less to say than I have to wear."

Lou Jacobi defined an actor as a guy who takes a girl in his arms, looks tenderly into her eyes, and tells her how great he is.

She sued him for divorce—and named his mirror as correspondent.

John Barrymore: One of my chief regrets during my years in the theater is that I couldn't sit in the audience and watch me.

Mrs. Patrick Campbell described Basil Rathbone: "He's got a face like two profiles stuck together." And another time she said about the man who played Sherlock Holmes: "He looks like a folded umbrella taking elocution lessons."

A fan club is a group of people who tell an actor he's not alone in the way he feels about himself.

Advertising

Dick Jacobs of the Joseph Jacobs Organization has a great way to convince you of the importance of advertising. "Doing business without advertising," says Dick, "is like winking in the dark at a pretty girl—You know what you are doing but nobody else does."

Herb Stiefel of Stiefel-Raymond was told by one of his clients, a food concern, that he was stopping all advertising to save money. "You might as well stop your watch to save time," Herb answered.

Did you ever notice that the man who writes the bank ads is never the man who makes the loans?

You do know that sometimes advertising can give you the wrong ideas. One girl I know swears that her living bra bit her.

Ben Eisenstadt of Sweet 'n Low tells me he got the idea for his sugar substitute when he asked a neighbor's little girl, "And what will you do, my dear, when you are as big as your mother?" And the kid answered, "Diet!"

Marvin Eisenstadt warns, "When dieting, remember—what's on the table is sure to wind up on the chair."

The Sweet 'n Low people now have a tonic for fatheads and a pill for fat mouths.

American Airlines has come up with some great advertising gimmicks. Wider seats for fat astronauts, lending toy libraries, and wardens for kids to keep them out of their mother's hair and their father's drink. Now you won't have to send the kids "outside" to play.

American advertises that they care about you. And they do. They are the cleanest and neatest airline—under each wing they have a deodorant pad.

On one 747 trip, from L.A. to New York I was sitting around the piano singing songs and swapping stories with some of the big guys in advertising at A.A., Bernal Quiros, Brian Dwyer, and Paul Gold.

Naturally, they all came up with flying stories. Bernal Quiros said, "In China, the space program was hit with a terrible blow when with only minutes to go before take-off the astronaut ate the fortune cookie that held the flight plan."

Brian Dwyer reminded us of the pilot on a plane who said, "I have good news and bad news. First the bad news—we're doing 750 miles an hour, 32,000 feet—but we're lost. Now for the good news—we're making very good time."

Naturally, I came up with some other good-news, bad-news bits. The agent called the actor and told him, "I have good news and bad news. First the good news. We can buy that beautiful estate in Beverly Hills that you like so much for only $380,000. Now the bad news. They want $200 in cash as a down payment."

Did you hear about the husband and wife who went to see the doctor? After examining the wife the doc told the husband, "I have good news and bad news. First the bad news—your wife has VD—And now the good news—you didn't give it to her."

Paul Gold came up with the story of the reporter who went to see one of the big generals at Cape Kennedy to find out how accurate their missiles are. "Well," said the general, "from Cape Kennedy we can hit targets in Miami, Fort Lauderdale, and Tampa."

"How about Soviet targets?" the reporter wanted to know. "Can you hit Russian targets?"

"Sure," the general answered. "If they're located in Miami, Fort Lauderdale, or Tampa."

Talk about honest advertising. I saw this sign in the window of an antique shop: COME IN AND BUY WHAT YOUR GRANDMOTHER THREW AWAY.

David Stone, the product manager for Instant Yuban Coffee says, "To sell something, tell a woman it's a bargain—tell a man it's deductible."

Yuban has a reverse-advertising story. They say it costs about 1/4 cent more for each cup of coffee. But think of the rich executive who has two secretaries—one for each knee. Imagine the cost of his coffee breaks.

Oscar Rose who sells Yuban for us on WEVD swears that a bum approached him and asked for twenty and one-fourth cents for a cup of coffee—"because I only drink Yuban."

Dick Rettig of Whitehall Laboratories is one of the giants who knows the meaning of good public relations. He sells Anacin but he gives you good advice to go with it. "The best way to avoid a cold," he explains, "is to drink water—lots and lots of water. Did you ever see a fish with a cold?"

Dick tells this story which has some kind of moral to it—figure it out for yourself. The lady walked over to the man standing on the corner and asked, "How many cigars do you smoke a day, sir?"

"Oh—about twenty, I would say."

"Twenty?—How much do you spend for them?"

"Oh, about fifty or sixty cents apiece."

"That's more than ten dollars a day. How long have you been smoking?"

"At least twenty-five years."

"Ten dollars a day for twenty-five years—You realize how much money that is?"

"I guess I do."

"Well—do you see that big office building across the street?"

"Yes."

"Well, if you never smoked a cigar in your life you might now own that fantastic building."

"Do you smoke, madam?"

"No—and I never did."

"Do you own that building?"

"No."

"Well, I do."

Harry Riley is the president of Sunshine Biscuits and is proud of the fact that his product is stacked as well as Raquel Welch. Being a brilliant, intelligent, and discerning executive he hired me to advertise Sunshine on my radio show. Would you say I was sort of a wise-cracker for Sunshine Biscuits? Okay, I'll go quietly.

Mr. Riley has always felt that any good product needs a good-will ambassador. And talking about diplomacy—Harry proves it. One widow asked Mr. Sunshine to guess her age and he answered, "I hesitate to answer—only because I don't know whether to make you ten years younger because of your looks—or ten years older because of your intelligence."

One TV station went on the air to say, "Quit smoking and you'll really be able to taste food." I know one man who took the advice. He quit smoking completely. "Now," he said, "I can really taste food —and I find I've been eating a lot of things I don't like."

The big-business man was complaining that, "Advertising costs me a lot of money."

"But," his friend said, "I never see your merchandise advertised."

"They aren't—but my wife reads other people's ads."

There's one thing in this country I can't figure out: Streets aren't safe, parks aren't safe, and subways aren't safe, but under our arms we have complete protection.

Advertising is 85 per cent confusion and 15 per cent commission.

You can wear this suit in the rain. It shrinks, but you can wear it in the rain.

Talk about progressive advertising: This department store ad offered in a local New York paper, "Maternity dresses—for the modern miss."

Africa

A man in Africa had a frightening experience. He lost his guide, wandered into the jungle, and suddenly he was surrounded by hostile natives. Then he remembered a trick he'd seen in an old movie. He scratched in his pocket for his cigarette lighter, pulled it out, flicked it once, and a big flame popped up. Then the chief spoke up. "It's a miracle," he said. "I've never seen a lighter that worked the first time."

"I once came across a tribe of wild women who had no tongues," the lecturer was saying. "Fascinating," squealed the lady in the first row. "How could they talk?"

"They couldn't ma'am—that's what made them wild."

The missionary was preaching to the African tribe, "We all must love each other."

"Moola Goola," hollered the natives.

"We all must live like brothers," the white man continued.

"Moola Goola," they all cried out.

The missionary was so pleased with his reception and said so to the chief of the tribe. "Thank you for coming," said the chief, "but be careful as you pass my cattle that you don't step in the Moola Goola."

Age

Dave Barry tells this: My mother-in-law is a widow. She is eighty-two years old. One night, just to get her out of the house, I arranged a date for her with a man who is eighty-five years old. She returned home from the date very late that evening, and more than a little upset. "What happened?" I asked. "Are you kidding?" she snapped. "I had to slap his face three times!" "You mean," I answered, "he got fresh?" "No," she replied, "I thought he was dead!"

Marlene Dietrich: I've been asked if a man pushing sixty should continue to exercise in order to maintain his physique. I always felt that pushing sixty is exercise enough.

Bernard Baruch on his eighty-fifth birthday: To me old age is always fifteen years older than I am.

Maybe it's true that life begins at forty. But everything else starts to wear out, fall out, or spread out.

There are three signs of old age—the first is your loss of memory—the other two I forget.

You're getting old when you don't care where your wife goes—just so you don't have to go along.

I'm at the age now when I go out with a girl I can't take yes for an answer.

He's so old he doesn't learn history—he remembers it.

"From birth to age eighteen, a girl needs good parents. From eighteen to thirty-five she needs a good personality. From fifty-five on, she needs good cash."

The ninety-year-old man married the nineteen-year-old girl. They were very happy for three months and then he passed on. It took three days just to wipe the smile off his face.

The bride was disconsolate in spite of the fact that he left her $35,000,000. Her friends tried to make her understand. "You are so young—You have a great life ahead—and $35,000,000—he had to go sooner or later."

"You don't understand," she sobbed, "he was the greatest lover. We lived next door to a church—and he used to make love to me by the sound of the church bells—Ding....Dong....Ding....Dong....If it wasn't for that damn fire truck he'd be alive today."

Middle age is when work is a lot less fun and fun a lot more work.

Statistics prove that at the age of seventy there are five women to every man. Isn't that the damndest time for a guy to get those odds?

I must be getting old. I threw out a *Playboy* calendar merely because it was last year's.

Did you hear about the beautiful young gal who married an elderly gent worth $85,000,000 and got "Get Will" cards from her friends?

She says she just turned thirty—but she must have made a U-turn someplace.

You're getting on in years when the girls at the office start confiding in you.

That Jackie-Ari marriage is something else—apparently some of those old Greek ruins still work.

Middle age is when it takes longer to rest than to get tired.

By the time a man is wise enough to watch his step—he's too old to go anywhere.

Zsa Zsa Gabor tells about the time her daughter, Francesca Hilton, then fifteen, asked, "Mommy, how old are you?" Replied Zsa Zsa, "I'm twenty-one, darling." Thoughtful pause, then, "Mommy, I have a feeling that someday I may be older than you."

Middle age is when you have stopped growing at both ends—and have begun to grow in the middle.

I'm at the age now where the battle of the sexes is none of my affair.

There's no fool like an old fool—You can't beat experience.

Flip Wilson tells the story about a traveling salesman who was passing through a small hick town in the West when he saw a little old man sitting in a rocking chair on the stoop of his house. The little man looked so contented the salesman couldn't resist going over and talking to him. "You don't look as if you have a care in the world," the salesman told him. "What is your formula for a long and happy life?" "Well," replied the little old man, "I smoke six packs of cigarettes a day, I drink a quart of Bourbon every four hours, and six cases of beer a week. I never wash and I go out every night." "My goodness," exclaimed the salesman, "that's just great. How old are you?" "Twenty-five," was the reply.

He was eighty and she was twenty when they got married. He explained his young bride simply. "I decided it would be better to smell perfume for the remainder of my life than to smell liniment."

The late film star Marie Dressler said, "It's not how old you are—but how you are old."

Of course I'm against sin—I'm against anything that I'm too old to enjoy.

A woman never forgets her age—once she decides what it is.

Dean Martin left a party in Hollywood explaining, "I have to go home now and burp my girlfriend."

The octogenarian went to the psychiatrist to complain about her husband's impotence.
    "And how old is your husband?" the doc asked.
    "He's ninety."
    "When did you first notice his disinterest in you physically?"
    "Well," she said, "the first time was last night—and again this morning."

Did you ever think that even back in the Stone Age, when women wrote down their ages, they were chiseling?

Wife: I don't think I look forty, do you, darling?
Husband: Not now, dear—but you used to.

You can stay young forever if you live modestly, get lots of sleep, work hard, pray daily, and lie about your age.

When a girl starts calling you sir—about the only thing you have to look forward to is your Social Security.

I wouldn't say she's old—but the last time she lit the candles on her birthday cake—it turned into a three-alarm fire.

Harry Hershfield made his first trip to Paris when he was past the Social Security age. He confided to his traveling companion Max Asnas that he wished he'd seen it forty years ago.

"You mean," Max asked, "when Paris was really Paris?"

"No," said Harry, "when Hershfield was really Hershfield."

The old man was letting his hands roam on the pretty young thing's body. "What are you doing," the girl asked, "taking a memory course?"

The two older gentlemen were sitting in their Fifth Avenue club. "Well," said the younger octogenarian, "what will we talk about tonight?"

"One thing," answered the older one. "Let's not discuss sex. What was, was."

I'm at the age now where I only chase girls if it's downhill.

A woman has reached middle age when her girdle pinches and the men don't.

When a pretty girl smiles at a man of twenty, he looks himself over to see what makes him so attractive. When a pretty young thing smiles at a man of forty, he looks around to see who the handsome fellow behind him is—but when a lady of any age smiles at a man of sixty, he looks down to see what's unzipped.

You've reached the point of no return when you would rather have a banker say yes than a beautiful girl.

Now that I have money to burn—my pilot light went out.

When a woman is twenty-one she believes in long engagements—When she's forty-one she doesn't even believe in long introductions.

He's got young blood—but he keeps it in an old container.

He's at the age now when he gets winded playing chess.

You have reached middle age when you are sitting at home relaxing, the phone rings and you hope it isn't for you.

You know you have reached middle age when weight lifting consists of just standing up.

I won't say he's old, but his Social Security number is 2.

He went to see his doctor on his eighty-second birthday and explained he wanted to get married. "Will I be able to expect an heir?" he asked. The doctor, after examining him, explained, "You're heir-minded—but not heir-conditioned."

Two octogenarians sitting at their club—one cracked, "Do you think there's as much love-making going on as there used to be?"
"Yes—but there's a new bunch doing it," wheezed the other.

Kids say everybody has their own bag. Of course, I'm getting to the age when my bag is a hot-water bottle.

I realized I had passed the middle age of no return when my wife told me to pull in my stomach and I already had.

An eighty-two-year-old man married a teen-ager. For a wedding present he gave her a "do-it-yourself" kit.

I asked one eighty-nine-year-old gentleman the secret of his long and healthy life. His answer was direct: "I never smoked, drank liquor, or ran around with girls until I was twelve years old."

The ninety-three-year-old man married the ninety-one-year-old lady and they spent the first three days of their honeymoon just trying to get out of the car.

Don't let age bother you—it's all in the mind. Now I'm past fifty—easy—but every morning when I get up I feel like a twenty-year-old—my luck, there is never one around.

The aging actress was so pleased with the birthday cake they wheeled on stage—If they put all the candles on it we all would have been overcome by heat. "The cake is just lovely," she gushed, "forty candles—forty brilliant candles—one for each year of my exciting life." After a moment of silence—one "friend" spoke up. "Forty?—You must have been burning them at both ends."

A reporter asked the late Lionel Barrymore if he still found acting as much fun as it used to be. "Look, son, I'm seventy-five years old," Barrymore snorted. "Nothing is as much fun as it used to be."

When Charlie got married at the age of eighty-one his friends were aghast—and when they learned his bride was only nineteen they exploded. One pal warned him: "Do you realize that sex with a young girl like that at your age could be fatal?"

"Well," Charlie answered, "if she dies—she dies—so I'll get another one."

"There are four ways you can tell when you're getting old," said eighty-seven-year-old Harry Hershfield. "First is when you forget names—Second is when you forget places—Third is when you forget to zip up—Fourth is when you forget to zip down."

Agnew

A funny thing happened to Agnew last week—he opened his mouth and a foot fell out.

No news—is Agnews.

I like Agnew—He has started more people praying—especially when he's playing golf and they are in the gallery.

If anything happens to Nixon the secret service men have orders to shoot Agnew.

One TV newsman said about Spiro Agnew's speech on TV journalism, "I'd like to have read it in the original German."

The Greeks had a word for it, but Agnew just can't remember it.

I am interested in finding out if Spiro Agnew has his prints in the sidewalk of Grauman's Chinese Theatre in Hollywood—He's so good at putting his foot in it.

Poor Spiro is having trouble brushing his teeth lately. His foot keeps getting in the way.

Airlines

One airline received this letter: "Gentlemen—May I please suggest that your pilots do not turn on the little light that says 'Fasten Seat Belts,' because every time they do—the ride gets bumpy."

One of the commercial airlines recently had a bit of trouble. The pilot had a chance to show his great courage. When both motors caught fire he strapped on his parachute and yelled to his passengers, "Don't anybody panic—I'm going for help!"

Bad weather made for a number of flight delays at an International Airport during one trip . . . Cindy was growing increasingly impatient. When a further delay was announced I walked up to the ticket agent and said, "I don't see why you people even bother publishing a flight schedule." The agent replied in his usual calm, professional tone, "Well, sir, we have to have something to base our delays on!"

I wasn't surprised at Castro's interest in the 747. "No wonder—it has three more bathrooms than Cuba."

El Al is the only airline where you don't have to worry about overweight—you're only in trouble if you're underweight.

Those plane schedules are very important—so we can tell how late we are!

The airlines sent out letters to all the wives of businessmen who used the special half-fare rates asking how they enjoyed the trip. Thousands replied, "What trip?"

With the new jets you can have breakfast in Honolulu, lunch in Tokyo, dinner in Hong Kong, and heartburn in India. The trouble with that jet lag is your timing is always off. Sit down to dinner, you're sexy—You go to bed, you're hungry.

Alimony

That's like pumping gas into another man's car.

Alimony is taxation without representation.

Alimony has one advantage—a husband no longer has to bring his paycheck home to his wife—He can mail it to her.

Marriage is the only business that pays money to one of its partners —after it fails.

Alimony is something that enables a woman to profit by her mistakes.

I don't believe it either—but one Texan was so rich—he was ahead in his alimony payments.

When a woman sues for divorce, there's only one thing she wants —everything.

You never realize how short a month is until you pay alimony.

America

"The thing that impresses me most about America is the way parents obey their children."
                                                    —Duke of Windsor

In America we produce more food than any other country in the world, and more diets to keep us from eating it.

America is still the land of opportunity. Everybody can become a taxpayer.

Most Americans I know drive last year's car, wear this year's clothes and live on next year's earnings.

Analysis

I went to a psychoanalyst for years—and it helped—now I get rejected by a much better class of girls.

"Yes," she explained to the analyst, "I'm a virgin—but I'm not a fanatic about it."

I realized after four years and $10,000 worth of analysis that if I'd had the $10,000 in the first place, I wouldn't have needed the analysis.

Animal Stories

The leopard complained to the analyst that "Whenever I look at my wife I see spots in front of my eyes." "Nothing to worry about, Mr. Leopard," said the doc. "But, Doc, she's a zebra!"

Phil Brito says his wife bought a parrot but as soon as she brought it home it started to use a stream of vile language. She took the bird back to the shop. "I don't want this bird. He keeps screaming for whiskey and uses the foulest language." Said the man, "Don't be too critical, lady, just be happy he doesn't gamble."

As the caterpillar said to the butterfly, "You'll never get me up in one of those things."

Did you hear about the widowed alligator? His wife is an old bag.

The male elephant watching a female elephant wiggle by: "Wow—a perfect 250 by 210 by 400."

This is Jack Carter's favorite horse story: A man went to a ranch to buy a horse, pointed at one and said, "My, that's a beautiful pony right there. What kind is it?"
"That's a Palomino," said the rancher.
"Well, any friend of yours is a friend of mine. I'd like to buy that pony," said the man.
The rancher replied: "I gotta tell you, sir, it was owned by a preacher man. If you want the horse to move, you say, 'Good Lord.' If you want the horse to stop, you gotta say 'Amen.' "
"Let me try that horse," said the buyer. He mounted and said, "Good Lord."
The horse promptly moved out and was soon galloping up in the mountains. The man was yelling, "Good Lord, Good Lord," and the horse was really moving. Suddenly he was coming up to the end of the cliff and, panic-stricken, he yelled, "Whoa, whoa." That didn't work and then he remembered and said, "Amen."
The horse stopped right on the end of the cliff and, wiping his brow with relief, the man said, "Good Lord!"

Ken Friedman says, "I have bad luck with pets. I just bought a centipede and it turns out that it has one hundred cases of athlete's foot."

Then there's my parrot. It comes from a tough neighborhood and refuses to talk without an attorney.

Lou Jacobi told of the football game in which elephants were playing bugs. The first half, the elephants beat the bugs 40–0; in the second half, the bugs came back and beat the elephants 85–40. The elephant captain asked the bug captain, "What happened? We were beating you 40–0 and you came back to beat us 85–40?" The bug captain said, "We put a centipede in the second half." The elephant captain asked, "Why didn't you put him in the first half?"
The reply was, "Well, he was putting on his shoes."

The dog walked into the agent's office and asked for a job. "My God," said the agent, "a talking dog—I'll get rich." His secretary said, "Don't be an idiot, dogs can't talk."—"But I just heard him —He talked—a talking dog."—"I told you—dogs can't talk—it's that wise guy cat of mine—he's a ventriloquist."

A middle-aged man, after retiring, decided he wanted to be a big-game hunter. He bought himself an outfit and went off to Africa. He was not in the jungle fifteen minutes when he saw a man-eating lion. The man got so excited he dropped the gun and ran. The lion gave chase and just as it got ready to pounce, the man fell on his knees and started praying. The lion saw this and fell on its knees also. The man looked up, and said, "Are you praying, too?" "Not me," replied the lion contemptuously, "I'm just saying grace before dinner."

A sweet young lady oyster was confiding to her girlfriend about her romance with a dashing young lobster. "He's dark, handsome, and real smooth. He took me to that secluded rock near the sound bar, looked into my eyes, whispered sweet nothings in my ear and . . ." As she uttered these last words, she clutched at her throat, "Oh, good heavens, my pearls."

The two explorers were going through the jungle when a ferocious-looking lion appeared on the track in front of them. "Keep calm," said the first explorer. "Remember what we read in that book on wild animals? If you stand absolutely still and look a lion straight in the eye, he will turn tail and run away." "Fine," said the second explorer. "You've read the book. I've read the book. But has *he* read the book?"

The vicar was taking tea with the old lady and was very impressed with her talking parrot.

"But tell me, dear lady," he said, "why does the parrot have a piece of string tied to each leg?"

"If you pull the string on the right leg," said the old lady, "he sings 'Onward Christian Soldiers.' And if you pull the other string he sings 'Nearer My God to Thee.'"

"What happens," said the vicar, "if you pull both strings at once."

"I fall on my ass, you old fool," said the parrot.

Anniversaries

Wedding anniversaries are the rest periods between rounds.

Henry Ford, when asked on his fiftieth wedding anniversary to give his formula for a successful married life, replied that it was the same formula he had used to make his automobile so successful: "Stick to one model."

Myron Cohen kills people with the story of the happy couple celebrating their twenty-fifth wedding anniversary at their sumptuous home on Long Island. Everybody was happy—that is everybody but the husband. He was glum. When his lawyer came in to congratulate him on his silver anniversary, the husband screamed, "You louze! You doidy dug! You bum! Remember when I waz married five years to dot doidy skunk, end I esked you waht would happen if I stick a knife in her—and you said I would get twenty years in jail? Vell, tonight I would have been a free man!"

Antiques

Pat Henry bought a statue of Venus de Milo. "I got it cheap," Pat said, "because it was an irregular—it had both arms."

He almost got killed. He walked into an antique shop and asked, "What's new?"

My friend bought an antique on credit. After three months he received a letter: "I gave you a genuine French desk that goes back to Louis the Fourteenth. If you don't send me the final payment immediately—it goes back to Shapiro's Antique Shop on the Fifteenth."

If George Washington slept in all those beds that the antique shops claim—no wonder they call him the Father of Our Country.

A smart dealer is a guy who is able to determine when a piece of junk becomes an antique.

Apartments

I never had any luck with apartments. I remember my first apartment. I just got married and I carried my wife over the threshold. She saw the apartment. She said, "Don't put me down."

Co-operative apartments are the greatest. Where else in the winter can you find the janitor banging on the pipes?

Rodney Dangerfield says, "In my apartment building all the tenants have the same pets—cockroaches."

Marvin Braverman says: It's a lifetime job in New York to get a decent place to live. I ran into this landlord. "I was passing the building," I told him, "and I saw a guy jump out the window. I figured maybe I could rent his apartment."

"No, that's already taken by the guy who pushed him out. What do you do for a living? Oh, you're a writer. Remember, we don't allow loud banging on the typewriter."

"I write very softly on a feather cushion."

"Gonna have any furniture? Any friends?"

"No furniture. I'll live in the closet. No friends, either."

"Okay. It's a forty-eight-hour lease. Raise your right hand. Do you, Marvin Braverman, take this apartment 4B for better for worse, in sickness and in health . . ."

When I moved into my apartment the renting agent told me there was a seven-mile view. I found out there's a seven-mile view . . . if I look up.

I was reading about Michelangelo, the Italian painter who spent seven years painting the ceiling of the Sistine Chapel. Seven years to get a ceiling painted? They must have the same landlord I do!

"Darling," he announced to his wife excitedly, "now we don't have to move to a more expensive apartment—the landlord just raised our rent."

Most of the new swank apartment houses don't allow children—and they're very strict, too. In one apartment building on Third Avenue, there's a woman who's so afraid of being evicted—she's in her fifteenth month.

Art

Picasso said it: "The world today doesn't make sense—so why should I paint pictures that do?"

There's only one way you can tell when a modern painting is completed: "If the paint is dry—it's finished."

Trying to figure out abstract art is like trying to follow the plot in a plate of alphabet soup.

Two five-year-old kids were looking at the abstract painting in the Guggenheim Museum. "Let's get out of here," one said, "before they say we did it."

Modern art is what you buy to cover a hole in the wall and then you find out the hole looks better.

I hung the picture because I couldn't locate the artist.

People are still buying fake oil paintings. You have to be so careful these days. I saw one guy trying to sell an "original Rembrandt." He said it was the only picture Rembrandt ever did in ball-point.

It's very obvious what Picasso is trying to say—he needs cash.

He who claims things aren't as bad as they are painted has never seen pop art.

Astronauts

You think you got trouble? I know one astronaut who got on a scale and his fortune said: "Beware of long trips."

We'll really be in trouble if the astronauts form a union—like the taxi drivers. Imagine having to pay them by the mile?

Two Jewish astronauts were talking. One said, "Forget the moon—everybody is going to the moon—we go direct to the sun."
  "But we can't go to the sun. If we get within thirteen million miles of the sun, we'll melt."
  "Okay—then we'll go at night."

When the astronauts found out they were allowed 110 pounds of recreational equipment—they requested Raquel Welch.

Atheist

An atheist is a man who has no invisible means of support.

The atheist says, "There ain't no such thing as hell." The Christian says, "The hell there ain't."

I am really sorry for the poor atheist who is doing good and feels grateful—but he has no one to thank.

b

Bachelor

He loves home-cooked meals—but he has a big choice of cooks.

As the widow said to the bachelor—"Take it from me—don't get married."

A bachelor is a guy who goes to work every morning from a different direction.

Never trust a husband too far—or a bachelor too near.

A bachelor past fifty is a remnant—There is no good material left in him.

A bachelor is a guy who doesn't have to leave a party when he starts having a good time.

Married man to good-looking bachelor: "How in the world have you managed to stay single so long?"
   Bachelor: "It's easy. Every time I look at television commercials I learn that women are anemic, have stringy hair, large pores, are overweight, and have rough hands."

Bald

Joe Garagiola is envious of men with hair: "To people like me—dandruff is a thrill."

This is a great way to defend your bald spot—or to introduce somebody with a bald head: "God made a lot of heads. Those he was ashamed of he covered with a lot of hair."

One thing about being bald—it's very neat.

Bald is great for a guy romancing a girl on the couch. When her parents come in—all he has to do is straighten his tie.

He's either bald—or that's the longest face I ever saw.

My mother told me I would come out on top some day—she's right —I'm getting bald.

He was so bald—he looked like a part with ears.

Bankruptcy

Three chaps had dinner together in a local restaurant the other night and when the time came to pay the check each grabbed for it. "I can charge it to business expenses," said the first. "I'll pay; I'm on cost plus," argued the second. "Give it to me," said the third, definitely. "I'm filing for bankruptcy next week."

"Did you hear about Frank? He went bankrupt—He's paying off sixty cents on the dollar."
"How does he feel?"
"Forty per cent better."

This guy has been going bankrupt for twenty-two years and always had a sign in his window, GOING OUT OF BUSINESS. Now he's opening another store for his son, so his son can go out of business for himself.

Banks

I got a friend who borrowed $10,000 and spent one year opening new bank accounts. He got free radios, TV sets, luggage, clocks, pots, pans, dishes—at the end of the year he gave the ten grand back—and opened his own discount house.

Some fellow held up a bank, he shoved a note to the teller that said, "This is a stickup! Hand over your cash." She shoved a note back to him that read, "Straighten your tie, stupid, we're taking your picture."

The holdup man goes into the bank and whispers to the cashier, "Give me all that money in a bag." The cashier says, "Here, take the books too, I'm $50,000 short."

Jim Farley, the president of Central State Bank, swears one depositor asked for him personally—he wanted a one-cent check cashed. "How do you want it?" asked the patient president. "Heads or tails?"

One woman to another: "Funny thing with checkbooks—once I've started one I can't put it down till I've finished."

The manager of the bank called my wife to tell her she was overdrawn $300. "Tell me," my wife asked, "what was my balance three months ago?" The manager looked it up and said, "Three months ago you had $1,200 to your credit."

"So tell me," my wife scolded, "when that was the situation—did I phone you?"

A local bank teller is worried, reports Pat Cooper. "The bank examiner's due tomorrow, and he's short two toasters and a set of dishes. . . ."

The trouble with most banks is that the man who writes the advertising is not the same guy who lends you the money.

My friend Ray Heatherton, the V.P. of the Franklin National Bank, was boasting that his bank is so big—they have a special window just for holdups.

Two retired bank thieves were talking about all the new branches that were opening, and one said that the stickup business sure has changed. "If we were to try to heist a bank now," he explained, "we'd need two shopping bags, one for the money and the other for the gifts."

I don't trust banks with counting money. If bankers can count, why do they always have eight windows and two tellers?

Barber

A hippie walked into a barbershop and his hair was down to his shoulders. He said to one of the barbers, "Are you the one who cut my hair?" The barber said, "I don't think so. I've only been working here for six months."

Business is so bad in the barbershops—one place on Broadway has this sign in the window: ONE BARBER—NO WAITING.

Advice: "When you go into a barbershop always pick the barber with the lousiest haircut—Remember, they cut each other's hair."

Jack Carter had survived a pretty close shave. When the barber was through, Jack asked for a drink of water: "I want to see if my neck leaks."

Barber: How would you like your hair cut?
Customer: In silence!

Beauty

Phyllis Diller was told she is beautiful on the inside. "Leave it to me," she complained, "to be born inside out."

A thing of beauty is a great expense.

Show me a man who doesn't turn around and look at a beautiful woman and I'll show you a man walking with his wife.

Every time I meet a beautiful girl—either she is married or I am.

Bible

Do you think the three wise men are the guys who got out of the stock market at the right time?

All the trouble started in the Garden of Eden when Eve bit into a piece of fruit. It was nothing compared to the trouble I had when I did the same thing in Mexico.

There are so many headaches in the world today—if Moses would come down from Mount Sinai now—the tablets he would carry would be aspirin.

Eve: Do you love me?
Adam: Who else?

The hardest thing for me to believe about the Bible is that there were only two asses in the ark.

Eve was created from Adam's rib—sometimes I wish he had kept his big side shut.

"Of course I haven't been going with another woman!" said Adam. "You know darn well you're the only woman here."
   Eve was still suspicious. That night she sneaked over to where Adam was sleeping and quietly started counting his ribs.

The eternal feminine problem is always: "What will I wear?" It probably began the day after the initial rebellion, when Eve looked up at the leaves of the fig tree and said, "I wonder which one I will wear today?"

This traveling salesman opened the Gideon Bible in his motel room. On the front page he read this inscription: "If you are sick, read Psalm 18; if you are troubled about your family, read Psalm 45; if you are lonely, read Psalm 92."

He was lonely, so he opened to Psalm 92 and read it. When he was through, he noticed on the bottom of the page the handwritten words: "If you are still lonely call 888-3468, and ask for Myrtle."

Eve to Adam as they were finding out about each other in the Garden of Eden: "But what are we whispering for?"

Joseph, the carpenter, hit his thumb with the hammer and cursed out loud. His son ran in from the other room and asked, "Did you call me, Dad?"

The kid said to the little girl next door, "Let's play Adam and Eve —You tempt me to eat the apple—and I'll give in."

Bigamy

The penalty for bigamy is two mothers-in-law.

The man in Alaska was arrested for bigamy. He had a wife in Nome, another in Fairbanks, and still another in Anchorage. The judge growled at the culprit, "How could you do such a thing?"

"Fast dog team," he replied.

This was an odd bigamist—He married his wife's sister so he wouldn't have to break in a new mother-in-law.

Birth Control

The Italians have no problem with birth control—they have been practicing it for five hundred years—Garlic.

My uncle Harry is furious about America sending $3,000,000 to India just to buy contraceptives: "Couldn't they just do what my wife does? . . . Pretend she's asleep."

Lee Tully says they now have a birth-control pill for men. They've been testing it for two years and after two years they found that not one man became pregnant.

A woman mixed her birth-control pills with saccharin. She now has the sweetest baby in the world.

Milt Moss knows this eighty-year-old woman who went to the doctor for a complete physical examination. The doctor said, "You're in perfect health." "Thank you, Doctor, but I also take birth-control pills," she explained. "What do you take them for?" he asked. "I take them to get rid of my headache." The doctor asked her to please explain. "I live with my granddaughter; a lovely twenty-three-year-old girl. Every morning we get up and have breakfast together. When she's not looking I take the birth-control pill and put it in her coffee —IT GETS RID OF MY HEADACHE.

Birthdays

If you want to know what your wife wants for her birthday—take a peek at what she bought.

Never forget your wife's birthday—just forget which one it is.

This is a great way to sneak out when you have forgotten your wife's birthday: "How do you expect me to remember your birthday, darling, when you never look any older?"

The tailor sent an angry letter to his customer with an enclosed bill that said: "This bill is one year old today," and the answer came back, "Happy Birthday."

He was so old that instead of candles they built a bonfire in the center of the cake.

Wife: Happy birthday, darling, I have a surprise for you.
Husband: Really, what is it?
Wife: Wait a minute, darling, I'll put it on.

Black (Is Beautiful) Humor

There is no gentle humor. Somebody or something must be abused to bring home the point. The black man was the first to do it to survive. Bert Williams was the first of the great black comedians to star on the stage. He was so successful that performers like Eddie Cantor, Al Jolson, Georgie Jessel, and Moran and Mack blackened up to do Negro comedy. Here are some examples of Williams' wit:

"If you have two wives, that's bigamy, if you have many wives, that's polygamy—If you have one wife—that's monotony."

Bert Williams told the story about the man who is brought before the judge for stealing a chicken. The judge couldn't understand how a man could steal chickens with dogs in the yard. "No use to explainin' to you judge," the old Negro answered. "If you tried it you would get eaten up or shot full of buckshot—and get no chicken either. If you want to engage in any rascality, judge, you bettah stick to duh bench whar you am familiar."

The put-down has been the black comic's trick to answer his hecklers: Sam Burns, a southern Negro, was refused entrance in a "white" church. The sexton told him to go to his own church and pray to God and he will feel much better.

The next Sunday he was back again. "Don't get upset," he said to the sexton. "I'm not forcing my way in. I just came to tell you that I took your advice and it came out fine. I prayed to God and he told me, 'Don't feel bad about it, Sam. I've been trying to get into that church myself for twenty years and haven't made it yet!' "

Black humor has come a long way since the lazy prototype. (Benjy says to a loafing black, "Would you like to make a dime?"—"No, boss —I'ze got a dime.")

Another stale one is about the Negro lady who has a man arrested for rape. They are both in court and the judge asks when the rape took place. "Yo honor," says the lady, "I don't exactly remember— but it seems it was just rape—rape—rape—all June, July, and August."

The put-down is used by white comics as well: Marty Allen making like Governor Wallace, answers questions: "Hello dere—I'm George Wallace."

"Tell me, Governor—What's the problem about being a write-in candidate for President?"

"The people who vote for me can't write!"

"Tell me, Governor Wallace, how would you campaign for the Negro vote?"

"By helicopter."

On one occasion the great white evangelist, Sam Jones, preached a sermon to a vast audience of black people. After he finished, a stout old lady waddled up to him, grabbed his hand and said passionately,

"God bless you, Brudder Jones—You is everybody's preacher—black and white—You may have a white skin, brother—but you sure have a black heart."

George Kirby: A young ninety-day-wonder lieutenant just arrived overseas walked up and said to the colored soldier, "Soldier, I'm talking to you—Where is my foxhole?" And the colored soldier said, "Baby—you're standing on it—take that shovel and start digging."

Slappy White: I remember the day I went into the army, all my friends and relatives took me to the airport. You should have heard all the screaming and the crying and the sobbing. Not them. *Me!* And when the sergeant asked me if I wanted a commission, I said, "No, I'm such a poor shot I'd rather work for a straight salary."

Redd Foxx: When I was in the service, there was one battle I'll never forget. I backed up so far I bumped into a general. He said, "Why are you running?" I said, "I'm running because I can't fly."

Black humor has always been a reflection of the times as well as the suffering:

> Here I is head bowed in shame
> Got a number instead of a name.
> I'se got to stay here the rest of my life
> All I did was to kill my wife.

In the same vein the husband is having an argument with his wife and he hollers, "Honey—out of my way before I lose my temper—and I'll go so far—it'll take two dollars to send you a postal card."

Now Black comics hit with their humor from a standing position rather than a kneeling one:

Dick Gregory:

The Presidency: When I ran for the office two years ago, I was the only real candidate for President. The others were running for sheriff.

The FBI: If a nine-year-old can find a dope pusher, why can't the FBI?

Nonviolence: It's a favor and not an obligation, and while I hate to admit it, it has helped the black's cause.

Looters: If you're going to shoot all the looters, make it retroactive and give the Indian a gun.

Spiro Agnew: He's the kind of cat who'd use the hot line to make a crank call to Moscow.

"Space Flights: I heard we've got lots of black astronauts; saving them for the first space flight to the sun.

Wiretaps: They've got so many bugs on my phone, I'm putting roach powder on it.

Washington, D.C.: It's the only place where a guy can hold up a bank and get mugged on his way to the getaway car.

All the new black comics have switched the army jokes to conform with what's happening.

Dick Gregory says he never will forget his first physical exam. The sergeant asked, "What were you in civilian life?" and Dick answered, "Deliriously happy."

Godfrey Cambridge tells about a white airplane traveler who "didn't want to sit next to a black brother—which is a hell of a way to start a plane ride. After all, we may go together." And in his story they almost do. The plane jumps, falls, rocks, and sputters. The white man trembling with fear, is less hostile and Godfrey feels he is making a friend through their mutual adversity. But once the plane is safely on the ground the white man ignores him. Godfrey is now really annoyed and snaps, "Then give me back my hand—and get the hell off my lap."

Dick Gregory says, "Segregation is not so bad. Have you ever heard of a wreck where the people in the back of the bus got hurt?"

Redd Foxx says, "Humor is the greatest weapon in breaking down race barriers." Redd remembers his father saying, "The garbage man is here—better have him leave some."

Always the black humor had to be defensive—or to put it another way—the black comic had to be a counterpuncher. Like the story of the black boy who wasn't too good in algebra. His white teacher told him he should be ashamed. "When George Washington was your age he was a surveyor." And the kid answered, "When he was your age he was President."

Today there's a new brand of black comic. He's clever—poised—informed—involved and tells it like it is:

"What's your handicap?" Sammy Davis was asked on the Golf Course. . . . "Are you kidding?—I'm a one-eyed black man who's Jewish. Any more questions?"

Flip Wilson says, "We've got to do something about the Indians? The Indians aren't ready yet. Now, quite often when I say that, people feel it's a harsh statement. But how harsh it is depends on how you look at it. Now let us ask ourselves this question, 'Do you want to build a $50,000 house and then have an Indian build a wigwam next door?'"

Flip Wilson: I was talking to this Indian—I recognized him because he looks like the guy on the nickel. When he made some smart crack about the Negroes, I read him a list of all the great black baseball stars, including Willie Mays, and I said, "I've never heard of any Indian hitting a home run," and the Indian got the nerve to say to me—"And I've never heard of anyone playing cowboys and colored people."

One of the great storytellers was an old pal of mine, Bill "Bojangles" Robinson. He made all audiences scream with the tale of the little black soldier who tried to leave camp and was stopped by the sergeant. "Where are you going?" "Out." "No you ain't." "Yes ah iz." "You ain't goin' no place," said the sergeant. "Look," said the soldier, "I got a mother in heaven, a father in hell, and a girlfriend in Harlem —and I'm gonna see one of 'em tonight!"

The subjects of black humor about whites has always shown what they consider worth ridiculing. Like the story of the black woman who is asked by a white man to change her seat on a northern bus. He says to her, "If I had you down South you know what I'd do to you?" She answers, "Yeh. You'd come rappin' on my door tonight, and I'd tell you *No!*"

For a long while humor was the only thing the Negro had to hit back with: Reporters asked a rural southern Negro how it felt to reach his hundredth birthday. "Well," he answered, "I'm a hundred years old today and I don't have an enemy in the world." "What rule did you follow to achieve that?" he was asked. "Well—I guess I outlived them all."

Bomb

The inquiring photographer asked me where I would like to be if the big bomb exploded. My answer was simple: "Someplace so I could say, 'What was that?'"

Books

Shecky Greene says he was asked to permit his biography to be written, but insists that it be authentic: "Something like, 'As told to his bookmaker.'"

Dedication: "To my wife—without whom I never would have been able to spend the money I made on my last book."

My book is in the fifth printing—the first four were blurred.

My book is a Book of the Month selection—but you can't make money selling one book a month.

Bob Orben just finished a book that is the saddest story ever told. It's the true story about a single girl who's expecting. She goes to another city leaving a phony forwarding address—checks into a small hospital using a phony name—doesn't write, phone, or tell her family or friends where she is—and gives birth to quintuplets.

The bore had the party underwhelmed with his exploits. "I write at least two books a year," he kept going on and on. "In fact, I just wrote for *Life* magazine."
    "That's nice," said a weary listener, "did they send it to you?"

"Have you read all of Shakespeare's plays?"
"Yes—unless he's written something new lately."

Speak no evil, see no evil, and hear no evil—and you'll never get a publisher to print your book.

The writer admitted that his greatest work of fiction was, "Filling out my income tax return."

Erich Maria Remarque: An author never finishes a book—he abandons it.

There's a new book out called *How to be Happy Without Money* —but it costs fifteen dollars.

Men who can read girls like a book—usually like to read in bed.

Bore

A bore is a man who never seems to have any previous engagements.

Bores are people who talk of themselves when you are thinking of yourself.

He lights up a room—when he leaves it.

They have parties—just not to have him.

He never opens his mouth unless he has nothing to say.

He's very cultured—he can bore you on any subject.

Boy Scouts

He was so in love with her that he offered her everything. "I'll build a home for you atop the George Washington Bridge. I'll get you sable linings for your mink coats. I'll buy you a platinum Cadillac. Just say the word."

"All I want," cooed the beautiful one, "is a solid-gold Boy Scout knife."

"But," said the stunned suitor, "you can have anything in the world."

"That's all I want," cooed the doll.

When he brought her the solid-gold Boy Scout knife, she beamed her thanks. "Is this all you want to make you happy?" he asked. "What are you going to do with it?" She opened a huge hope chest to put the knife inside, thereby revealing hundreds of similar solid-gold Boy Scout knives. "Why?" asked the bewildered lover.

"Well," she explained, "right now I'm very young and beautiful and everybody wants me, but when I get old and not so attractive, and undesirable—can you imagine what a Boy Scout will do for one of these?"

A group of Cub Scouts visited the local FBI office and viewed pictures of the ten most wanted men in the United States. One kid pointed to a picture and asked if that really was the photograph of the wanted person. The agent said yes. "Then why," asked the boy, "didn't you keep him when you took his picture?"

I actually caught a Boy Scout doing his good deed. He was helping a little old lady across the street, and she wasn't even a lady—it was a hippie.

Brides

A newlywed shouldn't expect his first few meals to be perfect—after all, it takes time to find the right restaurant.

Like the bride said on her honeymoon, "And that's what I've been saving myself for, for all these years?"

Bride to groom as they walk down the aisle, "Well—it won't be wrong now!"

Modern brides are wearing their wedding dresses shorter and oftener.

Brides aren't happy—just triumphant.

Budget

What's the big fuss about the Onassises spending $20,000,000 a year? They're still the only couple I know who stay within their budget.

So Jackie and Ari spend $20,000,000 a year—big deal—so does Rhode Island.

Definition of budget? A family quarrel.

Bum

The bum knocked on the door asking for something to eat. "Sure," said the lady of the house, "I'll give you something to eat—if you'll do the dishes afterward and mop the floor."

"Lady," the tramp answered, "I asked for a donation—not a transaction."

The beggar approached the lady and pleaded, "Please, lady, can you give me five dollars?"

"That's a nerve," the lady said, "five dollars?"

"Yeh—I want to quit early tonight."

A panhandler walked up to a man and asked, "May I borrow ten dollars till payday?" He was asked, "When's payday?" To which he replied, "How do I know? You're the one that's working."

The woman lectured the beggar. "How come I always see you around here half drunk?" He answered, "Because I run out of money, lady."

Burlesque

Men always claim they go to burlesque to see the comics. They then bring binoculars to see the comics better.

The stripper was so ugly they were hollering, "Up in front."

She does a very unusual dance—the only thing on her is the spotlight.

My father always warned me not to go to burlesque—There are things I wouldn't expect to see. He was right. The first time I went I saw my father in the first row.

She was barefoot—up to her chin.

Business

Sign on a store: DON'T BE FOOLED BY IMITATORS GOING OUT OF BUSINESS. WE HAVE BEEN GOING OUT OF BUSINESS LONGER THAN ANYONE ON THIS BLOCK.

Sign in the window of a vacant store: WE UNDERSOLD EVERYBODY.

Two business partners are conversing. "I can't understand why we're losing money," says one, "the President insists business is better than ever." Says the other, "Maybe he has a better location than we have."

Mickey Freeman tells this story: Two partners own a clothing store. They take turns minding it. Harry, the one who's at the store, calls his partner at home. He says, "You got to come on down here and congratulate me. I just made a terrific sale—sold that awful electric-purple suit with the big lapels." The partner goes to the store, sees Harry bandaged, bleeding, and says, "What happened?" "The customer's seeing-eye dog didn't like the suit," replies Harry.

The government is still trying to help small business. A little fellow used to make the rounds with a hand organ and a monkey. The government gave him a loan. Now he goes around with a steam calliope and a gorilla.

Two Seventh Avenue merchants were having their weekly cry about business. One said, "Now take June—please—what a month—only returns—horrible—and that was good compared to July—even the customers who don't pay weren't buying. . . ."

"Big deal," said his friend. "You think you got troubles—let me tell you something—yesterday I found out my son is a homosexual and my daughter is a lesbian! Now what could be worse than that?"

"August!" came the answer.

Things are so bad in the garment center—the manufacturers are laying off their sons-in-law.

The dress manufacturer sent this letter to one of his customers: "Dear Sir: After checking our records, we note that we have done more for you than your mother did—we've carried you for fifteen months."

"I have a hundred suits," the cloak-and-suiter was bragging, "and they're all pending."

"I buy a piece of merchandise for one dollar and I sell it for four dollars—you think 3 per cent is bad?"

The big boss stood up before his board of directors and stockholders and said, "This year's financial report is being brought to you in living color—*Red*."

Charlie Cohen and his son were traveling through Italy. They particularly loved Rome. The guide pointed out the Colosseum.

"You see," Charlie lectured his son, "this illustrates what I've always told you—when you haven't got sufficient capital—you don't start to build."

The businessmen were discussing a compatriot: "He used to work for me," said the first one. "I wouldn't trust him with my money. He would lie, steal, cheat—anything for a buck."

"How do you know him so well?"

"How? I taught him everything he knows!"

To get 10 per cent out of him you've got to be at least a fifty-fifty partner.

We're a non-profit organization—we don't mean to be—but we are.

Forget the depression—this bum went broke during the boom. He went bankrupt during his busy season.

"I'm sorry, sir," the manufacturer told the store owner, "I just can't extend you any more credit. Your bill is much bigger now than it should be."

"I know that," said the store owner. "So if you'll make it out for the proper amount, I may pay it."

Whenever the American businessman comes up with a new idea—a month later the Russians invent it—and two months later the Japanese copy it and sell it to us cheaper.

C

Cannibals

The two cannibals sat back and patted their stomachs. "That," one
said to his host, "was an absolutely delightful meal."

"I'm glad you liked it," said the other. "My wife certainly makes
wonderful soup. But I'm sure going to miss her."

Did you hear about the cannibal who was expelled from school?—
They caught him buttering up the teacher.

The missionary was captured by cannibals and thrown into the pot.
Just when he was ready to give up he noticed the cannibal chief fall
on his knees and start to pray. A ray of hope. "Are you a practicing
Christian?" the missionary asked hopefully.

"Of course," said the chief, "and be so good as not to interrupt me
while I'm saying grace."

Cars

In my neighborhood there are so many foreign cars that it has been
two years since anybody has been hit above the knees.

Dick Cavett said, "I don't like to drive those small cars. Every time I
stop at a light, I expect a little kid to come up and say, 'It's
my turn.'"

The truck driver pulled up alongside one of those tiny foreign cars
that was stalled on the highway and yelled, "Whatsa trouble, pal,
need a new flint?"

Jack E. Leonard got a bill for sixty dollars for an auto tune up and
snapped at the mechanic, "Who does your tuning up . . . Leonard
Bernstein?"

If you're out driving—just make sure you have a car.

I love those ads that say the only thing you can hear in a Rolls-Royce
is the clock. In my Rolls I hear everything but the clock—that
stopped.

I remember when $150 was the down payment on a new car—now it's the sales tax.

I think every new car owner gets two shafts—one in the car and the other in the warranty.

I got a friend who really has a problem—How to get his car started in the morning—and his wife at night.

A sign on the road: BE CAREFUL OF OUR CHILDREN—THEY'RE TERRIBLE DRIVERS.

Celebrity

A celebrity is someone who works all his life to become famous enough to be recognized—then goes around in dark glasses so no one will know who he is.

A celebrity is somebody who is known by many people he's glad he doesn't know.

A person who's bored by the attentions of people who formerly snubbed him.

Cemetery

"I can't find my husband's grave," the lady approached the caretaker at the cemetery. "His name is Charles Stein."

The caretaker looked at his records. "I'm sorry, we have no Charles Stein buried here. The only Stein we have is Sylvia Stein."

"That's Charles—He always put everything in my name."

This town is so healthy—they had to shoot a traveling salesman to start a cemetery.

On the tombstone for the old maid: "Who said you can't take it with you?"

The man was crying over three tombstones and explained, "They are my three wives—the first died from eating poisoned mushrooms —the second died from eating poisoned mushrooms—the third from a fractured skull."

"How come?" he was asked.

"She wouldn't eat the poisoned mushrooms."

Charity

Bob Hope, accepting still another plaque at a dinner, said that he had stopped letting such honors go to his head. "I just got a call from a fellow who said I'd been named Man of the Year by his organization because I was America's outstanding citizen, greatest humanitarian and so forth. It was going to be the biggest dinner, biggest civic reception ever. He set the date: April 19. I told him I was sorry, but I was going to be tied up that night. There was a short pause. Then he said, 'By any chance would you have Red Skelton's phone number?' "

The shady lady visited the local community chest and offered, "Honey, I'd like to donate five grand to the chest."

"Madam," said the chairman, "and I don't use the word loosely, we don't need that kind of money."

The cochairman poked him and said, "Take it, jerk—it's our money anyway."

The big-game hunter was lost in the jungle. He was missing for weeks. He built a little shelter and tried to stay alive. They sent a searching party, which got to the shelter just as he was ready to collapse from hunger and fever. The rescuers knocked on the door. "Who is it?" he asked weakly. "The Red Cross," came the brisk answer. "I gave at the office," the dying man said.

I know one charity which collected $3,000,000—and doesn't even have a disease yet.

Cheap

A comedian noted for his thriftiness was described: "He wouldn't offer to buy a round of drinks at an Alcoholics Anonymous meeting."

A girl at Roseland described her penny-pinching date: "He's tighter than a cummerbund around Jackie Gleason."

He's so cheap—if he was at the Last Supper he would have asked for separate checks.

He's always the first to put his hand in his pocket—and the last to bring it out again.

He tries to make every dollar go as far as possible—and every girl too.

He is so cheap that the only time he'll pick up a check is when it's made out to him.

"When it comes to picking up a check—he has a slight impediment of the reach." "He talks through his nose to save wear and tear on his teeth." "He tosses quarter tips around like manhold covers."

He is saving all his toys for his second childhood.

Jack Benny said, "I am Howard Hughes compared to an uncle of mine who is so frugal he bought his daughter a dollhouse with a mortgage on it."

This character is so cheap. His nurse told me he was mad because he got well before all the medicine was gone.

Cheap? His money talks with a stutter.

He has a physical handicap—he's hard-of-spending.

This cheap bum and his wife visited one of the circus airfields where they charge fifty bucks a plane ride just around the town. The couple seemed hesitant until the pilot approached them and propositioned them. "I'll take you and your wife up for nothing. It will be a rough ride—but if you or your wife lets out one single word—one sound—while we are up there—you pay double."

They accepted the proposition and up they went. It was really a rough ride—dives—loops—turnovers. Finally they landed. "You win," the pilot admitted, "not a word or sound out of you."

"No," the cheapskate said, "but I almost did speak when my wife fell out."

He is so cheap he refused to go on the first trip to the moon—he won't go anywhere out of town unless he can stay with relatives.

My aunt is a very economical woman. She replaced the light bulb in the refrigerator with a candle.

Cheating

The politician was late as usual. His opening line to his wife was, "I've just been talking to the senator and he agreed to do everything I want him to do."

"Well," sneered the wife, "first wipe the senator's lipstick off your lips."

I've heard all the alibis but this one takes the prize. She explained to her husband that more people drown in bathtubs than in the ocean or swimming pools—that's why he found her with a lifeguard in her bathtub.

The middle-aged lady had been reading all the stories about the permissive society and the free love, switching and cheating going on in the suburbs. She was interested. "Tell me," she asked the head of her women's club, "how do you start an affair?" "Always the same way," said the lady president. "First with Hatikvah, then the 'Star Spangled Banner,' and then the invocation!"

Mrs. A: I hear you're having an affair.
Mrs. B: That's true.
Mrs. A: So tell me—who's the caterer?

The husband came home and found his wife in bed with a midget. "I forgave you before," he screamed. "You promised only last week when I caught you, you would never cheat again."

"Now don't be angry, darling," she exclaimed. "Can't you see I'm tapering off?"

His wife has always talked about having a catered affair. He never paid any attention to her until he came home unexpectedly and found her in bed with the delicatessen man.

Sixty per cent of the men cheat in America. The rest cheat in Europe.

The couple checked into a motel in Philadelphia opposite a railroad station. In the morning the husband went to see some clients and left his wife in bed alone.

About 9:30 A.M. a train passed and the vibration knocked her out of bed. Ten minutes later another train passed and again the vibration knocked her out of bed. Fifteen minutes later the same thing happened. She finally called the clerk downstairs and told him what she thought of his motel. "I don't believe it," he said. "Come up and see for yourself," she screamed and hung up.

The manager came up full of apologies but still not admitting the lady's claim. "I'm lying in bed," she explained again, "and every time a train passed—the damn vibrations knocked me out of bed."

"I don't believe it," he repeated.

"Okay," she said, "lie down and see for yourself."

He was in bed five minutes when the husband came in. "What the hell are you doing in my bed?" he shouted.

"Believe it or not," the manager cried, "I'm waiting for a train."

The wife approached the girlfriend and asked her to release her husband or else. "Tell you what I'll do," the girl said, "let's be sporting about it. I'll play you one game of gin for him. If I lose I'll give him up—if you lose, you'll give him up—Fair enough?"

"Well," the wife hesitated, "sounds okay to me—but to make it more interesting—let's play for a penny a point."

The story is told of Noah Webster that he was embracing his chambermaid when his wife suddenly entered the room and caught him in the act. "Why, Noah," she said, "I'm surprised."

The great man of words quickly composed himself and said, "No, my pet, you are amazed. It is we who are surprised."

Two neighbors were drinking at the bar when one suddenly spoke up: "Do you like fat sloppy women who roll their stockings down below their knees?"

"I should say not . . ."

"Well, do you like women who always smell from garlic and have false teeth?"

"No, of course not—sounds horrible!"

"Then, tell me, my friend, why are you always trying to date my wife?"

Jack Carter tells the story: A man walks into a hotel and sees a woman in black sitting in a corner crying. "What's the matter?" he asks solicitously. "I'm going to miss him," she says and keeps on crying. The man asks who died. The woman says, "My husband. I knew he ran around, but I'm really going to miss him." The man asks, "When did he die?" "Tomorrow morning," the woman replies.

Adam was the only man who could be sure about his wife—and even then there was that snake in the grass who tried to make trouble.

It's Lon Ritchie's story about the jealous husband who was sure his wife had a boyfriend, so he hired a detective to shadow her and take movies of what he saw. A few weeks later the detective reported with the film. "Well, here it is," he said, "all the evidence . . . and with your best friend, too!"

He ran the film and the husband saw the pictures of his wife and his best friend as they ate lunch, took a swim, bowled, danced, and had a real good time. After a while the husband shook his head and said, "I just can't believe it, I just can't believe it!"

"But," replied the detective, "the evidence is all here."

"No," answered the husband, "that's not what I mean . . . I just can't believe that my wife could be so much fun."

Sam warned his best friend about marrying the local playgirl: "Do you realize this girl has partied every guy in your town?"

"So what—I come from a very small town."

"Did you hear about Sam getting shot when Tom found him in bed with his wife?"

"It could have been worse."

"How?"

"If it was the night before—it could have been *me*."

I heard about a man who had to stay home sick one day, and found out how very much his wife loved him. She was so excited. Every time a mailman or a delivery man arrived, she shouted, "My husband's home! My husband's home!"

I just hired a detective to watch my wife—not that she's unfaithful —I just want to know where she is when I am.

One woman told her lawyer she wanted a divorce.

"On what grounds?"

"My husband isn't faithful," she said.

"What makes you think so?" the lawyer asked.

"Well," she said, "I don't think he's the father of my child."

Children

The little girl walked into her mother's bedroom at three o'clock in the morning. "Tell me a story, Mommy," she whimpered. "For heaven's sake, it's three o'clock in the morning," cried the sleepy mother. "Tell me a story," demanded the tot. "Look," suggested the mother, "why don't you wait until four o'clock when your father comes home and he'll tell us both a story!"

Al Capp: Those parents who concern themselves with their children's problems are crazy. The problem of a nine-year-old kid cannot be solved in any way—except by becoming ten.

S. J. Perelman: Nowadays you don't know how much you know until your children grow up and tell you how much you don't know.

I walked into my daughter's room the other night and said, "What about the prayers?" She said, "I'm saying them." I said, "I don't hear you." She said, "I'm not talking to you."

Tiny Tim's favorite children stories:

A Boy Scout, as of course you know, is supposed to do one good deed each day.
"What good deed did you perform today?" once asked a neighbor of a small Scout.
"Oh," said the young hero, "Mother had only enough castor oil for one dose, so I let my sister take it!"

Little Marie was sitting on her grandfather's knee one day, and after looking at him intently for a time, she said,
"Grandpa, were you on Noah's Ark?"
"Certainly not, my dear," answered the astonished old man.
"Then why weren't you drowned?"

Little Lydia had been given a ring as a birthday present, but, much to her disappointment, not one of the guests at dinner noticed it. Finally, unable to stand their indifference, she exclaimed, "Oh, dear, I'm so warm in my new ring!"

Mother was instructing little Gertrude in regard to her manners, as she was being dressed to return her friend's call.
"If they ask you to dine, say, 'No, I thank you, I have dined.'"

But the conversation turned out differently from what she had anticipated.

"Come along, Gertrude," invited her little friend's father, "have a bite with us."

"No, I thank you," came Gertrude's dignified reply. "I have already bitten."

A lady who had just received an interesting bit of news said to her little daughter,

"Marjorie, dear, auntie has a new baby, and now mamma is the baby's aunt, papa is the baby's uncle, and you are her little cousin."

"Well," said Marjorie, wonderingly, "wasn't that arranged quick?"

The teacher asked what a sweater was and one kid answered, "It's something I have to put on when my mother gets chilly."

Little Harry was asked by his Sunday school teacher, "And, Harry, what are you going to give your darling little brother for Christmas this year?" "I dunno," said Harry. "I gave him the measles last year."

A little four-year-old girl and a three-year-old boy walked hand in hand up to the front of their neighbor's house. "We are playing house," the little girl said when the neighbor opened the door. "This is my husband and I am his wife. May we come in?" The lady was enchanted with the scene. "Do come in," she said.

Once inside she offered the children some lemonade and cookies, which they graciously accepted. When a second glass of lemonade was offered, the little girl refused by saying, "No, thanks—we have to go now—my husband just wet his pants."

Everytime I found a girl that I liked, I brought her home, but Mamma always said, "I don't like her, she's not for you." Then I found a girl that looked like Mamma, talked like Mamma, and walked like Mamma. I brought her home, but lost out again—Papa didn't like her.

Here's a problem for a PTA discussion:
"Should parents strike back?"

"I'm trying something new," the young mother was saying. "This summer I'm sending my dogs to camp and my kids to obedience school."

There was a fascinating story in the paper recently. A nine-year-old girl played a chess tournament in Prague against fifteen of the world's greatest chess champions, all at the same time!

Would you believe it? She lost every game!

When a youngster hears a bad word, it goes in one ear—and out of his mouth.

"None of my kids are dropouts," my neighbor was bragging, "but they caused quite a few dropouts among the teachers."

Christian Science

If the cost of medicine and doctors keeps going up, we'll all have to become Christian Scientists.

My mother-in-law is a good Christian Scientist who says her prayers first thing every morning and has been doing it for many years. Lately I noticed that she has been reading the newspapers first. "Are prayers less important?" I asked. "Not at all," she explained. "I'm just looking to see what I have to pray about."

Christmas

I'm sorry to say my wife is not talking to me since last Christmas —I promised her everything—then I gave her Arpège.

It's gonna be a typical American Christmas at our house this year. The tree comes from Canada, the ornaments from Japan, the lights from Taipei—and the idea comes from Bethlehem.

I gave my wife a gold watch for Christmas and she was surprised —She was expecting a chinchilla coat.

I gave my wife a twenty-five-dollar gift certificate for Christmas and it made her very happy—she used it as a down payment on a mink coat!

This guy received an envelope from his boss: "I am enclosing a little gift. Try it for size. If it's too small, don't return it because I can't get it in a larger size." Enclosed was a check for $25.

Victor Borge says Santa Claus has the right idea—visit people only once a year and you'll always be welcome.

I know a guy so cheap that on Christmas Eve he fires three shots in the air and tells kids that Santa Claus just committed suicide.

Flip Wilson says, "When I was a kid I lost respect for Santa Claus. You see, everywhere I went I kept seeing the old boy in a different store. How can you respect a guy who can't hold a steady job?"

With inflation the way it is today, I went out and paid fifty dollars for a Christmas tree and brought it home—My wife wore it as a corsage.

May you have a Christmas you'll never forget—and a New Year's you won't remember.

I wanted to get my wife a bra for Christmas. It is a little embarrassing the way the salesgirls look at you. When they ask you the size, you're torn between pride and reality.

One guy said he wants a size 7¼ bra—The salesgirl asked him how he measured—He said with his hat.

Red Skelton tells the story of the wealthy farmer who was not only rich but had a lot of money. He went to church on Christmas and after the services he said to the reverend, "That was a damn good sermon —damn good!"
    The minister was pleased but suggested, "It would be nicer if you didn't use such terms in expressing yourself."
    "Can't help it, Reverend—but I still think it was a damn good sermon—that's why I put $500 in the collection basket."
    "The hell you did," said the minister.

Now you know how Santa feels—Living in a whole world of takers and no givers.

Santa Claus is not rare any more. He wears that wild red outfit— boots, beard, a bag on his shoulder—and he only works one day a year. Do you know how many teen-agers and hippies this fits?

With inflation today, I can't believe the prices they are getting for Christmas trees. It's true that only God can make a tree—but I wish he would investigate his salesmen.

The soldier boy was so unhappy. "But this is Christmas"—I tried to cheer him up—"Santa Claus and all that."

"What Santa Claus?" he cried. "Twenty years ago I asked Santa for a soldier suit—now I get it."

Church

A minister asked a little girl what she thought of her first church service. "Well," she said, after giving the matter some thought, "the music was nice, but the commercial was too long."

When the topless girl tried to enter the church the vicar stopped her at the door. "But, Vicar, you can't stop me from going to church," she protested. "I have a Divine right."

"They're both divine," he said, "but that is not the question—you'll have to go home and put on something that is more respectable."

"There are so few people going to church these days," the chorus girl was saying. "In fact, in my church there are so few in the congregation, when our minister says 'Dearly Beloved' I feel like I got a proposal."

Sign over collection box in the vestibule: GIVE GENEROUSLY—REMEMBER—YOU CAN'T TAKE IT WITH YOU—SO WHY NOT SEND IT ON AHEAD?"

"I will not give you the blessing this Sunday," the minister said to the congregation. "I don't feel you need it. The Lord said 'Blessed are the poor' and judging by the size of the collection, that covers all of you."

"How come I never see you in church any more, Timothy?"
  "There are too many hypocrites there, father."
  "Don't worry, son, there's always room for one more."

The minister reprimanded one of his congregation who always sat in the first row and fell asleep as soon as the sermon started. "You should feel complimented," the congregant explained. "If I didn't trust you—I couldn't sleep."

There are more old sinners than there are old preachers.

Chutzpa

The bravest man I ever knew once took a taxi to the bankruptcy court and invited the driver in as a creditor.

The crook with the greatest chutzpa I ever knew is the one who held up a bank with a nylon stocking over his head. He held up the first cashier and made him hand over $50,000. Then he proceeded to the next cashier and tried to open an account with the money.

Circumcision

Eddie Cantor sent this telegram to producer Irving Thalberg after the birth of his first son: CONGRATULATIONS ON YOUR LATEST PRODUC-TION—I'M SURE IT WILL LOOK BETTER AFTER IT'S BEEN CUT.

A surgical operation that has become a catered affair.

Circus

The Barnum & Bailey Circus was playing Bridgeport, Connecticut, and the local paper sent their best reporter to interview the world-famous Tom Thumb, Barnum & Bailey's brilliant dwarf. The reporter found the room at the hotel and knocked on the door. It was opened by a towering giant who filled the doorway. "I'm a reporter," said the young man. "I want to interview Tom Thumb." "Good— glad to see you," said the giant. "I'm Tom Thumb—come on in." "You're nuts," said the reporter, looking up at the giant. "Tom Thumb's a dwarf." "Well," said the giant, "this is my day off."

He married the tattooed lady at the circus because of his insomnia. Now when he can't sleep at night he stays up and looks at the pictures.

The fat lady at the circus married the India rubber man—and in three weeks he erased her altogether.

Ad in *Show Business:* "Lion tamer—looking for tamer lion."

It was a bad year for the circus and the owner called all his troupe together to make his sad announcement. "I'm sorry to say there is only enough money to pay off three of you this week—Samson the strong man, Benny the bone crusher, and Ivan the knife thrower."

Ad in *Show Business:* "Wanted—human cannon ball—must be able to travel."

Cleaners

Robert King says, "The cleaners lost one of my best suits last month and to my surprise I received a bill from them. When I phoned to ask about it they informed me that they were sure they'd cleaned the suit before losing it."

Cold

It's so cold in my house even the janitor is banging on the pipes.

It was so cold when I was born, a penguin brought me instead of a stork.

It was so cold that the hens were laying eggs from a standing position.

It was so cold I was looking for a girl with a high fever for a roommate.

There is nothing as cold as a woman who has been refused a mink coat.

It was a perfect marriage—he was old and she was frigid.

She likes the cold weather—if it weren't for the goose-pimples—she'd have no figure at all.

College

When the father questioned his son's marks at school, the answer was, "I don't care what anybody says, I'm just as smart as the next guy—who also flunked."

Two young college kids were having a slight argument talking about their relationship. "I don't mind your mother living with us," the fellow was saying, "but I do wish she'd wait until we get married."

Larry Gore tells of a friend's son who is a conscientious objector. He refuses to go to a college and fight.

When my nephew goes back to college he can't decide what to take. It's a tossup between the library and the dean's office.

The president of the college left like he came—fired with enthusiasm.

The trouble with the college kids today is their sex habits. Too many youngsters start experimenting with their fingers crossed—which happens to be the wrong part.

They take only top students in this college—must have "A" in Pot.

He is well informed about anything he doesn't have to study.

The mother went to see the analyst and asked, "Tell me—I got a daughter in college—she doesn't use drugs—she's not pregnant—she doesn't drink—she got the highest marks in her class and she writes to us every day—tell me—where did we go right?"

My kid goes to an Ivy League college—now he can write on toilet walls in Latin.

The personnel manager looked over the application of the college graduate: "I see you've never been in jail—Didn't you take any interest in college activities?"

The old man was bragging: "My son just made the Yale Picket Team."

One way to stop a student-protest movement is to make it a required course.

"I've dated the entire football team and I haven't made love to one of them," said the senior. "I'll bet it's that shy right end," answered her roommate.

A: When your son finishes college, what will he be?
B: About 40.

Cookbook

When Rosemary Wilson wrote the *Beautiful Wife's Cookbook*, Earl cracked, "They are making it into a TV series called 'The Survivors.'"

I love Rosemary, but when she was on my radio show I said, "Rosemary Wilson's cookbook comes with 200 assorted get-well cards."

Cooking

Joan Rivers admits she's a terrible cook: "Yesterday I tried to make ladyfingers—and they turned out all thumbs."

Joan says her favorite recipe is TV dinner—and her second favorite recipe is to warm it up.

"The last time my husband had a hot meal was when a candle fell in his sandwich.

"I never realized how bad a cook I was until Betty Crocker threw a rock through my window.

"I once served hors d'oeuvres on a Ouija board. The board spelled out, 'Don't eat the hors d'oeuvres.'"

Joan Rivers swears she made orange juice for her husband every single day on their honeymoon—and then she lost the recipe.

One guy complained about his wife's cooking: "I broke a tooth on it—and that was just the coffee."

You've heard about people who can't boil water. My wife can—she calls it soup.

Every time I meet a girl who can cook like my mother, she looks like my father.

Bob Hope says Phyllis Diller has the only dining-room table with a garbage disposal for a centerpiece.

Phyllis admits she's a lousy cook. "In my house we have Alka-Seltzer on tap."

Don Adams says his mother was such a lousy cook, she brought him up on radio dinners.

Pat Cooper says, "My wife broke our dog of begging from the table—she let him taste it."

It still takes many housewives hours to prepare dinner. Do you think it's easy getting some packages out of the freezer?

Show me a beautiful, sexy wife who doesn't like to cook and I'll show you a couple who eat out a lot.

My wife discovered a great way to keep all her dishes, pots, and pans sparkling clean. She never uses them.

I won't say my wife is a bad cook—but the other night I sent her out to dinner and she burned the Diners' Club card.

My wife has come up with a great formula to keep food costs down—it's her cooking.

My wife is really a lousy cook—The other night we had to call a repairman to fix our TV dinner.

I won't say my wife is a bad cook—On the other hand, I will say it. She cooks for a cookbook called: *Condemned by Duncan Hines.*

My wife always has an excuse. I bought her a foreign cookbook and now she says she can't get parts for the meals.

I told my wife that for a new and exciting meal she should try the Galloping Gourmet's cookbook—so she boiled it.

One thing—she's a fast cook—She serves three-minute eggs in one minute and cooks minute rice in thirty seconds flat.

Thelma Lee says: "There are some men who think we women run home from club meetings and put TV dinners on the table. First of all I happen to be a very good cook, and my food melts in my husband's mouth—while it's defrosting."

You think the government has space problems—we women have the space problems with the crummy freezers we're forced to use. You can't buy what you like to eat, you have to buy what fits. And I measure before I go shopping. I say, well, I have 2 inches here, 4 inches there. So I even found myself saying to the butcher, "I would like a chicken 2 by 4 by 7. And I would like you to take his left leg and wrap it around his neck, and if my calculations are right, I can take four meatballs and put them under his armpit into the freezer!"

Pat Cooper

I saw a hippie having his reflexes tested. A doctor hit the fellow's knee with a flower.

The movie house in my home town showed second-run pictures. They were on TV first.

I complained to the landlord about my new terrace apartment. The sidewalk was blocking my view.

I walked away from a Las Vegas laundry machine for five minutes and somebody won my wash.

Liberace is afraid of the dark. When he goes to sleep he leaves his jacket lit.

I visited a Las Vegas hospital; the condition charts list the odds on the patients.

Courts

"The court will give you three lawyers because of the importance of this case," the judge said.

"If it's all the same to you, your honor," the criminal said, "just get me one good witness."

This is the only country in the world where they lock up the jury and let the prisoner go home every night.

Woman to judge: That's my side of the story—now let me tell you his.

Defendant: As God is my judge—I did not take the money.
Judge: He isn't—I am—You did.

The scared defendant asked the irate judge what was the maximum penalty for bigamy.

"Two mothers-in-law," was the answer.

Woman juror to eleven exasperated men jurors: "If you men weren't so stubborn, we could all go home."

Lawyer: I'd like a new trial for my client.
Judge: On what grounds?
Lawyer: My client has dug up some money I didn't know he had.

A young man was brought before the judge for robbery. The case against him was strong but he heard nothing from the defense. The judge turned to the alleged robber and scolded, "Well, what have you to say for yourself? Where are your witnesses? Don't you have any witnesses in this case?"

"No, your honor," the prisoner said quietly, "not me—I never take along any witnesses when I commit a robbery."

Credit

A large number of people are trying to keep up with the Joneses—and a number of creditors are trying to keep up with them.

Credit: A device that enables you to start at the bottom—and go into a hole.

My car has something that will last a lifetime—monthly payments.

These days, if somebody pays you in cash you get suspicious. You think maybe his credit is no good.

It's great to take a loan. At least you know somebody's gonna call you.

Education is a wonderful thing—If you couldn't sign your name—you'd have to pay cash.

We don't live within our income—It's all we can do to live within our credit.

Credit Cards

Did you hear about the new credit cards for wives? It self-destructs after $100.

She likes guys who lay their cards on the table: Diners' Club cards—American Express—Master Charge.

The out-of-towner asked Joe Kipness of the Pier 52 Restaurant if he honors any of the credit cards. Joe smiled. "We not only honor them, but we also love and obey them."

What this country needs is a credit card for taxpayers.

My friend has so many credit cards, he was bankrupt for six months before he knew about it.

Credit card: A convenient way to spend money you wish you had.

Eat, drink, and be merry—for tomorrow you may lose your credit card.

Credit card: Instant debt.

Many a man is poor today because his credit card was good yesterday.

Crime

New York City pushed up theater time to 7:30 P.M. so people shouldn't be up too late because of the crime on Broadway. The restaurant owners complained that it hurt their business. "The only ones it helps are the muggers—they now get home earlier."

The crook pulled a gun on the cashier in the Chinese restaurant and said, "Give me all the money you got in the register—to go."

Woody Allen's apartment was robbed so many times he finally put up a sign which said: WE GAVE ALREADY!

The guy stayed later than he thought. His friends warned him, "With so many crimes in the neighborhood—start running when you leave here, and don't stop till you get home." The next day he called from the hospital—beaten and bloody—"I did what you said—I ran and ran, and I caught up with a mugger."

Everybody is conscious about crime in the streets. I asked one guy on Seventeenth Street and Broadway how I could get to Twenty-third and Lexington. "Easy," he explained. "You turn left on the next block and if you make it . . ."

The FBI claims that organized crime in America has a yearly take of over $50,000,000,000—and it's going higher. What I want to know, is it going public?

Stanley Myron Handelman says, "My house was burglarized about ten times. Finally I figured I'm really going to get this guy. So I made believe I went out, turned off all the lights and then hid in the closet. This guy thought I was out, came into the house, and he stole two candles, my silverware, and a portable TV set. And the guy is really wise. He thinks he's gonna get away. But this time I got a complete description of him. He was average height and build and he was wearing a rubber mask of Charles de Gaulle."

Guy says, "Mrs. Snyder, your son just held up a bank and he shot the teller and he killed two people in the bank. He ran outside and shot a police officer, then scaled a fence and broke into a building and attacked a woman on the third floor before we caught him." And she says, "I'm surprised. He's never that way at home."

Every politician is hollering about "our boys" in the penal institutions being treated badly. The whole idea is to make the prisoner feel at home—I guess so he'll want to come back again soon.

The big idea is to give him a home away from home. One warden really went a little too far—He had an inmate's wife make a slip cover for the electric chair.

Crime is getting so bad in some big cities—even the muggers travel in pairs.

I was going to read that report about the rising crime rate, but someone stole it.

A jeweler called the police station to report a robbery. "You'll never believe what happened, sergeant. A truck backed up to my store, the doors opened and an elephant came out, broke my plate glass windows, stuck his trunk in, sucked up all the jewelry, and climbed back into the truck. The doors closed and the truck pulled away."
The desk sergeant said, "Could you tell me for identification purposes, was it an Indian elephant, or an African elephant?" The jeweler asked, "What's the difference?" "Well," said the sergeant, "an African elephant has great big ears, an Indian elephant little ears." And the jeweler said, "Come to think of it I couldn't see his ears, he had a stocking over his head."

Central Park had a very slow night last Saturday, so these two muggers—mugged each other.

Dick Cavett picks on New York City: Like the time he told about being at the Shakespeare Festival in New York's Central Park, where crime is not unknown. He was watching a production of *Julius Caesar*. When Caesar got stabbed, eight people got up and left. Explained Cavett, "They didn't want to get involved."

I figured out why they're building the subway under Central Park. The subway is equated with pickpockets and perverts while the park is associated with pushers and muggers. This is New York's way of getting it all together.

I know how New York's Forty-second Street got its name. It's called Forty-second Street because you can only last forty seconds without getting into trouble.

Crime is booming. A guy I know serving a term for burglary is eating his heart out because he's missing a very good year.

Stick-up man: "Your money or your life."
Mike: "Take me life—I'm saving me money for me old age."

What a tough neighborhood I live in! In my neighborhood, no one ever asks you what time it is. They just take your watch.

He spent three months forging a check—only to have it come back from the bank stamped, "Insufficient Funds."

"Hand over all your money or I'll blow your brains out," the thief said to the New Yorker. "Go ahead and shoot," the victim said. "You can live in this town without brains—but not without money!"

I live in a rough neighborhood. My kid goes to the only school where the school newspaper has an obituary column.

Even cops in my neighborhood are afraid. The police station on my block is the only police station where the front door has a peephole in it.

I'm not worried about crime in the streets, but in my neighborhood they make house calls.

There's a new thing now—Topless Muggers—They do it that way so you won't remember their faces.

The grocer was robbed so many times he put a sign in the window of his store: ATTENTION, CROOKS, WE GAVE ALREADY!

The guy had a friend, another delicatessen owner, who had been robbed so many times, that he thought up a way to get even. He made one robber his partner.

"If he's my partner I can steal from him," explained the storekeeper.

Walking home from work one night, my uncle was approached by a bum who pleaded, "Please, sir, if you don't mind, sir, can you spare the price of a meal? I have no work, no decent clothes, I have nothing in the world except this knife and this gun."

A stranger confronted a man on a dark street and asked, "Sir, have you ever been awarded a black belt in Karate?" The other man said no. The first one then said, "In that case, this is a stick-up."

Critics

Robert Benchley: It was one of those plays in which all the actors unfortunately enunciated very clearly.

George Jean Nathan: He writes his plays for the ages—the ages between four and twelve.

G. B. Shaw sent Winston Churchill two tickets for the first night of his *Pygmalion* with the note: "Here are a couple of tickets for the first night. Bring a friend—if you have one."

Mr. Churchill replied: "Sorry, I cannot come to the first night—but will come to the second—if there is one."

A critic is a man who knows the way—but cannot drive the car.

Drama critic Clive Barnes, reviewing a Broadway play: "I realized it was not a particularly distinguished play when, at the intermission, I found myself rushing up the aisle for a cigarette outside. It was not until I got out there that I remembered that I don't smoke."

The cast was well balanced—they were all rotten.

One of the shortest musical criticisms on record appeared in a Detroit paper: "An amateur string quartet played Brahms here last evening—Brahms lost."

Another pithy review lasted much longer than the play called, *Dreadful Night*. The account: "Dreadful night: PRECISELY!"

Irving Hoffman critikilled a play. The producer went to his publisher and complained that Mr. Hoffman has very bad eyesight. "I may not see very well," Irving answered later, "but there is nothing wrong with my nose."

Go to any public square—and see if you can find one statue erected to a critic.

The worst review I ever read. This actor did a one-man show and the critic wrote: "There were too many in the cast."

Heywood Broun about a play: "He opened at 8:30 sharp—and closed at 10:50 dull."

Alexander Woollcott: "The scenery was beautiful but the actors got in front of it."

The show had two strikes against it—the seats faced the stage.

Percy Hammond demolished one show. In closing he said, "I have knocked everything except the knees of the chorus girls—and God anticipated me there!"

Dorothy Parker said about Katherine Hepburn, "She runs the gamut of emotion from A to B."

Heywood Broun was once sued by some actor called Stein for calling his performance "atrocious." The next time Mr. Broun reviewed Stein, he brushed him with, "Mr. Stein's performance was not up to his usual standard."

John Chapman said about a Mae West show, "Miss West has one more bust than she needs."

Don Rickles was discussing a new movie. "I came in late—but I wish I had missed it from the beginning."

d

Dancing

Dancing is a rough thing for me. I got two left feet, and it's hard for me to find a girl with two right ones.

What bugs me about ballet is the fact that no matter how much I pay for seats and no matter how close I am to the stage—I can never hear a word they're saying.

If you're over forty, do yourself a favor and stay out of discothèques. At this age it's no longer dancing. It's committing suicide one bone at a time!

Dating

Fannie Flagg says, "I had a terrible time fighting off a blind date last night. He thought I'd given him the go-ahead because the second I saw him I turned green."

My blind date looked much better over the telephone.

Morty Storm reports that he has no trouble making dates with girls. "My trouble is that they don't show up."

Bob: How did you do last night?

Frank: Great—I finally persuaded her to say yes.
Bob: Congratulations! When is the wedding?
Frank: Wedding? What wedding?

"No more drinks," she said shyly. "I only drink to be sociable, and I'm feeling sociable enough right now—So let's go to bed."

Rodney Dangerfield explained the time he got no respect on a blind date. "I waited on the corner until this girl Louise walked by . . . I said, 'Are you Louise?' She said, 'Are you Rodney?' I said, 'Yeah,' and she said, 'I'm not Louise. . . .'"

"My daughter is getting married," the woman announced, "and I hope she'll make her husband as happy as she's making *my* husband."

Death

Two corpses were laid out in the same room at the funeral home. One night when everybody left, one corpse sat up and asked the other, "What did you die from?"—"Cigarettes," he answered, "I just smoked too many cigarettes."—"What kind did you smoke?"—"Raleighs," he answered. "At least, did you save the coupons?"

"Hell, yes! How do you think I got this coffin?"

Two friends were talking about the death of a man who owed them both money. They agreed it was too late to collect. "Isn't it funny," one said, "they say you can't take it with you—but you sure can take somebody else's."

Honoré de Balzac, the French novelist, was fond of the good life. When a stingy old uncle died and left him a great deal of money, Balzac's wit would not permit him to mourn; instead he informed his friends of the news by announcing, "Yesterday, at five in the morning, my uncle and I passed on to a better life."

Who says you can't take it with you? My broker just opened an office at Forest Lawn.

Bob Hope said if he died and returned to earth, he would like to ask for just three things—Al Smith's tolerance—Cardinal Cooke's heart—Dean Martin's kidney.

Two pals were talking about the good old days.

"Almost all our friends are gone," said Tom, "but the one I miss the most is Frank."

"Why Frank?" his friend asked.

"Because I married his widow."

When one famous phony died Red Skelton went to the funeral to find a huge crowd with people fighting to get into the funeral parlor. "Well," said Red, "it only proves what they always say—give the public something they want to see—and they'll come out for it."

Demonstrations

Remember the good old days when a demonstrator was someone who sold you potato peelers?

We now have a law that prohibits outside agitators from crossing state lines . . . I sent a copy of it to my mother-in-law.

The demonstration turned into a riot. One guy staggered out of the crowd carrying the limp form of a girl. "Here," said a cop, "hand her to me—I'll get her out of this." "The hell with you," said the guy. "Go and get one of your own."

Do you go back far enough to when a teen-age protest was just a girl who said "No"?

Every place you go—all over the world—the college kids are demonstrating about something. Picketing and complaining. They are learning to be the greatest mothers-in-law.

Remember the good old days when a demonstrator knocked on your door and tried to sell you a vacuum cleaner?

Dentist

I asked my dentist to put in a tooth to match my other teeth—he put in a tooth with four cavities.

The dentist said to his beautiful blond patient, "Honey, we can't go on meeting like this. You have no more teeth left."

The next time you go to your dentist, try double-parking—that'll give you something to keep your mind off the pain.

I can never forget the Smith and Dale routine every time I go to a dentist's office:
    Doctor: "Don't worry—I'm painless."
    Patient: "Well, I'm not."

The modern dentist lives up to his claim, "It won't hurt a bit"—until the bill arrives.

The male patient complained to the dentist that he was in terrible pain, but he insisted on saving the tooth.
    The dentist put on his white coat, adjusted the light on his forehead, started his drill, and said, "Okay, now open your mouth and we'll see what we can do." Just then the patient grabbed him below the belt. "What the hell are you doing?" the dentist screamed. "Now,"

the man said quietly, not letting go, "we're not going to hurt each other, are we?"

Diet

I was on a cruise recently. And like almost every cruise I've been on there were these adorable elderly little women. On this cruise there were two, in their mid-seventies. They were still wearing the muumuus they got when they were on their Hawaiian cruise. Well, they sit down to have coffee. And you know those little Sweet 'N Low packs you find in sugar bowls? As a rule one of these packets is too much for one cup of coffee. Now one of the women kept on opening packet after packet into her coffee. Finally her girlfriend said, "What are you, crazy? Just because it's free? Do you realize what you're doing? If you keep that up, you'll get artificial diabetes!"

Joan Rivers, who's dieting, boasts she lost two pounds last week. "But I cheated a little—before I got on the scale I shaved my head."

"You know what my diet's done for me?" . . . "Yes, it made you a bore—you never talk about anything else."

Even marriages change. Ten years ago I put my wife on a pedestal. Yesterday I put her on a diet.

Either she goes on a diet or we'll have to let out the couch.

The biggest thing to remember when you are dieting—what you see on the table must wind up on the chair.

You want to please a woman—tell her she lost weight. You want to displease a woman—tell her she needed to.

More diets begin in dress shops than in doctors' offices.

You can eat as much as you want of anything you don't like.

Marty Ingels says he's been trying a new diet drink—two parts scotch and one part Metrecal. "So far I've lost five pounds and my driver's license."

One woman got up in her weight-watching class and announced, "I just got rid of 175 pounds of excess flab—I divorced my husband."

A woman charged her husband with mental cruelty so severe that she lost thirty pounds. "Divorce granted," said the judge. "Not yet," the woman pleaded. "First I want to lose another ten pounds."

He went horseback riding to lose weight and it must have worked. The horse lost thirty pounds.

Marty Allen says, "I've been losing weight and losing weight and I just found out why. My wife got a new rubber mattress, and at night I toss and turn and that's what's doing it. I'm erasing myself."

Phyllis Diller

Phyllis Diller has a style all her own—masochistic humor.

My cooking is so bad my kids refer to breakfast as morning sickness.

I once baked a rum cake that gave Fang a hangover.

Today my alphabet soup spelled "UGH."

I got my first laugh when my mother entered me in a baby contest.

When I was a kid and we used to play Post Office. I was the Dead-Letter Office.

I joined an astrology club and every week we meet and discuss the stars. This week we're discussing Paul Newman.

My mother-in-law buys her coats in a carpet shop. She wears a 9 by 12.

If Fang had a brain operation, it would be minor surgery.

Fang came home loaded one night, went into the closet, and said, "Third floor, please."

Fang is such a drag. He took his suit to the cleaners to be cleaned and depressed.

The only way I can get Fang out of bed in the morning is to wear a black dress and a veil, and sit on the edge of his bed and cry.

The doctor looked my body over. I said, "Is there any hope?" He said, "Yes. Reincarnation."

If I wore a peekaboo dress, it would be like turning in a false alarm.

Do I believe in witchcraft? I'm the result of it.

My sister-in-law is so skinny that she has a striped dress with only one stripe.

I found a great new weed killer, but it stains the carpet.

Fang is so dumb. When he won his letter for high school, the coach had to read it to him.

Fang had a terrible accident. He found a job.

Fang said if they had used my figure for the hourglass, the day would be very short.

Fang will not go on a picnic. He says we have the whole thing at home: bugs, dirt, tainted food. At our last picnic we wanted to play horseshoes, but his mother refused to go barefoot.

When Phyllis was about three months pregnant, her neighbor asked her bluntly, "Are you going to have another baby?"
  "No," answered our heroine, "I'm just carrying it for a friend."

Diplomat

A diplomat praises married life while he stays single.

"A real diplomat is one who can cut his neighbor's throat without having his neighbor notice it." —Trygve Lie

A diplomat thinks twice before saying nothing.

A diplomat is a guy who can convince his wife she looks fat in a mink coat or that she looks vulgar in diamonds.

I asked one diplomat what his favorite color was and he said "Plaid."

The definition of a diplomat—he talks interestingly for an hour and doesn't say anything. Or, it's the art of skating on thin ice without getting into deep water.

A diplomat is a person who can be disarming even though his country isn't.

Divorce

There is only one quick relief from cold misery—a divorce.

The sexy wife of a busy husband recently won a divorce, charging her hubby with lack of attentiveness. "If anything ever happened to me," the stacked missus claimed, "my husband wouldn't be able to identify the body."

"I'd divorce him," said the bitter wife, "if I could find a way to do it without making him happy."

Shecky Greene explained California's community property laws. "Everything you have is divided fifty-fifty—your wife gets half and her lawyer gets the other half."

People get married before they know each other—and then get divorced when they do.

My marriage ended because we were incompatible. My wife hated me when I was drunk—and I couldn't stand her when I was sober.

They got divorced because of illness—they got sick of each other.

Some great philosopher said about divorce—I forget the philosopher's name—In fact, I forget what he said—but I say—divorce is useless. You get married for lack of judgment—you get divorced for lack of patience—then you remarry for lack of memory.

They separated because of religious differences. She worshiped money—and he didn't have a dime.

Two guys talking. One said, "I got married because I was tired of going to the Laundromat, eating in restaurants, and wearing socks with holes."

The other guy said, "That's funny; I got divorced for the same reason."

Doctors

My doctor is one in a million. He put me on my feet in no time. Made me sell my car to pay his bill.

Being a doctor is the world's greatest profession. In what other business can a man tell a woman to take all her clothes off and then send her husband a bill.

"My right foot hurts, Doctor."
   "Don't worry. It's just old age."
   "But I've had my left foot just as long—why doesn't that hurt?"

Doctor: Look, Mr. Cohen, the best thing for you is to stop smoking, stop careening around the night spots, stop drinking, and cut down on all those sweet and fattening foods.
Patient: "Doctor, honestly I don't deserve the best. What's second best?"

I am a little nervous about going to see a doctor when I realize that doctors are usually described as practicing.

The doctor was taking a stroll with his wife when they came face to face with a gorgeous blond package. She gave him a special greeting. "Who was your blond friend?" the wife asked a few minutes later. "Oh, just a young lady I met professionally," he answered nonchalantly.
"Professional?—really?—Yours or hers?"

I wouldn't say he was a bad doctor. In fact, he was a good diagnostician—he diagnosed your condition by feeling your purse.

A specialist is a doctor whose patients can only be ill during office hours.

Doctor: If I thought an operation was necessary, would you have enough money to pay for it?
Patient: If I didn't have the money to pay for it, would you think the operation was necessary?

"The operation was successful," the doctor told his nurse. "I'm happy to say I did it in the nick of time—another few days and he would have recovered without it."

Doctor: You seem to be improving—I know your leg is still swollen, but I wouldn't worry about that.
Patient: If *your* leg was swollen I wouldn't worry about it either.

The first two things a doctor learns at medical school: Always write your prescriptions illegibly and always write your bills clearly.

Any doctor can tell you the difference between an itch and an allergy. It's about twenty-five dollars a visit.

The doc said to his patient, "I've got bad news and good news. Bad news is I amputated the wrong leg—took off the good one. Good news is your bad leg is getting better."

The nurse to doctor: "That patient, Mr. Finekuchen, who wouldn't respond to treatment, won't respond to his bill either."

The doctor asked the airline pilot when he last had sex. "That was—let's see—1955," the pilot said. "So long ago?" the doctor asked. "That's not so long," said the pilot. "Right now"—looking at his watch—"it's only 2140."

Sam Levinson tells about the man who called his doctor for an appointment. The nurse suggested a date three weeks off. "But I may be dead by then!" . . . "That's okay—you can always cancel the appointment."

My doctor only charged ten dollars for my X rays but he talked me into wallet-size 8 by 10 glossies for thirty-five dollars.

The noted doctor opened the patient's stomach and a bunch of butterflies flew out. "Say," the doctor said, "this guy was telling the truth."

A doctor opened his waiting-room door to a roomful of patients and asked, "Who's been waiting the longest?" "I have," said his tailor. "I delivered your suit three years ago and haven't been paid yet."

Patient tells doctor he has trouble with his ears. Says he coughs all night but can't even hear it. The doctor prescribes some medicine and the patient asks, "Will this make me hear better?" "No," said the doctor, "but it'll make you cough louder."

The elderly doctor sent his patient with a note to the young doctor in the office across the hall: "This will introduce Mrs. Gloria Oshin—She has been married for three years but has never achieved satisfaction. I was hoping you could help her."

Harassed surgeon to medical students watching a delicate operation: "Will the wise guy who keeps saying 'oops' please leave!"

It's Henny Youngman's favorite doctor joke.
Doc: I am happy to tell you that you will probably live to be ninety.
Patient: But Doctor, I *am* ninety!
Doc: See—what did I tell you?

My doctor was writing a prescription with a thermometer. I said: "How can you write with a thermometer?"
   "Oops!" he said. "One of my patients must be walking around with my fountain pen stuck in him!"

The doctor said, "Lady, in order to determine what's wrong with you, I'll have to give you a complete examination. Please get completely undressed." The woman looked at him coyly and said, "Doctor, you first."

The miracle drugs are the greatest. Now a doctor can keep the patient alive until he pays his bill.

Doctor to beautiful young patient: "I don't see anything wrong with you so far—Keep undressing!"

Pat Cooper says his doctor ordered him to stop smoking. The doctor added, "And since you're quitting, I'll give you five dollars for your gold lighter."

Talk about inflation—My doctor sent me a get-well card and in it was a bill for twenty dollars.

Their prescriptions are so hard to read—but their bills are always loud and clear.

The doctor lost all his money in Las Vegas—He even gambled away the house and car. He knew he couldn't go home to his wife, so in desperation he decided to hold up a bank. But his luck continued— nobody could read his holdup note.

My doctor told me, "Nobody makes house calls any more—except plumbers, TV repairmen, and burglars."

"I'm doing what I can," the doctor explained to the patient, "but you know I can't make you any younger."

"The hell with that," said the impatient patient. "I'm not interested in getting younger—I just want to get older."

"I'm sorry," the doctor said to the stripper, "I don't have a brochure of scars to show you. You'll just have to take pot luck."

Draft

Two fellows meet and one says, "The government has no right to draft me, give me a uniform and a gun and take me to a far place and have me shoot a man I don't even know." And the other says, "The government doesn't do that at all. The government does not have you shoot a man you don't know. True they draft you, true they give you a uniform, and true they take you to a far place. Then they put you fifty feet away from the enemy who's also got a gun. Then they let you use your own judgment."

Boy: Mom, why do I have to wear lipstick?
Mom: Quiet—we're coming to the draft board now.

Draft board: The world's largest travel agency.

I just received a notice from my draft board—They burned my draft card.

If they ever draft women, it'll be no problem to get them to fight . . . the sergeant will just have to yell "Charge!" and "Green stamps!"

The doctor on the board passed the new soldier with flying colors. The boy ran to see the doctor that night. "Isn't it funny," he screamed at him, "you have always found something wrong with me when I paid you twenty dollars a visit."

I think the draft board should take only married men. They are the only ones who know how to take orders.

Drinking

James Thurber said it: "One martini is all right, two is too many, and three is not enough."

He does not drink to his wife—he drinks because of her.

Talk about embarrassing moments. I saw a friend of mine really get loaded. He walked over to a gorgeous redhead at a party, introduced himself, and suggested she go home with him—and she did—she was his wife.

I got my uncle so drunk last night it took two bellboys to put me to bed.

I better stop drinking—I can't remember what I'm trying to forget.

He was a good soldier, but when he was drinking he was a monster. After a few visits to the brig, the captain decided to have a talk with him. "You're a good soldier," the captain said. "You could be sergeant someday, you might even become a lieutenant if you could only drop the liquor bit."

"You're right, Captain, but when I've had a few drinks I'm a captain."

If you drink like a fish—swim—don't drive.

The drunk approached the girl at the bar. "I'll let you kiss me if you tell me what I've got in my hand." "A six-hundred-pound alligator," says the doll. "That's close enough," says the drunk.

The drunk came home at seven in the morning and the wife was waiting for him. "They arrested me," he explained, "because I didn't want to wake you when I got home. I thought I'd take off my clothes and shoes before going upstairs." . . . "How could you get arrested for that?" she asked suspiciously. . . . "Well, when I got upstairs I found out it was the elevated subway station."

Two drunks were riding a roller coaster, when one turned to the other and said, "We may be making good time, but I've got a feeling we're on the wrong bus."

And speaking of drunks—two men were drinking in a bar, and suddenly one of them fell on his face. His buddy looked down and said, "That's what I like about you, Sam, you know when to quit."

Then there's the friend of mine who used the new martini-flavored toothpaste. He has 40 per cent more cavities, but couldn't care less.

"The Dean Martin Show" is in the top three, right behind Four Roses and Southern Comfort.

The drunk's hands were trembling when he went to see the doctor. "My God," said the medic, "how much have you been drinking lately?"
    "Not much—I spill most of it."

The fourth drink, and he said, "Y'know, one more drink and I'll feel it."
    And she said, "Y'know, one more drink and I'll let you!"

Summer is the time of the year when all TV series have reruns, except "The Dean Martin Show"—it has refills.

The lady was complaining about her husband's drinking. "We'd be rich today—if whiskey came in deposit bottles."

I wouldn't say he drinks a lot—but he is the only guy in the world who doesn't see anything unusual about the Tower of Pisa.

The bus conductor asked the drunk if he got home okay last night.

"Naturally," the poor soul said. "Why shouldn't I?" "Well, when you got up to give a lady your seat, there was only the two of you in the bus."

Two drinking pals were having dinner at Danny's Hide-a-way and really having a great time when one picked up the untouched plate of spaghetti in front of him and poured the contents on the bald head of his buddy—who didn't seem too pleased.

"Now, just why did you do that?" he asked, "Why the hell would you go and pour all your spaghetti over my head—and I just had it shined, too."

"Oh, I'm sorry," he blurted out. "I thought it was macaroni."

The temperance lecturer demonstrated the evils of drink by putting two glasses in front of him—one with water and the other with whiskey. He then produced a couple of worms which he put in the water. They swam around happily. He took them out and put them in the whiskey, and after a few wriggles they both died.

"That," explained the lecturer, "is what happens to your insides when you drink whiskey." He made his point. On his way out the little old lady stopped him and asked what brand of whiskey he had used. "Because," she said, "I've been bothered with worms for years."

Dean Martin was born with a silver olive in his mouth.—Twice a year Dean goes to the Red Cross and donates a fifth of blood.

There is a difference between a drunk and an alcoholic—the drunk doesn't have to go to meetings. . . .

The drunk was stopped by a policeman as he staggered about the street at three o'clock in the morning.

"Can you explain why you're out at this time?" asked the policeman.

"If I could," said the drunk, "I'd be home by now."

Ice has great healing powers—it's a great pain reliever, especially when used in a glass of scotch.

Customs are different in various parts of the country. In Omaha, the mother announces the engagement. In Hollywood, the press announces the pregnancy.

He was called the town drunk. And that's not so bad, till you realize he lived in New York City.

With the price of liquor today—beggars can't be boozers.

Two drunks were weaving along the railroad tracks. One said, "I never saw so many steps in my life." The other said, "It's not the steps that bother me, it's the low railing."

The poor soul weaved into a local tavern, put his head on the bar, and asked for a double Bourbon.
"Don't be silly," said the barkeep, "you can't even lift your head."
"Okay," said the drunk amiably, "then give me a haircut."

Drinker's advice: "Never drink when you're driving—you might spill some."

The lush came home late and explained to his wife that he had just bought something for the house. "What did you buy for the house?" she asked. "A round of drinks," he answered.

Conditions were not good when Roosevelt ran for President, and this was his favorite story: A fellow was a big drinker. And he went to the doctor and said, "I can't hear and I can't see good." The doctor asked, "Are you a drinker?" "Yes, I'm a heavy drinker." "That's why you can't see and hear so good. You've got to stop drinking." A month later the doctor runs into the fellow and he's drunk again. "Didn't I tell you that drinking would interfere with your seeing and hearing?" he asked. "Doc, what I've been drinking is so much better than what I've been seeing and hearing lately I decided to keep it up."

A drunk walked into an Automat, got change, then stopped in front of a slot marked "Cheese Sandwich." He dropped in coins, got a sandwich . . . dropped in more coins, got another sandwich. After he had collected twenty sandwiches, the manager came over. "Don't you think that's enough?" he asked. "What!" cried the drunk, "you want me to quit in the middle of a winning streak?"

The shy character noticed a low-cut blonde sitting next to him alone at the bar. He gathered all his courage and sent a drink to her. She silently nodded her thanks. He repeated the same gesture six times. Finally, the drinks in him spoke up and he got up all the courage he could muster and mumbled, "Do you ever make love to strange men?"
"Well," she smiled, "I never have before—but I think you've talked me into it—you clever, silver-tongued devil, you."

A full-blooded Indian got a job as a bartender but he was fired after five minutes—a customer asked for a Manhattan and the Indian charged him twenty-four dollars.

The drunk walked up to the parking meter, put in a quarter, and saw the dial go to sixty. "How do you like that?" he said. "I weigh an hour."

The brave fireman fought his way through the flames and rescued the man lying on the burning bed. When he carried him to safety he noticed the man was loaded. "Look what you did," he said to the drunk. "I hope that teaches you not to smoke in bed."
"Who was smoking? It was on fire when I got in."

Drive-in

I know a man so rich he goes to drive-in movies in a taxi.

Just think what a drive-in theater would be called if there was nothing on the screen.

The Catholics have a drive-in confessional. It's called the "toot and tell."

He was watching a movie at the drive-in theater with his girlfriend and somebody threw a brick in the window and hit her in the chest. It broke four of his fingers.

A drive-in is better known as a passion pit.

You go to a drive-in theater and what do you see—sex, perversion, sodomy, and then you look at the screen.

Driving

My wife is such a bad driver—every time she loses control of the car, it goes back on the highway.

I gave my wife a car. She loves it so much, she's taking it to England. She wants to see what it's like to drive on the left side of the street —*legally*.

My wife is the world's worst driver. If she were an Arab, she'd come home with a dented camel.

My wife has a terrible sense of direction. She even goes against the traffic when she gets on an escalator.

The cop signaled the wife to the curb. "Okay," he sneered, "why didn't you signal what you wanted to do?" "Because," she answered, "there's no signal for what I want to do."

Drugs

Greenwich Village is a very unique place. Where else will you find signs that say KEEP ON THE GRASS.

They now have LSD with Platformate—you take the same trip but you go three miles farther.

For a business trip—try LSD in your IBM.

Henny says his wife is hooked on LSD—Lox, Salami, and Danish.

Dull

This actor was so dull he was upstaged by the scenery.

He's so dull he could go on color TV and come out in black and white.

His life is so dull he looks forward to dentist appointments.

He died at twenty but he was buried at seventy.

You take him with you when you want to be alone.

Dumb-dumb

The drunk was floundering down the alley carrying a box with holes on the side. He bumped into a friend who asked:
  "Whatcha got there, pal?"
  "A mongoose."
  "What the hell for?"
  "Well, you know how drunk I can get and when I get drunk I see snakes and I'm scared to death of snakes—that's why I got this mongoose—for protection."
  "But," the friend said, "you idiot—those are imaginary snakes."
  "That's okay," said the drunk, "so's the mongoose."

My brother-in-law lost his job working a bank's hidden camera. He tried to get a holdup gang to stand closer together.

My nephew bought an inexpensive dictionary—it's not in alphabetical order.

The irate husband screamed at his wife, "The bank just returned this check for $100!"
"Isn't that just great," she gushed. "What should I buy with it this time?"

Bob Barker tells about a man who went home and complained to his wife. "I saw Tim Murphy downtown this morning and he didn't even speak to me. I guess he thinks I'm not his equal." His wife responded, "Why that stupid, brainless, conceited, good-for-nothing, moronic Tim Murphy! You certainly are his equal."

The train came to a sudden stop and the lady was thrown from her seat to the floor. "My goodness!" she said to the conductor. "What on earth happened?"
"We hit a cow," he explained.
"Was it on the tracks?"
"No, lady," said the conductor wryly, "we had to chase it across a field."

She thinks intercourse is the time spent between classes.

He's so dumb he thinks Shirley Temple Black is a Negro synagogue.

This dumb chorine says she's glad New York has seven TV channels. "I can keep switching till I find a weather report I like."

Phyllis Diller confides that nothing she does turns out right. "For instance, there are my twins—one is eighteen and the other is twenty."

He's the only person I ever knew who got up on the wrong side of the bed in a Pullman.

Most fishermen are superstitious—especially these two who hired a boat for a day's fishing and came back loaded with fish of all kinds. The guy at the pier congratulated them. "Thanks," one of them said. "We'd like the same boat again tomorrow." "Lucky for you, eh?"
"No—we put a chalk mark on the side to show us where we were fishing today."

She thinks statutory rape means doing it standing up.

She is so dumb that when she rented a furnished room, the landlady left the VACANT sign up.

She's so dumb she takes off her sweater to count to two.

Lady: I want to mail this package parcel post.
Clerk: Anything breakable, ma'am?
Lady: No—but keep it right side up—it's a can of paint without the cover.

A farmer was driving his horse laboriously along a dusty road. He came to a man sitting beside the road and pulled his team to a halt and called out, "How much longer does this hill last?"

"You ain't on no hill," the stranger called back. "Your hind wheels is off."

A man was staring at another man in the subway. "What are you staring at?"

"I beg your pardon, but . . . I . . . er . . . if it wasn't for the mustache, you know, you'd look just like my wife."

"But I have no mustache."

"I know, but my wife has."

A: It's raining—open the umbrella.
B: Wouldn't do any good—it's full of holes.
A: So why'd you bring it?
B: I didn't think it would rain.

1st guy: They fired my girl from her job at the bank.
2nd guy: Yeah? How come?
1st guy: Well, when customers brought in money, she'd always say, "For me?"

"Fishing?"
"No, drowning worms."

"What do you think of LSD?"
"I think he'd make a great president."

Victor Borge says, "My uncle was run over by a steam roller. He's in the hospital in rooms 22 to 29 flat on his back."

"I ran a hundred yards in six seconds."

"But that's not possible—the world's record is more than nine seconds."

"I know a short cut."

I may have to find a new maid. When I lose the button off my shirt, she sews up the hole.

Mistress: It feels much colder in here—has the temperature dropped?
Maid: Yes mum, I'm sorry, I was cleaning the thermometer and I dropped it.

A friend told me one way to make housework easier was to use paper plates—I found they clog up my dishwasher.

Woody Allen's hobby is to relax in a tub. "I stay there for hours," says Woody. "Sometimes I even fill it with water."

e

Earthquake

Bob Hope was ready with his earthquake jokes. "Imagine if there was no earthquake," he told his writers. "I'd be stuck with all these earthquake jokes.

"Caltech called it moderately severe. Mayor Yorty called it a disaster, and the Chamber of Commerce announced that real estate is just fluctuating again.

"John Wayne played it cool. Put all his kids in a circle.

"My zip code changed three times and I was still in my bed.

"My milkman delivered three quarts of whipped cream.

"Engelbert Humperdinck wound up with both his sideburns on one side.

"To you easterners, the best way to describe an earthquake is just imagine two mountains doing the funky chicken."

Economy

"Do you have any reliable rule for estimating the cost of living?"

"I sure do. Take your income—whatever that may be—and add 25 per cent."

Every child born in the U.S.A. is endowed with life, liberty, and a share of the government debt.

The trouble with today's economy is that when a man is rich, it's all on paper—when he's broke it's cash.

"If all the world's economists were laid end to end—they wouldn't even reach a conclusion. . . ." —George Bernard Shaw.

An economist always knows more about money than the people who have it.

We're living in a great economy—I never spent so much taxes in my life.

Ego

The husband was primping in the mirror before leaving for his big speech. "I wonder how many great men there are in the world?" he mused.

"One less than you think," said his wife.

He shaves in cold water because hot water steams up his mirror.

Every year on his birthday he sends his mother a telegram of congratulations.

The nicest thing about an egotist—he never goes around talking about other people.

An egotist is a man who thinks he is everything you think you are.

An egotist is a self-made man who worships his creator.

Epitaphs

On a gravestone in the North of Scotland:

> Dry up your tears and weep no more
> I am not dead but gone before
> Remember me and bear in mind
> You have not long to stay behind.

From a Scottish graveyard:

> Here lies I, Martin Elginbrodde
> Have mercy o' my soul, Lord God,
> As I wad do, were I Lord God,
> And ye were Martin Elginbrodde.

Inscription on the tombstone of an old maid: And they say you can't take it with you. . . .

> Here lies our Elvira Cohn
> To virtue quite unknown
> Rejoice—be happy—have good cheer
> At last she sleeps alone.

If, after I depart this vale, you remember me and have some thought to please my ghost, forgive some sinner and wink your eye at some homely girl. —H. L. Mencken.

Mrs. Billy Graham said if she had to select the words to be inscribed on her tombstone, she would borrow these from a road sign: END OF CONSTRUCTION—THANKS FOR YOUR PATIENCE.

A *Hippie:* Don't dig me, man, I'm real gone.

A *Waiter:* At last God caught his eye.

To a Husband from His Dear Wife: Rest in peace—till we meet again.

Ethnic Humor

I used to do a bit in vaudeville with the five-times world boxing champ Tony Canzoneri. Tony explained that there are certain things you can't do in the ring any more. "This you can't do." He demonstrated by putting his thumb in my eye. "And this is not allowed," he said as he hit me below the belt. "And, of course, you should never do this," he said as he kicked me in the shin. "And most important," he added, "no biting," which he demonstrated by taking a bite of my ear.

It's the same thing with ethnic humor. You use jokes like the following at your own risk. I record them here to show you the jokes, gags, and anecdotes that the ethnic groups are fighting.

Recently, New York State's Commissioner of Human Rights bemoaned the "alarming increase" in ethnic humor and warned that he was "prepared to proceed against offenders under the antidiscrimination law."

Like my pal Canzoneri, I put these jokes here to warn you or alert you. If you insist on doing them at public gatherings—make sure you keep moving—don't be a target.

The unkempt Arab rug peddler was making his way down a Parisian boulevard trying to sell his wares. "Will you buy a carpet, monsieur?" he pleaded to a passing tourist.

"No, no!" snapped the tourist, drawing back. "They stink!"

The Arab drew himself up in proud indignation. "How dare you say that!" he cried. "I'll have you know, monsieur, that my carpets do not stink! It's me!"

How do you tell the bride at a Polish wedding? "She's wearing something old, something new, something borrowed, something blue, something pink, something purple, something orange, something yellow . . ."

"What is matched Puerto Rican luggage?"
"Two shopping bags from the same store."

"How can you tell the difference between a Jew and an Italian?"
"The Jew is the one in the Italian suit."

Did you ask the difference between a French woman, an English woman, and a Jewish woman's reaction when she is kissed in bed by her husband?

The French woman says, "Oo la la, Pierre, your kisses are oo la la."

The English woman says, "Jolly well done—I say, Winston, your kisses are jolly well done!"

The Jewish woman says, "You know, Sam, the ceiling needs painting."

They were hanging an Italian, a Jew, and a Pole. The Italian was first. The noose was loose and he slipped out, fell in the water, and swam away. The Jew was next. The noose was loose for him too, he slipped out, fell in the water, and swam away. The Pole cried out to the executioner, "Please—tighten that noose—I can't swim!"

The little Jewish boy wanted to play with the gentile kid next door who said, "My father won't let me play with you because you're Jewish." The boy answered, "That's all right—we won't play for money."

Or the switch of the Catholic kid who bragged to the Jewish kid, "My priest knows more than your rabbi!" The Jewish kid answered: "Sure, why not? you tell him everything."

The Scotsman, the Welshman, and the Englishman were left legacies by a friend on condition that each should put five pounds in his coffin.

The Englishman put in a five-pound note. The Welshman put in a five-pound note which he borrowed from the Englishman. The Scotsman took out the two five-pound notes and put in a check for fifteen pounds, payable to bearer.

Three days later he was astonished to learn that the check had been presented and cashed. The undertaker was an Irishman.

Pat read so much about the evils of drinking that he gave up reading.

It all reminds me of my favorite story of the two pals having a gab session and one says, "Did you hear about the two Jews that got off a bus and one says to the other—"

"What is wrong with you?" interrupted his buddy. "Why must it

always be two Jews? Two Jews—always we tell stories to abuse the
Jews—They have enough trouble—Why don't you pick on some other
nationality for a change?"

"Okay," said his friend, "if that's how you feel about it. Two China-
men got off the bus and one said to the other—"Are you coming
to my son's Bar Mitzva?"

"What would you call a six-foot-four Negro with a knife in his hand?"
"Sir!"

"Why do Italians talk with their hands?"
"Because they can't stand each other's breath."

Yom Kippur is the one day of the year when the Jewish people fast.
Levy was surprised to see Cohen eating in a restaurant—and oysters
yet! "Oysters? On Yom Kippur" queried Levy with raised eyebrows.
"What's wrong?" answered Cohen. "Yom Kippur has an *r* in it."

Cross a Jew with a Pole—he's a janitor but he owns the building.

The woman was bragging about her son Mark. "He's a lawyer—and
making a lot of money."
"How about your son Max? What happened to him?"
"He became a rabbi."
"A rabbi, how nice. How is he doing?"
"By me—that's not a business for a Jew."

Sammy Davis, Jr., tells the story of the Negro lad who goes to heaven
and St. Peter stops him at the gate.
"We only have heroes in here," says St. Peter.
"But I'm a hero."
"What heroic thing did you do?"
"I was married to a white girl on the steps of Biloxi, Mississippi,
City Hall at twelve noon!"
"When did this happen?" St. Peter asks.
"Two minutes ago!"

In Israel they have a slogan in the navy that goes: "Don't give up
the ship—sell it."

"How do you tell a bride at an Irish wedding?"
"She's the one in the maternity dress."

"How was the limbo invented?"
"A Puerto Rican sneaking into a pay toilet."

Sammy Davis, Jr., says that years ago he got on a bus in the South and was told by the bigot driver to go sit in the back.

"But I'm Jewish," Sammy protested.

"Get off altogether!" shouted the driver.

These lines were thrown by their own people—so don't holler:

Comedian Corbett Monica, Italian, says: "I'm trying to bring peace. I want the Italians and the Arabs to go to war. Nobody'll be hurt." He also says as soon as Italy heard that the Israelis were attacking Egypt, Italy surrendered.

One Polish man tells this one on the Poles. The couples insist on getting married in bathtubs because they want a double ring ceremony.

A Puerto Rican comedian whose name escapes me opens his show with: "I'm late because we had an accident at the house, eight were hurt. The bed broke."

Show me a Jewish boy who doesn't go to medical school and I'll show you a lawyer.

Ahmed decides he needs a new brain, so he goes to the Cairo brain bank. The caretaker shows him the bottled brain of a German mathematician, for $600. "Too expensive," Ahmed says. The caretaker leads him to the brain of an American nuclear physicist, for $900. "Much too expensive," Ahmed replies. Finally the caretaker offers him the brain of an Egyptian general, for $9,000. "Why should I pay that kind of money for the brain of an Egyptian general?" Ahmed protests. "But sir," the caretaker explains, "this brain has never been used."

Quoting Irwin C. Watson: I've been thinking that if I had to have a heart or a brain transplant and I was able to pick my donor, whose heart or brain would I want? And I decided I would want the heart or the brain of a bigot whether he be black or white—because I'd want a heart or brain that hasn't been used.

I dreamed that Governor Wallace died and went to heaven and instead of St. Peter meeting him some voice boomed, "Hello dere."

Fifty Puerto Ricans were arrested for sleeping in Central Park. They pleaded not guilty. Their defense was that they were having their room painted.

"Do you know what happened when the Ajax white knight came to Harlem?"
"He was mugged."

A nymphomaniac is a Jewish girl who will go to bed with a guy after she's just had her hair done.

Did you hear about the new Italian university?
It's called Whatsa-Matta-U.

How do you tell when an Irish patient is getting better? When he tries to blow the head off his medicine.

I knew a southern bigot who happened to be a bed wetter. He used to go to his Klan meetings in rubber sheets.

How do you make a Hungarian cake? First you steal two eggs . . .

The missionary from good old England was trying to convert the Hindu to Christianity. "Tell me, wouldn't you like to go to heaven when you die?" The Hindu was not impressed. "Heaven can't be very good," he said, "or the British would have grabbed it years ago."

"Go with your sister?" the tourist said to the Mexican boy. "I won't even drink your water!"

What do 1776 and 1492 have in common? Give up? Adjoining rooms at the Poland Hilton.

Bob Considine tells the story about restaurateur Toots Shor, who learned to cope with problems early in life. As one of the few Jewish boys in a predominantly Catholic neighborhood in South Philadelphia, he found that his efforts to make friends with other kids were sometimes rebuffed—to the extent that they would chase him home like a pack of wolves closing in on a toothsome rabbit.

Toots learned to outwit them in a novel way. He discovered that by taking a short cut through any Catholic church in his line of flight, he could gain a few yards and usually get home safely. "Those bums would have to genuflect when they passed the altar," Toots recalls, "and I didn't even break my stride."

Two black salesmen checked into a hotel in Georgia. One suggested they call room service and have them send up a couple of white broads. "Are you nuts?" the other screamed. "You gonna ask for white girls in Georgia?"

"What's wrong? I want to love them—not go to school with them."

How do you keep a nice Jewish girl from having sex? Marry her.

Why does a Jewish wife close her eyes when having sex? She hates to see her husband having such a good time.

The British are the most diplomatic people in the world. Who else could smile at you when they serve you that coffee?

A Jew and a Christian were arguing about their heritage. The Jew said indignantly, "Why, when your ancestors were picking up acorns in the forest—mine already had diabetes."

A Catholic girl and a Jewish boy fell madly in love. But their religious beliefs interfered. The Irish Catholic mother advised her daughter to "sell him a bill of goods. Teach him the beauty and joys of Catholicism—make him be a Catholic." The girl did. She sold him and sold him, and the wedding date was set. One day before the marriage the girl came home and sobbed. "The marriage is off."

"Why," said the mother, "didn't you sell him?" And the girl answered, "I sold him. . . . Now he wants to be a priest."

An Israeli was bragging to his neighbor on the phone about Moishe Dayan. "The hell with Dayan," said the man.

"Well," said the man from Tel Aviv, "how about Golda Meir, you got to admit that she's great."

"The hell with Meir," he said.

"Tell me—what nationality are you?" the Jewish gentleman asked quietly.

"I'm Irish," he said proudly.

"Then, the hell with Ella Fitzgerald," he said finally.

It was a chip-in party—a reunion of old friends. The Englishman brought a cooked turkey; the Irishman brought a case of whiskey; the American brought a Virginia ham—and the Scotsman brought his brother.

Pat Henry, the comic, a disciple of Frank Sinatra, is of Italian descent. He said of the demonstration organized by Joe Colombo to protest discrimination against Italian-Americans: "What shrewd planning that was. The dais alone represented eight hundred years off for good behavior."

Etiquette

Etiquette is yawning with your mouth closed.

Etiquette is making your company feel at home even though you wish they were.

Executive

A good executive is a man who will share the credit with the man who did all the work.

He doesn't believe in wasting time with secretaries. He uses the old saying, "If at first you don't succeed—fire her."

He's a perfect executive; when he's dictating to his secretary, he always ends a sentence with a proposition.

"I have so many problems," said a corporation executive, "that if anything happens today, it'll be two weeks before I can worry about it."

Exercise

Exercise kills germs—but we can't figure out how to make the damn things exercise.

A couple noticed that they weren't feeling as perky as they should so they decided to consult a doctor. The doctor examined them and, finding nothing organically wrong, advised them to get more exercise. So the husband went out and bought himself a set of golf clubs, and a lawn mower for his wife.

Who knows from exercise—I get winded pulling my toothbrush out of the hole.

The only exercise I get is putting my cufflinks in my shirt.

When I feel like exercising, I lie down until the feeling goes away.

"Why are you lying down? Are you tired?"
"I'm lying down so I don't get tired."

Chauncey Depew said it. "I get my exercise acting as a pallbearer for my friends who exercise."

"When I was a youngster I thought nothing of a ten-mile walk."
"Well, I don't think much of it myself."

What kind of exercise—I get winded turning on the television set.

f

Family

My wife didn't come from a big family—she brought most of them with her.

Molly Picon was telling me on my radio show that her mother raised her and ten other children in a small three-room apartment.
"How did she manage?" I asked.
"She took in boarders," she explained.

It's Gypsy Rose Lee's immortal line: "I'm descended from a long line—that my mother fell for."

I once introduced a man in Indonesia as the "Father of the Year." He actually had twenty-three children. When he was asked to speak he said, "I'm pretty tired—I'm usually in bed by this time."

A recent survey proves what we always suspected—the people who live longest are rich relatives.

Farmer

The politician was trying to appease a group of angry young farmers because he was a bit behind schedule in his promises:
"If you put a bull into a field one night," he declared, "you wouldn't expect to get a lot of newborn calves in the morning, would you?"
"No," a voice replied from the back of the hall. "But you'd certainly expect to see a lot of contented faces."

The driver of the car was really honest and when he hit the rooster wandering on the road he stopped and went around to see the farmer.
"I'm sorry—but I killed your rooster and I'd like very much to replace him."
"As you say," said the farmer. "Go around the side and you'll find the hens in the back."

The ad appeared in a farmer's journal: Farmer, age 41, would like to meet with woman about 30 who owns a tractor. Object: Marriage. Please send picture of tractor.

I asked one farmer if he ever shot craps. "No," he said, "because my wife doesn't know how to cook 'em."

The farmer was asked why he married for the sixth time. "To tell you the truth," he explained, "for the little bit a woman eats—I wouldn't be without one."

"It's our anniversary tomorrow, Clem," said the farmer's wife, "our silver anniversary—Don't you think we ought to go out and kill a chicken?"

"Why kill a chicken now for what happened twenty-five years ago?"

When the farmers went on strike—this one farmer was so serious about it—he couldn't even go to see a topless show.

Fashion

Times have changed: When my grandmother was a girl she didn't use mascara or nail polish or wear a wig. Not when she was a girl —but she does now.

I saw a woman with a hat that looked like a birthday cake. The only trouble she had was keeping the candles lit on rainy days.

Sophia Loren: "I don't like those loose dresses—I think tents are strictly for Boy Scouts."

The newest thing in women's hairdos is men!

One lady shopper to another: "These new fashions are for the birds —I haven't seen a thing I'd want to get thin for."

This season the girls are wearing hot pants. That's jockey shorts with a hem.

Joan Rivers says her husband gave her a household hint on what to do with her old clothes: "Wear them."

Fashion note: Women will be wearing the same thing in brassieres this year.

If women dressed to please their husbands—they'd wear last year's clothes.

A woman's dress should be like a barbed-wire fence—serve its purpose without obstructing the view.

A woman's dress should be tight enough to show that there is a woman inside it but loose enough to show that she is a lady.

She was wearing a dress with an Italian look—there were wine stains all over it.

My secretary announced the other morning, "I'm going to quit wearing pantsuits if every Tom, Dick, and Harry is going to wear them."

Joan Rivers explains why she finally decided to wear the midi, "If you're going to look ugly—you might as well look this year's ugly."

She was using a soft, feminine material to make a dress. "See," she said, holding the dress up to herself to show her husband. "Won't it be pretty when it's finished?"
   "But you can see right through it!" the husband exclaimed.
   "Not when I'm in it."

The designer of see-through blouses and hot pants suggested this jingle to the advertising agency, "I'll be seeing you—in all the old familiar places."

She was so ugly—she wore a see-through dress but nobody wanted to.

No wonder they call it high fashion, just take a look at the price tags.

Smith went in to complain to his tailor that he couldn't sit down in his new trousers.
   "But you asked for them to be skin-tight," said the tailor.
   "True," said Smith. "But I can sit down in my skin—I can't in these trousers."

I always get a kick going to Paris with its exotic perfumes—its see-through blouses—its hot pants—but that's enough about the boys —now let's talk about the girls.

His pants are so tight they wear out on the inside.

His trousers are so tight he has to trim his toenails to put them on.

Fannie Flagg says she hopes jodphurs come back into style: "They're the only pants that go out the same place I do."

Woody Allen admits he is the world's worst dresser. In spite of his millions he still prefers corduroys and sneakers to bankers' grays or

Madison Avenue blacks. Woody explains his wardrobe like this: "The other day I opened my closet door and discovered a moth had eaten my sports coat. He was lying on the floor, nauseous."

Overheard in a local boutique: "But, madame, looking ridiculous is the fashion this year."

Fat

He's so fat, whenever he boards a boat it becomes a submarine.

He's so fat, when he just sits on a bar stool he has a hangover.

I won't dare say she's built like a truck—but I did notice that nobody ever passes her on the right.

She brags that she's got the figure of a girl. That's true—a fat girl.

She's not really fat—she's just short for her weight! She should actually be about 8 foot 6 inches.

Here are some "Fat" commercials I created for Sweet 'n Low:

I know a girl with a great figure—39 by 22 by 38 and that's only her left leg—She needs Sweet 'n Low.

If you cast a giant shadow and kids run to you to stay in the shade —try Sweet 'n Low.

Girls—the more snacks—the tighter the slacks.

If you bought a Bikini for a ridiculous figure—you got to reduce.

If you're worth your weight in gold and you're very rich. . . .

Either my aunt goes on a diet—or they are going to have to let out the living room.

If my uncle doesn't go on a diet—they will have to let out the car.

If you have to wear a stretch bathrobe—you need Sweet 'n Low.

If they wrote a show about you trying to get into a Volkswagen called "Mission Impossible"—you need Sweet 'n Low.

If she looks like a model for duffel bags—you know she needs Sweet 'n Low.

I wouldn't say my aunt is fat—but once at a bus stop three people tried to board her.

She is so fat—when she wears white hot pants—she looks like a bandaged whale.

Totie Fields says she was even heavier when she got married: "In fact, on our wedding night when George carried me over the threshold he had to make two trips."

Someone tried to describe hefty comedienne Totie Fields: "We'll put it this way—she's having her portrait done by Rand-McNally."

She is the only person I know who has an unlisted dress size.

She's on the critical list at Weight Watchers.

This guy is partial to statuesque girls: "Thin may be in, but fat's where it's at."

Jackie Vernon, who dieted off seventy-three pounds, says of his former flabbiness, "It used to be that when I got on a scale I got two fortunes. . . ."

She's so fat her husband was married to her for eight years and never saw all of her.

He's so fat he has to sign up for group insurance—by himself.

Joan Rivers claims she was so fat as a child that "Whenever I played post office—they sent me bulk rate."

She's so fat the photographer charges her group rates.

I'm not saying my aunt is fat, but—if she falls down she rocks herself to sleep trying to get up.

She is so big—the only thing they had in her size in the store was the dressing room.

She has gotten so big:
    They had to let out the windshield in her car.
    She has to wear a stretch bathrobe.
    They had to let out the sofa.
    They had to let out the kitchen.
    She's a model for slip covers.
    She's a model for duffel bags.
    She's a model for tents.

Father's Day

Henny Youngman says his wife gave him a present for Father's Day: The bills for Mother's Day.

Father's Day is always a tense situation as one father put it: "What if they gave me something I can't afford?"

W. C. Fields

"A woman drove me to drink, and I'll be a son of a gun, but I never even wrote to thank her."

"I arrived in Hollywood with twenty-six dollars in my pocket and three years later I was broke!"

"If at times I appear to be a little unkind, try to understand that at heart I'm vicious."

"Some of my best friends can't be trusted."

"I'm completely free of prejudice . . . I hate everyone equally."

"I got that guy so drunk last night—it took three bellboys to put me to bed."

Fighters

Rocky Graziano was managing a fighter who kept pleading that he wanted to fight Slugger Callahan. "I told you a thousand times," Rocky explained, "I can't get you a fight with Slugger Callahan! *You're* Slugger Callahan!"

This fighter was knocked out so many times, he sold advertising on the soles of his shoes.

Kid Slugg was breathing heavy between rounds. "Am I doing him enough damage?" he asked his second.
　"No—but keep swinging—the draft might give him a cold."

This fighter was catching everything but he wouldn't let them throw in the towel. "How am I doing?" he asked his second after a disastrous eighth round.
　"Pretty good—but as it stands now, you'll have to knock him out to get a draw."

Max Baer was being ribbed by his pal Slapsie Maxie Rosenbloom about the licking he took from champ Joe Louis. "That Louis sure knew he was in a fight," Baer said. "For a while there I gave that Louis a terrific scare."

"You sure did," said Slapsie. "He thought he killed you."

Figure

These days when a girl walks the straight and narrow—she's usually built that way.

She was wearing a peekaboo blouse—just one peek and they booed.

George Kirby says, "Twenty years ago my wife had a million-dollar figure, and she's still got it. Only now when she walks it's like it's all in loose change."

I introduced Jane Russell this way: "Here she is—the two and only. . . ."

She is an expert touch typist. She has to be—her figure is 45-23-36 and she can't see the keys.

She has to wear falsies—just to look flat-chested.

The bigger they are the dumber they can afford to be.

About Jane Russell: "She looks like a chiffonier with the top drawer pulled out."

One woman wrote away for one of those bust developers—now she is so big they had to let out the windshield in her car.

Fishing

The two buddies went fishing but by the time the afternoon was over, one was ready to stab the other. "I don't understand it," he cried. "I have been fishing longer than you. I have a much better rod. I throw my line better, and you're getting all the fish."

"I play hunches," the other explained. "When I get up in the morning, if my wife is lying on her left side, I fish on the left side of the boat. If she is lying on her right side, I always fish on the right side."

"Suppose she's lying on her back?" his buddy snarled.

"Then I don't go fishing."

Wives are like fishermen. They complain about the one they caught and brag about the one that got away.

His wife was shivering in the rowboat while her husband was fishing. "Tell me again," she cried between blue lips, "how much fun we are having—I keep forgetting."

He was disgusted. He hadn't caught a fish all day when the woman approached and asked, "Fishing?"
"No," he answered, "I'm drowning worms."

He was a fanatical fisherman who just couldn't give up a weekend without it. He drove five miles down the road to a place marked "private" and went through a gate with the legend, KEEP OUT— TRESPASSERS WILL BE PROSECUTED, then to the river where there was a big sign planted, NO FISHING ALLOWED. He was on his way home when he was approached by a stranger who asked, "Have a good day?"
"Couldn't be better—I got a couple of hundred pounds of the finest bass you ever saw in the back of my car—by the way, who are you, sir?"
"I'm the State Game Warden—and who are you?"
"I'm the biggest damn liar in these United States."

As usual, the Texan was bragging about his fishing. The Australian countered that he caught a fish in his home town that was eight inches.
"Isn't that small?" the Texan squelched.
"In Australia," he answered, "we measure 'em between the eyes."

"I had a dream I was alone in a boat with Raquel Welch."
"Really, how did you make out?"
"Great—I caught an eight-pound bass."

Flying

I'm not superstitious or afraid of flying, but why did the plane I was in last week, upon take-off, have to fly under a ladder?

There's still a bit of risk in aviation—the taxi ride from the city to the airport.

He won't fly on account of his religion—he's a devout coward.

Foreign

AFGHANISTAN

As judge of his village, Mullah Nazardin was trying a case. Listening to the plaintiff, he said, "You are right." Listening to the defendant, he said, "You are right." The clerk of the court bent down and whispered to the judge, "But, Mullah, they can't both be right." To which Nazardin replied, "You are right, too."

Mullah was attending the funeral services of the richest man in the village. Because he was weeping bitterly, a man inquired sadly, "Was the deceased one of your dear relatives?"

"No," said Mullah sorrowfully.

"Then why are you crying?" asked the stranger.

"Because I'm not one of the relatives," answered Mullah.

ARABS

Egypt might have lost the war—but they look like a cinch in the olympics.

They tell of an Arab army deserter—He left his unit to stand and fight.

Sadat asked Kosygin if he would supply arms for the next Israeli-Arab fight. "Of course," said the Russian leader. "Find out what Dayan needs."

The Arabs claimed the war was unfair, "because Israel has three million Jews and we don't have any."

ASIA

"What price would you put on my value as king?" asked the egotistical conqueror.

"Fifty dirhim," Mullah replied.

"Why, you dog," cried the king, "this towel alone is worth fifty dirhim."

"I know," said Mullah, "that is why I bid so high."

"At what age were you first married?" Mullah was asked.

"I don't know exactly," he answered, "but I do know it was before I became wise."

Mullah was asked by a villager, "How many hours of rest do you get each day?"

"She sleeps a few hours after lunch and a few hours at night."

"Who is she?" asked the confused villager.

"My wife."

"I didn't ask about your wife, I asked how many hours rest you get?"

"The same thing. The only time I get any rest is when she is asleep."

AUSTRALIA

The Australian loves to tell jokes perpetuating the myth that he's the laziest man alive. A swagman was lying in the sun by a country road when a passerby saw a deadly snake dangerously close to his feet. "Mind you there, mate," he yelled, "there's a snake near your foot." The swagman slowly lifted his head. "Which foot, mate?" he yawned.

CAMBODIA

One of the clean favorites is about the visitor to the zoo who noticed one of the keepers sobbing quietly in the corner. On inquiry he was told that the elephant had died.

"Fond of him, was he?" the visitor asked.

"It's not that," was the reply. "He's the chap that's got to dig the grave."

CHILE

"Yes, but has the dog a pedigree?"

"Señora," said the street seller, "if that dog were to speak it wouldn't talk to either one of us."

CHINA

A woman went to court and sued a man. She said, "I went to the well to draw water, and this man came from behind and assaulted me."

The judge asked, "Then why did you not run away?"

"I was afraid that if I stood up and went away, it wouldn't be finished."

A maidservant happened to belch in front of her master, who became angry and was going to strike her, but, seeing her wide hips, his anger suddenly abated, and he took his pleasure with her. The next day, when he was in his study, there was a knock on the door. It was the maidservant. "What is it? What do you want?"

"Please, sir, I belched again a little while ago."

God, he make the universe and then he rested. He then make man and then he rested again. He next make woman—and nobody have rested since.

Wouldn't it be crazy if Red China does split the atom and finds a fortune inside which reads, "Red China is wonderful—but only on a white tablecloth."

I'd like to see Taiwan and China in the UN—The big fight is who is going to be in Column A?

What's the big deal about two Chinas? In the Catskills they always had two Chinas—one for meat and one for dairy.

They should not allow Red China in the UN. You know the Chinese; once they vote—an hour later they want to vote again.

Any country with a population of 800 million that says its favorite sport is ping-pong—will lie about other things too.

ENGLAND

The English have answered hecklers way before Churchill lit his first cigar. When the distinguished prime minister was a youth, he was making a speech in a market square and was suddenly hit by a large cabbage. Brushing away the debris he said, "I asked for the gentleman's ears—not his head."

The English are supposed to have a backward sense of humor. There is an old fable that an Englishman laughs at a joke three times: Once when he hears it, once when it's explained to him, and once when he understands it. This is strictly a legend and untrue. They have a great sense of humor. It's true that English humor could be droller and perhaps more subtle; some say less stuffy. "I hear they buried your wife," one lord said to the other. "Had to. Dead, you know," the other answered.

She gave birth to twins—one at two and the other at seven—in England everything stops for tea.

Two Britishers were crossing on the *Queen Mary*. After a few short ones and a couple of longer ones they left the bar and went topside looking for dates. A while later one of them was back in the bar with a "live one" when the other staggered up. "Beg pardon, old bean," he mumbled, "but would you mind awfully changing ladies? Due to the whiskey and the fog, I seem to have gotten hold of an old aunt of mine."

A German and a Russian were on a river in Germany. The German was fishing in the West Zone, and was catching fish right and left —well, not left—but the Russian in the Red Zone wasn't having any luck at all. He yelled to the German, "How come you manage to catch so many fish?" and the answer came back, "Over here the fish aren't afraid to open their mouths."

FIJI

In Fiji they have a tribe that can actually walk on fire. They say anybody can do it if they give up sex and coconuts for two weeks. I refused to try. I'd miss the coconuts too much.

FRANCE

The ardent honeymooning of her eighty-year-old groom was exhausting the young bride. During a momentary lull, while he was shaving, she sneaked out and staggered into the hotel coffee shop downstairs. "I don't get it," her friend the waitress exclaimed. "Here you are, a teen-age bride with an ancient husband, and you look a wreck! What happened?"

Yelled the young bride, "The old goat double-crossed me! He told me he saved up for sixty years—and I thought he was talking about money."

A well-known citizen of Paris met his ex-wife at a cocktail party, and, warmed by the libations, suggested they have another go at connubial bliss.

"Over my dead body," said the lady haughtily.

"My error," said the erstwhile spouse. "I see you haven't changed a bit."

Three French boys, six, seven, and eight years old respectively, were running down a Parisian alley when the six-year-old stopped and hollered to the others, "Hey, fellas, come here. A man and a woman are fighting in that house—I can see them through the window."

The seven-year-old looked and said, "You dumb-dumb, they're making love."

And the eight-year-old said, "Yeah—and badly."

You never have to worry about getting robbed at night in Paris—the shopkeepers grab it all during the day.

Goldberg: I wish I came to Paris forty years ago.
Adams: You mean when Paris was Paris?
Goldberg: No—When Goldberg was Goldberg.

Air France doesn't show movies—just postcards.

Things must be getting tough in France—I just got a postcard from Paris and there was writing on it.

Nanette is a girl of few words—those words are francs, dollars, and pounds.

In France, the postman isn't the only working person who has to walk the streets to pick up the male. The local traffic in sin makes Broadway look like an Abbey.

Nanette: Darling, where did you get that mink coat? I've been struggling for years to get one.
Odette: Darling—you mustn't struggle.

Sign in French Shop: ENGLISH AND FRENCH SPOKEN—CASH UNDERSTOOD.

GERMANY

"My wife disappeared yesterday and I asked you to try and find her. Don't trouble any more."

"Has she returned?"

"No. I have thought it over."

German weather broadcast: "Tomorrow will be sunny. That's an order!"

HUNGARY

A girl answered the doorbell to find a tax collector. "Ma, the tax collector is here," she shouted to her mother upstairs. "I'll be right down," the mother called down. "Give him a chair." The girl shouted back, "A chair won't do—he wants all the furniture."

INDIA

"I shot this tiger here in India. It was a case of me or the tiger."
"Well, the tiger certainly makes a better rug."

A man threw a rupee to a blind beggar, who expertly retrieved it. The man was astonished. "I thought you were blind!"
"No, sir, I am not that blind beggar who usually sits here. Today he has gone to see the cinema."

Tourist: Are you content to spend your life walking around the country begging?
Beggar: No, lady. Many's the time I've wished for a car.

INDONESIA

A pest met a cabinet member at the Indonesia Hotel in Djakarta and gushed, "You know, I passed your house this morning."
"That was kind of you," said the minister. "Thank you."

IRELAND

Father Murphy was too busy to listen to Pat's confession. "We have hundreds in the church today," he explained. "I'm sure it's no big emergency—you haven't committed a murder since last time. See you tomorrow."
On his way out he met Dolen and said, "Go home—they're only taking murder cases today."

Pat: I've been drinking whiskey all week to cure my sinus.
Mike: I can give you a cure.
Pat: Who asked you?

"If one could only teach the English how to talk and the Irish to listen—life might be civilised."   —Oscar Wilde.

Pat staggered down the corridor looking for the legend spelled AA. "Izh dish Akoholocks Anonomish?" he asked the man at the door. "Yes, sir—do you wish to join?"—"No, shir—to resign."

Paddy had a great idea. After a tough time with the income tax boys he sighed. "Look—why don't you keep the income and give me the tax?"

Mr. Patrick Mulligan was dictating his last will and testament. "Put Brenden down for 250 pounds—put Shamus down for 500 pounds —put Timothy down for 1,000 pounds. . . ."

"But," his puzzled lawyer interjected, "where is all this money coming from?"

"To hell with 'em," Patrick exclaimed. "Let them work for it like I did."

The famous Irish author George Moore was asked on his eightieth birthday to explain how he managed such a long life. "Easy," he said. "I believe it is due to the fact that I never smoked, drank, or touched a girl—until I was ten years old."

Pat walked into a bar in Dublin, his face beaten to a pulp. "And who did that to you?" asked the bartender.

"I had a fight with Mike Shannon!"

"What?" asked the bartender. "You let a little guy like that beat you up? You ought to be ashamed of yourself, a little good-for-nothing runt like that Mike!"

"Hold on there," said Pat. "Don't be talking disrespectfully of the dead."

The judge was reprimanding the prisoner. "You have been brought here for drinking."

"Okay, lesh get started."

"Whiskey has killed more men than bullets."

"Yeah, but wouldn't you rather be filled with whiskey than bullets?"

The three mugs grabbed Tim in the alley and after a rough battle they got him strapped down and took twenty cents from his pocket.

"Now what the hell was the idea of putting up such a battle for a lousy twenty cents," one of the holdup men asked disgustedly.

"Sure and I thought you were after the fifty bucks I got in me sock."

It has been said that an Englishman thinks and speaks—a Scot thinks twice before he speaks—and an Irishman speaks before he thinks.

An Englishman thinks seated—a Frenchman, standing—an American, pacing—and an Irishman, afterward.   —Austin O'Malley.

"I've made me will," said Clancy. "All me fortune goes to the doctor that saves me life."

Pat: Those damn scientists—now look what they've gone and done!
Mike: You mean goin' to the moon?
Pat: No—those idiots fooled around until they come up with somethin' besides whiskey to cure a cold.

Show me the man who has kissed the blarney stone—and I'll show you a fella with a sex problem.

Do you think if an Irishman gets drunk he should be called Irish stew?

The Irish are always talking about the wee people. I don't know if they mean a leprechaun or somebody with a kidney problem.

The Irish always fight among themselves—to be sure of having worthy adversaries.

The Irishman explained his long life. "Moderation is the key," he said. "Especially drinking. I have made two rules. First—never to take whiskey without water—and never to take water without whiskey."

"I love these places with sawdust on the floor," said the visitor in the little bar. "Sawdust, my eye," said the bartender, "that's yesterday's furniture."

ISRAEL

General Rabin explained why his men fought so well in the Six-Day War: "I told them that the war was a serious business, and that I wanted them to act like businessmen. They did. When I said 'charge,' they overcharged."

The worst thing to do in Israel is to read mystery stories—you know the murderer immediately.

Who cares if it's true?—It is funny—An Israel gasoline company advertises this way: "So we don't have a tiger in our tank—we got something much better—a boiled chicken."

The Jews are known to be tardy when it comes to meetings and functions, so their humor often reflects it. I heard one radio announcer in Haifa announce, "When you hear the chimes it will be exactly 5 P.M.—or a few minutes later."

President Nixon suggested to Prime Minister Golda Meir that the two countries trade two top generals. "I'll take Moshe Dayan and Yitzhak Rabin," Nixon said.

"Good," Golda replied. "We'll take General Motors and General Electric."

Levi Eshkol (onetime prime minister of Israel): "Put three Zionists in a room—and they will form four political parties."

Chaim Topol: "In our country we don't believe in miracles—we *rely* on them."

Golda Meir told off the United States about those jets they wanted to buy. "But we sent you $100,000,000," the State Department said, and Golda retorted, "So when the Arabs attack—what do we do? Write them a check?"

An Arab officer, harassed by an Israeli sharpshooter on a steep hill, sent his entire platoon to knock off the Jew. Shortly, the platoon returned minus several men. The sharpshooter was still in action. "Why have you come back?" the officer demanded.

"We are sorry, effendi," spoke up an Arab noncom, "but there were *two* Jews."

When an air-raid siren went off in Tel Aviv a woman was annoyed that her husband was slow in leaving the apartment, so from the stairs she shouted, "Come on, Harry!"

"I'm coming," replied her husband, a denture wearer. "I've just got to get my teeth."

"Never mind your teeth," shouted back his wife. "What do you think they're dropping—pastrami sandwiches?"

The newspaperman confronted Golda Meir about her insistence on meeting the Arabs in face-to-face negotiations. "Even divorces," he challenged, "are arranged without personal meetings."

"I'm not interested in divorce," said the Prime Minister. "I'm interested in marriage."

My wife, Cindy, admired a paratrooper in Haifa and asked, "How many successful jumps have you made?" "Oh," said our modest hero, "every one of the jumps must be successful."

ITALY

Marry for money and you'll probably earn it.

A woman's visit to Italy isn't complete unless she gets pinched. The last time I was there, I went up to a group of the street-corner Romeos and asked if one of them would pinch my wife. They told me they were on strike. They're trying to get hospitalization benefits.

Josephine to her girlfriend: "Do you think thirty years is too great a difference in age between a woman and a man if he is a director of a bank?"

JAPAN

A diplomat was in America and met an American woman at a reception. She did not know him and asked sweetly, "What 'nese are you—Japanese, Chinese, or Javanese?"

"I'm Japanese, madam. What 'kee are you? Monkee, donkee, or Yankee?"

A tourist, after a meal in a Japanese restaurant, hollered, "No wonder they make you take your shoes off—after you eat this stuff you really wanna kick the hell out of them."

MEXICO

The bullfighter was bragging to Groucho Marx,
   "I've met at least two hundred bulls."
   "You must be the envy of every cow in Spain," marveled Groucho.

NEPAL

The Gurkhas were the toughest guerrilla fighters of all in World War II. A Nepalese soldier in Patan told me this story: One division that had just joined the paratroopers was instructed to jump when they reached five thousand feet in the air. The hardiest of the Gurkhas refused, saying, "We don't mind jumping five hundred feet, but five thousand feet is too much even for us—" "But," said the captain, "if you jump five hundred feet you won't have time to open the parachute."

"Oh," grinned the Gurkhan leader, "if we have parachutes we don't mind jumping five thousand feet."

POLAND

In Warsaw, two strangers were admiring a new car. One exclaimed enthusiastically, "A handsome machine, no? Another triumphant exhibit of Soviet ingenuity and initiative." The other man said, "That's an American car. Can't you tell one when you see it? Didn't you know that?" The other said, "Yes, I know it—but I don't know you!"

RUSSIA

A Russian worker came home and found his wife in the arms of another man. "What kind of wife are you, idling around the house and amusing yourself on Lenin's birthday—and he isn't even a party member."

A Russian who lived in Germany many years accepted an offer to return to his native land. He decided to go alone and then have his wife and two-year-old daughter, Anna, join him after he got settled. Three months later, his wife received his first letter. He wrote, "It's wonderful here. Even more so than I expected. I'm so anxious to have you here with me. However, I would suggest that you postpone your trip till Anna gets married."

The six-year-old boy was asked by his teacher if he knew the size of the Communist party. "About five feet," he answered.

"How do you get five feet?"

"Well, my father is six feet, and every night he puts his hand to his chin and cries, 'I've had the Communist party up to here!' "

Russia really has practiced disarmament. It's disarmed Czechoslovakia, Hungary, Rumania, Poland . . .

Russia's biggest joke is China. It all began, the Soviet jest says, when Mao Tse-tung cabled to Gromyko: STARVING. SEND GRAIN.

Gromyko replied: SHORT OF GRAIN OURSELVES. CAN'T SEND ANY. TIGHTEN YOUR BELTS.

Whereupon Mao Tse-tung cabled back: SEND BELTS.

Russia is where you are allowed to go anywhere they please.

Excerpt from a Moscow broadcast: "Boris Tamaroff, our greatest athlete, has just broken all existing records for the hundred-yard dash, the mile run, and the five-mile run—all in a single day. Fortunately for all you sports fans out there, this magnificent athlete was captured and returned to his home in Siberia."

"I can't understand why the Russians are so unfriendly," Henny Youngman says. "Two drinks of vodka and I like *everybody*."

A man was sentenced to death for defeatism in Russia because he was caught repeating that the Kremlin was short of ammunition. The doomed man asked if he was to be hanged or shot. Hanged, he was told. "See?" he replied. "Short of ammunition."

An American and a Russian were debating the merits of their respected countries. "In the United States," said the American, "we have freedom of speech."

"We have freedom of speech in the U.S.S.R., too," retorted the Russian.

"In this country," said the American, "I can walk up to Nixon and call him a jerk."

"That's nothing," replied the Russian, "in my country, I too can walk up to Kosygin and say, 'Nixon is a jerk!' "

SCOTLAND

Front-page news: A Scotsman gave a waiter a tip—the horse came in last.

They stopped the crime wave in Scotland by putting a sign over the jail saying: ANYONE CAUGHT AND PUT IN JAIL WILL HAVE TO PAY HIS BOARD AND LODGING.

He's a true Scotsman—he saved all his toys for his second childhood.

The minister asked for a good response to his collection appeal and then he noted that some parishioners were putting buttons in the plate instead of money. "If ye're still determined tae put buttons on the plate," he pleaded, "please bring your own buttons—Dinna clip them off the cushions!"

The Scotsman went on a holiday and took with him a clean shirt and a pound note—when he returned he hadn't changed either of them.

On a Saturday night in a Scottish village, members of the Salvation Army were saying prayers and singing hymns. At the intermission a young Army lass went up to an elderly Scotsman and held out the familiar tambourine.

"Will you give a shilling to the Lord?" she asked.

"Hoo auld are ye, ma lassie?"

"I'm just sixteen."

To which the old man replied, "Weel, I'm seventy-nine, an' I'll be seein' Him before you, so I'll just hand it tae Him maself."

A Scot who was a bad sailor was crossing the Channel. He went to the captain and asked him what he should do to prevent seasickness.

"Have you got a sixpence?" asked the captain.

"Aye," replied Sandy.

"Well, hold it between your teeth during the trip."

The old Scotsman was asked by a friend what he thought of his nearest neighbor. He replied,

"Och, weeel, he's a decent-like lad, but he's no' exactly a temperance man. He was sittin' there juist drinkin' an' drinkin', until I could scarcely see him."

The lady of the farm house was not renowned for her generosity in pouring drinks. She handed her shepherd a drink and remarked that it was extraspecial, being fourteen years old.

The old shepherd raised his glass solemnly and said, "Weel, ma lady, there's one thing for sure. It's verra small for its age."

A Scot died and left his brother all the money that his brother owed him.

Mac asked his friend Scot for a cigarette. "But I thought you quit smoking," said Scot, reluctantly pulling out the Winstons.

"Well—I've reached the first stage—I've stopped buying them."

A true Scot never sends his pajamas to the laundry unless he has a pair of socks stuck in the pocket.

Young Sandy McTavish came home from school one day and announced to his father that his teacher said he needed a new world atlas. "Ah well," said the old man, "ye can jist wait till the world's a bit more settled."

A Scotsman came to America and checked into a hotel in New York for the night. The clerk at the desk noticed that, in addition to his luggage, he carried a large cord of rope.

"I beg your pardon," said the clerk, "what is the rope for?"

"I always travel wi' that," said the Scotsman. "It's ma fire escape in case of an emergency."

"Very well, sir," answered the clerk. "I'm afraid that guests with their own fire escapes have to pay in advance."

Sandy must have been drunk or a little tetched when he dropped a coin in the Salvation Army tambourine. Twenty minutes later he was approached again. "Oh, no," said the Scotsman, "I gave—I made my contribution."

"You're a good man," said the Salvation Army gal. "You can't do too much for these people—God will repay you a thousandfold."

"Could be," said Sandy, "but I'll just wait till the first transaction's finished before I start on the second."

Now, what about the three Scotsmen who were found drowned in the lake? It seems that they had bet a shilling each as to who would stay under the water the longest—winner take all.

TURKEY

Goha took his eight-year-old son to the market to buy a sheep. Everybody knows that the value of a sheep depends upon the amount of fat which it stores in its tail. Goha proceeded to massage and weigh in his hands the tail of one sheep after another until his son asked, "Father, why do you do that?" Goha replied, "I must do so before I decide what sheep to buy."

"Father," said the boy, "our neighbor was in our house yesterday. I think he wants to buy mother."

Abu Nawwas was approached by a neighbor. "I understand that you have vinegar that is forty years old. Could you give me some?"

"I'm sorry," Abu replied. "It wouldn't be forty years old if I kept giving it away."

Fortune Cookies

Someone opened a fortune cookie in a Chinese restaurant the other day and it said, "Better tip big. We've got the bomb, too!"

Married men, he have two ages: when they want to be faithful and are not, and when they want to be unfaithful and cannot.

My friend Ah Wong he say he would like to drown his troubles—but he say he not can get wife to go swimming.

Never start argument with woman when she is tired—or when she is rested.

Kindness one thing you cannot give away—it come back to you.

A real loser is guy who opens fortune cookie and finds a summons —or a draft notice.

The message in the fortune cookie read, "You will meet cute red-head. You will give her money. She is our cashier."

Friends

A few months ago a friend of mine was in financial trouble and of course I helped him the best I could. "I'll never forget you," he promised. And he didn't. He's in trouble again and he just called me.

A friend is someone you can always count on to count on you.

If you ever need a friend—buy a dog.

You can always depend on three faithful friends—an old wife—an old dog—and cash.

A friend in need—is a pest.

Joe Frisco

There are hundreds of Joe Frisco stories; in fact, they have become a legend. My favorite is the one where Joe had hit upon lean times. It became his custom to stand in front of the Brown Derby hoping to find an old acquaintance who might buy him a meal. Almost everybody loved Joe and when they saw him outside the Derby they would say, "Hey, Joe—how about a cup of coffee?" or "Won't you join me for a cup of java?" After a couple of dozen of such invites Joe remarked, "D-d-d-don't anybody e-e-ever eat m-m-meat in there?"

When the stuttering comic first came to Hollywood from the vaudeville stages of the east, a friend took him on a tour. "Look at that scenery," his pal squealed, "those beautiful hills—look at that beautiful Pacific Ocean!"

"Y-yeah," said Joe, "b-b-but you can't put k-k-ketchup on it."

It was Frisco who said about Hollywood: "This is the only t-t-town where you wake up in the m-m-morning and listen to the b-b-birds coughing."

g

Gambling

He lost everything at the casinos in Vegas. He tried every one in town and each was a disaster. All he had left now was a Kennedy fifty-cent piece. He kept tossing it in the air—à la George Raft—as he walked along the street trying to figure out a way to get another stake—when his coin slipped out of his fingers and fell into a grating in the middle of the street.

Our hero was after it like a shot, but before he could grab it he was hit by a taxi and carried off to the hospital with a broken leg.

He was out in a couple of months, and with the settlement from the insurance company he started back to the casinos. On the way, he limped past the same grating where he lost his coin. He started to look down to see if he could find it when he was hit by another taxi, and he was back in the hospital with his other leg broken.

"How could you get knocked down twice in exactly the same place?" the nurse asked. "I mean, what in the world made you go back to that stupid grating?"

"That was my good luck charm," he explained, "and I didn't want to lose it."

Show me a man in Las Vegas who can lose $5,000, get up from the table and laugh, and I'll show you a shill.

This guy in Las Vegas was running up and down putting dimes in parking meters saying, "I love this outdoor gambling."

The only way to double your money in Las Vegas is to fold it and put it in your pocket.

You can't win in Las Vegas. I know a guy there who only made mental bets—he lost his mind.

A gambler proudly boasted to a friend that he'd been to a psychiatrist who'd helped him with his gambling problems. "I used to go to the track every day," he told his friend. "Now I only go there when it's open."

It's Myron Cohen's story about the four guys who are playing gin rummy. One of them loses $800 and drops dead right at the table. So out of respect to the deceased, they finish the game standing up. . . . However, the situation now presents a problem: somebody must tell his wife. Nobody wants to, of course. So they draw lots. One of them is selected, and the other two ask him to be careful breaking the news; to be gentle. He says, "With me you've got nothing to worry about." So he goes to the man's house, rings the bell. The door opens and he says, "Lady, your husband just lost $800 playing gin." She says, "He should drop dead." He says, "He did!"

You couldn't lose at the track if you could ever find a horse that goes as fast as your money.

Las Vegas is a wonderful town. You can't beat the climate, the food, or the crap tables. I even lost money on the stamp machine.

Nobody forces you to gamble. Nobody forces you to have sex either —but it's more sociable.

You want to make money in Vegas? When you throw the dice—throw them as far away as possible.

That dumb wife of mine blew my racetrack money on the rent.

Garbage

Advice: In case of a garbage strike, gift wrap your garbage and leave it in your car—and somebody'll steal it.

Our garbage man is getting more like our doctor every day—now they both refuse to make house calls.

Pat Cooper says, "The garbage on my block wasn't removed for so long it's called a landmark."

"I saw somebody throw a bag of garbage out of a window in Miami —and it was hijacked to Cuba."

Citizen: I never saw so much litter on the street.
Cop: It's the mayor's fault. He had 100,000 leaflets distributed asking people not to leave litter about.

It's been such a bad week for me that even my garbage was stolen —and with my luck, the police will find it and return it to me.

He's so rich he has monogrammed garbage.

Gas Stations

I can't figure out gas stations. In the office the cash register is wide open and the safe is wide open—but the men's room is locked.

Generation Gap

We spend the first half of our lives trying to understand the older generation—and the second half trying to understand the younger generation.

The generation gap is the difference between a ukulele and an electric guitar.

Gentleman

A gentleman is a guy who steps out of the shower to go to the bathroom.

God

"Oh, Lord"—Sam Rabinowitz offered his prayer—"help me in my business. You help complete strangers—so why not help me?"

This story has been told about Sukarno, DeGaulle, LBJ, and even Sinatra: Madame Sukarno, in bed one night, said, "My God, it's cold," and Sukarno replied, "Darling, in bed you may call me Papa."

I don't know if it's true, but it's funny anyway. DeGaulle said pompously to LBJ, "Sir, my mission to save France came to me directly from God." And the President answered, "Funny thing—I don't remember giving you any such mission."

"Please God," the horseoholic prayed before he put down his first bet of the day, "I know I shouldn't gamble—but this one time— *please*—let me break even—I need the money so badly."

Golf

Bob Hope praised Jackie Gleason's golf prowess. "He can putt and drive like a champ. In fact, he can do everything but bend over and tee up the ball."

Bob Hope's not happy about his golf game. "I wear Arnold Palmer shirts, Arnold Palmer pants, and Arnold Palmer shoes—but I play like Betsy Palmer."

They were having their daily golf argument. "You're always talking about golf—golf—golf—That's all I hear from you—golf—and you even forgot the day we were married."

"I remember it like yesterday," he consoled her, "and you know what a lousy day we had yesterday. The truth is I do remember the day we were married. It was the day after I made that hole in one."

"My friend plays a wild game of golf. He got up to the first hole—hit one into the woods. On the ninth he hit one in the lake. On the next hole he hit a new ball into the woods again. I said, 'Why don't you use an old ball?' He said, 'I never had an old ball!' "

"Say, caddie, why do you keep looking at your watch?"
"It isn't a watch, sir, it's a compass."

If you break one hundred, watch your golf. If you break eighty, watch your business.

I found something that can take five points off your game—an eraser.

When Spiro Agnew addresses a golf ball, it's to whom it may concern.

Bob Hope said, "Vice-President Agnew should be sent to Viet Nam with a number-three wood."

Bob noted that Palm Springs, California, where Agnew hit three tournament fans with wild drives, is now known as "Agnew's Fault."

He said that on one of the V.P.'s drives, Agnew got "a Birdie, an Elk, a Moose, and a Mason," adding, "It's hard to concentrate when the entire gallery is saying the Lord's Prayer."

St. Peter and St. Thomas were playing golf. St. Thomas' first drive on a 600-yard hole was a hole in one.

St. Peter got a bit irritated. "Okay, Tom," he said, "let's knock off the miracles and play golf."

A golfer got so disgusted with the way he was playing that he heaved his putter into the trees, then took each and every one of his clubs and smashed them to bits. He stomped into the clubhouse, took a razor blade from his locker, and cut his wrists. A friend walked over

h

Habits

Mrs. Traum was so happy. "I've cured my husband of biting his nails."

"After all these years?" I said. "Tell me how."

"I hide his teeth," she revealed.

Want Ad: Pretty girl, college graduate, good typist, wants job as secretary—no bad habits—willing to learn.

"I just can't break my wife of the habit of staying up till four or five in the morning."

"What the hell is she doing?"

"Waiting for me to come home."

Happiness

Happiness is a man with a wife to tell him what to do—and a secretary to do it.

You want to make someone happy today?—Mind your own business.

A guy is never happy until a girl comes along and makes him miserable.

Dr. Albert Schweitzer: "Happiness is nothing more than good health and a bad memory."

Happiness is midway between too much and too little.

They say that money doesn't bring happiness, but I'd like to be able to find out for myself.

Health

Emil Cohen tells about the man who meets a friend he hasn't seen for a long time and asks, "How do you feel?"

"Terrible. I have hardening of the arteries, high blood pressure, dizziness, arthritis, bronchitis."

"I'm sorry to hear that—what have you been doing?"

"Same thing I've been doing for the last twenty years. Still selling health foods."

"And last but least," the lawyer read the will aloud, "to my nephew, Charlie, who has always told me that health is more important than wealth, I leave the entire contents of the closet in my study—my sunlamp."

Mark Twain said it: "The only way to keep your health is to eat what you don't want, drink what you don't like, and do what you'd rather not."

Hearing

Three little old ladies—loving but deaf, met at the supermarket.
"Beautiful day," said one.
"No—it's Friday," said the other.
"Me, too," said the third. "Let's have a cup of tea."

My friend was bragging about his new hearing aid. "I can hear a leaf drop a block away. A drop of water is like an explosion. I can hear the tears in the apartment next door. It's the greatest hearing aid in the world."
"What kind is it?" I asked.
"It's a quarter to nine," he answered.

Hecklers

One good way to save face is to keep the lower half shut.

Next time you give your old clothes away—stay in them!

There's a bus leaving in five minutes—get under it.

Find yourself a home in a wastebasket.

I don't know what I'd do without you—but I'm willing to try.

If you had your life to live over again—don't do it.

Do you have a chip on your shoulder—or is that your head?

Sammy Davis, Jr., to a pest: "If you're ever in California, sir, I do hope you'll come by my house and use my pool—I'd like to give you some drowning lessons."

Jack E. Leonard annoyed by a noisy ringsider, finally exploded. "Sir, I have a terrible toothache that's killing me—but compared to you it's a pleasure."

Milton Berle had a practice of picking on somebody at the ringside smoking a cigar. Pretending to wave the smoke away, he would groan, "What are you smoking? An old army blanket? Don't you ever inhale?"

F. Hugh Herbert was ready for him and shouted back, "Not while you're in the room!"

Why don't you phone me sometime, so I can hang up on you?

Don Adams says he has a sure way of squelching a night-club heckler. If someone is giving him trouble, he signals for an off-stage phone to ring, then he feigns answering it, turns to the heckler and says, "Pardon me, sir, it's your doctor. Your spare mouth is ready."

Milton Berle quieted a ringside woman heckler by saying, "You did the same thing to me in 1946—I never forget a dress."

It's all right to drink like a fish—if you drink what a fish drinks.

In your case, brain surgery would be only a minor operation.

Thelma Lee was heckled by some bore who yelled, "Hey, baby, take off your clothes." She squelched him with a line from *Kismet*, "Don't work up an appetite if you have no teeth."

Some overexcited broad screamed at the great Dizzy Dean, "If I were your wife I'd give you poison," and he answered, "If you were my wife I'd take it." This line has been credited to everybody from Winston Churchill to Rin-Tin-Tin, but it sounds like our Dizzy.

I hear they just redecorated your home—put new padding on the walls.

Some day you'll go too far—and I hope you stay there.

I won't ask you to act like a human being—I know how good you are at imitations.

Hippies

I went to one weird hippie wedding. The bride didn't throw her bouquet—She smoked it.

The hippie bride was bragging to her hippie groom that their new apartment will have one bath. "Do we really need that many?" he asked.

The hippie couple had their apartment redone in early slob.

I noticed a hippie on Sunset Strip who was wearing one shoe. "Lose a shoe?" I asked. "Nope," he grumbled, "but I found one."

Hippie girl to hippie boy: "Of course I love you. What a dumb question—I love everybody."

There are now over fifty thousand hippies who dress alike, look alike, smell alike—And what's their big beef?—Conformity.

Most of them haven't had a bath in so long they are on the critical list of Lux.

If you look at them they got that far off look—and if you ever smell them you know why they are far off.

Hippies say they want to love everybody—and they miss very few.

A hippie was walking down the street with a cigar box under his arm when he met another hippie who asked, "Hey, man, what's cookin'? Where you goin' with that cigar box?"
"I'm movin'."

This is Jack Carter's favorite hippie story:
A married couple of hippies was blessed with a child through natural birth. A friendly policeman helped them deliver the child in the park and as the officer brought the little babe to life by slapping it gently on the rear, he heard the screams of this hippie couple yelling, "Police brutality, police brutality!"

Hijacking

Everybody is so nervous now. On one champagne flight everytime the cork popped—the pilot changed course.

Did you notice they rarely hijack a 747. They know they can't feed that many in Havana.

About that new plane, the 747: It's so large it takes four hundred passengers, twenty crew members and a dozen guys to hijack it.

i

Indians

Did you ever realize that the American Indians are the only ones ever to be conquered by the United States and not come out ahead?

Jack Carter's story: A man walking along the highway sees an Indian lying down with his ear to the ground. He goes over, and hears the Indian say, "Small wheels, Cadillac, color green, woman driving, two children in the back, a California license plate." The man says incredulously, "You mean to say you can tell all that by just putting your ear to the road?" The Indian says, "Ear, nothing; that car ran over me a half hour ago."

I can't understand why the Indians want to reclaim five thousand miles of California. They'd never be able to send smoke signals in the smog.

Dick Capri says his wife is an Italian Indian: Sort of Siouxcillian.

John Wayne says he defeated so many Indians in his movies he gets hate mail from Jane Fonda.

Inferiority

"No one can make you feel inferior without your consent."
—Eleanor Roosevelt.

Inflation

"The cost of living," says Lee Tully, "is ridiculous. I asked for fifty cents' worth of Swiss cheese and they wrapped up eight holes."

The price of a penny postcard went up from a nickel to six cents.

Inflation means you never had it so good—or parted with it so fast.

You can console yourself with one thought—the money you don't have isn't worth much anyway.

What used to cost five dollars to buy—now costs twenty-five dollars to fix.

I shop at a friendly grocer. They not only deliver—they arrange financing.

The young housewife picked out three apples, an orange, two pears, and a banana and handed them to the grocery clerk.
"That'll be $4.75," he barked.
She handed him a five-dollar bill and started to walk out.
"Wait, you forgot your change," he called to her.
"That's okay," she said sweetly. "I stepped on a grape on the way in."

We're told that money isn't everything. The way things are going it soon won't be anything.

Even inflation has it's bright side. Now there's hardly enough candy in a five-cent candy bar to be fattening.

I wanted to join an organization that fights inflation—but they raised their dues.

We have the highest standard of living in the world. Too bad we can't afford it.

The bride was near tears as she explained to her mother that, although she had followed the recipe explicitly, there hadn't been enough meat to go around. Her mother spotted the trouble quickly. The recipe in Grandmother's faded handwriting, began: "Get about fifty cents' worth of rump roast . . ."

Sign in supermarket: NOBODY UNDER $21 ADMITTED.

Sure two can live as cheaply as one—but now it costs twice as much.

What goes up—must keep going up.

Flip Wilson: The cost of living is going up—and the chance of living is going down.

Fannie Flagg: Women who complain about inflation should go to Italy. That's where a girl really feels the pinch.

I handed a bill to the cabdriver and asked, "Do you have change of a dollar?"
"Are you kiddin', mister," he barked. "These days a dollar *is* change."

Inflation is really here. I gave my nephew a nickel and the kid asked, "What is this, a medal?"

"Darling," the husband announced happily, "I got good news. We don't have to move to a more expensive apartment—the landlord just raised our rent."

Inflation: Mini money.

Inflation: That's when you pay a quarter for a nickel penny candy.

A dollar doesn't go as far as it used to—but what it lacks in distance —it makes up in speed.

Who says kids don't know the value of a dollar? They must—that's why they ask for ten.

Look at it this way. If the buck really loses its value—think how good you will feel when you send your ex-wife her monthly alimony check!

There is one consolation in inflation: The money you haven't got isn't worth as much as it used to be.

In the good old days what you paid for a car—you now pay for the insurance.

My insomnia is so bad, I can't even sleep when it's time to get up.

The doctor told his patient after a thorough examination, "You're sound as a dollar." The patient got panicky. "Please, doctor, don't scare me like that."

It now takes twice as much money to live beyond your means as it used to.

Insult

Wilson Mizner about Hollywood producer Jack Warner: "He has oilcloth pockets so he can steal soup."

Have you ever wondered where people in hell tell each other to go?

You're a real magician—You just made an ass out of yourself.

He's suffering from bottle fatigue.

You know I'm forming an attachment for you—It fits right over your mouth.

Don Rickles blasted a ringsider: "The shnook wears a wash-and-wear suit—and gets a gravy stain on his silk tie."

If there's ever a price on your head—take it.

You have a ready wit—Let me know when it's ready.

Groucho: I never forget a face—but in your case I'll make an exception.

Don Rickles saw Ernest Borgnine in his audience and yelled, "Look at that face! Quick, call up Allstate—I think I've found an accident."

Don't get such a big head. Remember, even a pair of shoe trees can fill your shoes.

Wife: When I was sixteen I was chosen Miss America.
Husband: In those days there were very few Americans.

Go jump in the ocean and pull a wave over your head.

Find yourself a home in a wastebasket.

There's a girl I would like to take home to mother—*Her* mother.

The lush blonde turned blond lush was the pest of the night. I looked down at her plunging neckline and sneered, "Be careful, honey, or you'll spill that dress all over your drink."

Director Billy Wilder listened to an actor sing, and told him, "You have Van Gogh's ear for music."

A prominent entertainer paid $1,000 for a toupee and Pat Cooper marveled, "Even Jesse James didn't have a price like that on his head."

You can write the story of his life on a piece of confetti.

The comic's wife told the agent she was going to have a baby. "Wonderful," he said, "I hope you have a better delivery than your husband."

Insurance

The lady sent a letter to the insurance company: "I'm happy to announce that my husband who was reported missing—is now definitely deceased."

"But lady, you can't collect the life insurance on your husband—he isn't dead yet."

"I know that—but there's no life left in him."

Jack Benny likes to play on the fact that he keeps his back toward the check. "It's true I have a slight impediment of the reach when a check comes," he said. "In fact, I don't want to tell you how much insurance I carry with Prudential—But all I can say is—when I go—they go."

My car had a fifty-dollar debatable policy.

My father-in-law is in the insurance business. He sold me a twenty-year-retirement policy—At the end of twenty years—*he* retires.

He sold me group insurance—but the whole group has to get sick before I collect.

Intellectual

That's a guy who thinks he has found something more interesting than girls.

Inventions

Irwin C. Watson tells this story: Talking about Women's Liberation brings to mind the people who always say that behind every successful man there's a woman. Well, once I went to check up on this and I found some interesting stories. You know that when Thomas Edison was getting together what was then called the incandescent lamp, he spent thirteen years trying to find the right filament, the right gas, and the right container to make this thing glow. And once, about three in the morning, he finally made it glow. And he ran out of the barn, across to the house, up three flights of stairs to his wife's bedroom and said, "Darling, look!" And she woke up and turned over and said, "Would you turn off that light and come to bed!"

He crossed a carrier pigeon with a parrot so it could deliver messages verbally. The first day he tried it out, it turned up three hours late. "What kept you?" asked the inventor.

"It was such a lovely day—I decided to walk," the bird explained.

Billy Falbo comes up with some great inventions: Did you hear about
the guy who crossed a carrier pigeon with a woodpecker so that
when messages are delivered, it can knock on the door?—Crossed
a dog and a hen and got pooched eggs?—Crossed an electric blanket
and a toaster and got a machine that pops people out of bed?

j

Jail

I entertained the inmates at Greenhaven State Prison. The guys loved me. They even voted me an honorary sentence.

It's easy to do a show in jail. That's one audience that won't walk out on you. Never worry when they walk out on you. It's when they walk towards you that you should worry.

A college football team arranged a match with the guys at Sing Sing Prison to help them in their rehabilitation program.

As the two captains were about to toss for sides, the college captain said: "Hey, just a second—you've got fifteen men on your side."

"I know," the Sing Sing captain smiled. "That's why we're in prison—we cheat."

Jealousy

"What's the matter, ma'am?" said the maid, finding her mistress in tears.

"I've just discovered that my husband is having an affair with his secretary."

"Nonsense!" snorted the maid. "You're only saying that to make me jealous."

Juvenile Delinquents

America will never be invaded. Our juvenile delinquents are too well armed.

The delinquents of today are the same as the delinquents of fifty years ago—only they have better weapons.

Strike your child every day—if you don't know why—*he* does.

He could go to any reform school in the country on a scholarship.

When he goes to school, the *teacher* plays hookey.

Never give your kid his full allowance. Keep some to bail him out.

Our juvenile delinquents today are well educated. When they write dirty words on the toilet walls, they're in Latin.

k

Kids

What's the use of teaching your kid to talk when in a few years you'll wish he'd shut up.

Teacher asked an eleven-year-old pupil why he didn't do his homework. "I did," he replied. "Only I made it into a paper airplane and it was hijacked to Cuba."

The neighborhood kids were in front yards when a fire truck zoomed past, with the station mascot sitting on the front seat. The children began discussing the dog's duties.
"They use him to keep the crowd back at a fire," said a five-year-old girl.
"No," said another, "they carry him for good luck."
A six-year-old boy brought the argument to an abrupt halt. "They use the dog," he announced firmly, "to find the fireplug."

"Tell me, son, do you like your new nurse?" "No," said the youngster, "I hate her. One of these days I'm gonna grab her and bite her on the neck like Daddy does."

A Sunday school teacher asked, "Who was the first man," and one youngster volunteered that it was George Washington. "It was Adam," the teacher said. "Oh," the kid answered, "sure—if you count the foreigners."

Archie Campbell says his little boy, ten years old, came home from school and said, "Daddy, what is a sweater girl?" Being quick on the draw, as a good father should be, he said, "Well, son, a sweater girl is a girl that works in a factory where they make sweaters." Then, looking at the boy, he said, "By the way, where did you get a question like that anyway?" The son replied, "Never mind that question, where did you get that answer?"

Dick Van Dyke collects kid stories. Here are some of his favorites: A girl thought it would be nice if God helped her with her arithmetic, but her mother said, "God can't help you with your math . . . ask Him to give you more patience to do your studies."

The girl looked puzzled and then said, "Oh, God doesn't know the New Math either?"

Some kids seem to regard God as a celestial Santa Claus. Four-year-old Betty slipped into bed without saying her prayers one night, explaining to her mother, "There are some nights when I don't want anything."

In a classroom, a teacher asked, "Why do you suppose we no longer offer burnt offerings to God?" A boy answered, "Air pollution."

Kids of kindergarten age love any kind of story, from Superman to the Good Samaritan. One teacher told me she was relating the Good Samaritan story to her class, making it as vivid as possible so the children would realize what was happening. Then she asked the class, "If you saw a person lying on the roadside all wounded and bleeding, what would you do?"
    A thoughtful little girl broke the hushed silence. "I think I'd throw up," she said.

One of my favorite stories comes from Fort Worth, Texas, where the First Baptist Church of Forest Hill was holding a special Mother's Day service. The pastor was giving corsages to the oldest mother, the mother with the most children, the youngest mother, and so on, while a five-year-old girl became more and more concerned because her mother hadn't received anything. Finally she whispered loudly, "Don't worry, Mother. If they give one for the fattest mother, maybe you'll win it."

My little nephew is practicing to be a hippie. "I can hardly wait," he told me, "to be old enough to shave—so I can grow a beard."

Rodney admits his father wasn't very fond of him: "He taught me to look both ways when crossing the street—up and down."

The three-day-old baby was screaming in his crib while his older brother of five watched with interest.
    "Has he come from heaven?" Johnny asked his mother.
    "Yes, dear."
    "No wonder they threw him out."

The old man asked his precocious six-year-old how he liked the new little girl next door.
    "W-e-l-l," said the kid, "she's no Elizabeth Taylor—but she's nice."

David, the six-year-old boy, was beginning to ask embarrassing questions and Mom and Pop couldn't get themselves to explain. So they got the elder boy Martin to explain the facts of life by first telling him about the birds and bees.

That night in bed Martin gave David his first lesson: "Look, David, do you know what it is that Mom and Pop do at night in bed?"

"Sure I do," said David.

"Well—it's exactly the same with the birds and bees."

In the presence of the camp owner and two counselors, the parents were signing the necessary documents to send their boy to camp. . . . Watching was the younger brother, who finally looked up with tears in his eyes and asked, "Daddy, why are we selling Robert?"

Jackie Kannon claims today's kids can talk their way out of anything: "My son had C's and D's on his report card, and he insisted they were vitamin deficiencies."

"Can any of you children name the fifty states?" the teacher asked her third-grade students. One clever youngster called them out in alphabetical order.

"Wonderful," exclaimed the teacher, "I certainly could not have done that at your age!"

"Sure," hollered one kid, "and then there were only thirteen of them."

The little boy was complaining to his father about his mother. "She makes me go to bed when I'm wide-awake—and wakes me up when I'm sleepy."

The youngster asked his father if he could do any work around the house to help make himself some extra money. The old man told him he couldn't think of anything. "If that's the case," said the kid, "how about putting me on welfare?"

A seven-year-old boy was being taught the proper way to ask a girl for a dance by the teacher in the dance-instruction class. A half hour later the kid asked the teacher, "Now, how do I get rid of her?"

Freddie Roman reports: "My wife has really pushed our kid. I think it's great that mothers want the best for their kids. But there's such a thing as overdoing it. My son's ten years old and I still remember the birth announcement my wife sent out. 'Mr. and Mrs. Freddie Roman proudly announce the birth of their son, Dr. Alan Roman.' "

An eight-year-old girl walks into a bakery shop and says, "My mommy found a fly in the raisin bread." And the baker says, "Bring back the fly, I'll give you a raisin."

The five-year-old boy says to his friend, "My father can beat your father." The friend says, "Big deal. So can my mother."

Kindness

You always remember a kind deed—especially if it was yours.

Kissing

Two models were comparing boyfriends. "Sometimes I'm suspicious of him," said one. "He kisses my hand."

"Oh, but that's the way a man with experience kisses," the other answered.

"I don't know—a man with experience should have better aim than that."

Never let a fool kiss you—or a kiss fool you.

A kiss is like faith, hope and charity. For a girl it's faith—for a married woman it's hope—and for an old maid it's charity.

"Where did you learn to kiss like that?"
"I used to blow the bugle in the Boy Scouts."

I learned to kiss by blowing up footballs.

"Never kiss a shoemaker with your eyes closed—he could have a mouthful of nails."   —Bob Sylvester.

1

Landmarks

Some conservation groups are fighting to preserve old buildings in their original form. I know a landlord who's been doing that for years.

Las Vegas

Freddie Roman tells it: People don't know what to do first when they come to Las Vegas. It's really funny to see a couple from Los Angeles come to Las Vegas for the weekend. They go to an early show, a lounge show, have dinner, a little blackjack, a little craps, then they go to a late show, a late late show, an early show. Now it's six in the morning, the husband's hands are shaking. He says: "Honey, let's go to bed." She says, "Wonderful, who's appearing there?"

Las Vegas is a strip of lights surrounded by slot machines.

Las Vegas is the only town where Western Union has messages already printed for sending home for money.

Lawyers

Lawyer: I worked out a deal—it took a lot of hard work and a lot of patience and time—but I think I worked a settlement that is fair for both sides.
Client: Fair to both sides? What the hell do I need a lawyer for that—that I could have done myself!

Divorces are arranged so lawyers can live happily ever after.

A lawyer tore excitedly into court and asked that a new trial be granted a client found guilty the day previous. "I've uncovered new evidence," declared the lawyer.
   "Of what nature?" asked the judge.
   "My client," the lawyer told him, "has an extra six thousand dollars. I only found out about it this morning."

"I swore to tell the truth," the witness said to the judge, "but every time I do some lawyer objects."

The story is told of the lawyer's wife who was complaining about the way their home was furnished. "We need chairs, a dining room set, and a new lamp." "Listen," her spouse told her, "one of my clients is suing her husband for divorce. He has a lot of money and as soon as I finish breaking up their home, we'll fix ours."

Tombstone: HERE LIES A LAWYER AND AN HONEST MAN. And who'd ever think there'd be room for two men in that one little grave?

Lawyer: A person who helps you get what's coming to him.

The lawyer called a plumber to do some repairs. The plumber billed him at the rate of seventy dollars an hour. The lawyer told the plumber, "Even as a lawyer I don't make seventy dollars an hour." The plumber replied, "Neither did I when I was a lawyer."

A convict sits in his cell awaiting murder trial. In walks a well-dressed lawyer. The lawyer said, "I'm the very best, you have nothing to worry about. I'm going to prove that you are completely insane or were in Europe at the time of the murder; also the witnesses are paid off and my uncle is the judge for your case. Meanwhile, try to escape."

A divorce lawyer is the referee in a fight who winds up with the purse.

A lawyer saves your business and your estate from your opponents and keeps it for himself.

Joe E. Lewis

Joe E. was committed to booze and gambling as a way of life. He continued to have twenty or thirty scotches a night despite doctors' warnings. But as Joe E. said, "I know more old drunks than old doctors.

"I tried going on the wagon once. It was the most boring ten minutes of my life.

"I'll only go on the wagon now if it has a bar on it."

At the late show in any night club he worked, he opened with, "You're my kind of people—drunks."

Joe E. explained his drinking: "You're never drunk if you can lie on the floor without holding on."

Once when a friend said, "Dean Martin took your drunk routine," he replied, "Yes, and he does it very well."

"I went on a diet and quit drinking—in fourteen days I lost two weeks."

"People say I'm never sober. Why, I've been sober four times today."

"Show me a friend in need—and I'll show you a pest."

"Show me a drinker who can hold his liquor—and I'll show you a man with a kidney condition."

Joe E. loved everybody and trusted everybody, "except a camel—or anyone else who doesn't take a drink once in a while."

"The recession didn't bother me—I went broke during the boom."

Joe E. met Harry Truman at the White House. The President asked him if there was anything he could do for him. "Well," said our Joe, "I've had some bad horses lately, Mr. President, can you get me an advance on my Social Security?"

Life

Tallulah Bankhead: The one thing I regret about my past is the length of it. If I had my life to live over again—I'd make all the same mistakes—only sooner.

Milton Berle's philosophy of life: "Life is very simple. The first thing to remember about life is—don't worry about it. Really, there are only two things to worry about; either you're successful or you're not successful. If you're successful, there's nothing to worry about. If you're not successful, there're only two things to worry about; either you're healthy or you're unhealthy. If your health is good, there's nothing to worry about. If your health is bad, there're only two things to worry about. Either you're going to live or you're not going to live. If you live, there's nothing to worry about, and if you don't live, why you've only two things to worry about. Either you're going to heaven or you're not going to heaven. If you go to heaven, there's nothing to worry about, and if you go to the other place, you'll be so doggone busy shaking hands with all your old friends, YOU WON'T HAVE TIME TO WORRY."

Tom Jones told me he lives every day like it's the last day of his life. When I told this to Harry Hershfield who is eighty-six, he said, "I live every day like it's the first day of my life."

Abraham Lincoln

When he lived in Springfield, a neighbor saw Lincoln walking out of his house, carrying one small son under each arm, the boys splitting the air with their wails. The man asked, "What is the matter?" Lincoln answered ruefully, "Just what is the matter with the whole world. I've got three walnuts and each wants *two*."

Lincoln had also found humor effective in the courtroom. Defending a client accused of assault and battery, he cross-examined a witness to the fight. Although the scrap was practically bloodless, the witness was so overcome by his own rhetoric that he claimed the set-to covered an acre of ground. Lincoln let him have his say, then mildly inquired, "Now don't you think that was a mighty small crop of fight to raise on such a big farm?" The jury found this very funny. It also found for Lincoln's client.

Lincoln loved to laugh. He said he lived by his humor—and "I would have died without it."

Another time, after a case went to the jury late at night, Lincoln met the opposing attorney at the courthouse next morning and asked how the case had turned out. "It's gone to hell!" his opponent answered glumly. "Oh, well, never mind," Lincoln comforted him. "You can try it again there."

Lincoln answered one of the stuffier Todds who wanted an "e" added to their name because of the national importance of the Lincolns.
"I don't think that will be necessary," he said. "God seems to get along all right."

When he was told that General Grant was drinking too much, he remarked, "Find out what kind of stuff he's drinking and feed it to all my generals."

Luck

Henny Youngman tells of a poor fellow, a real hard-luck guy he and some friends wanted to help out. The sad man had a lot of pride, so they decided the best way to avoid embarrassment for him would be to hold a raffle and make all the tickets the same number as his, so he couldn't possibly lose. Shaking the stubs up in a hat, one of the group held it out for him to draw. The number he pulled out was 6⅞.

You think you're unlucky? Did you hear about the single girl who is pregnant—so she goes to a small town far away from the big city and leaves a phony forwarding address. Then she checks in at a small hospital using a false name, of course. She doesn't tell a soul where she is—neither family nor friends—and then she gives birth to quintuplets.

This guy is so unlucky—he opened a fortune cookie and found a summons.

This guy is so unlucky—he opened a fortune cookie and found his draft notice.

The question is always being asked by some people—is it really bad luck to have a cat walk behind you? And I think it all depends on whether you're a man or a mouse.

I've had bad luck with both my wives—the first divorced me and the second won't.

He had tough luck. He had a check for ten dollars and the only person who could cash it was a fellow to whom he owed nine dollars.

It's always bad luck when thirteen people are drinking at the bar—and you are picking up the check.

On doctors: I went to a doctor for a kidney condition. Of course, you never know how a doctor will deal with kidneys. You don't have to get 100 per cent in every subject to be a doctor. You can get 65 in one subject and 90 in another and you're a doctor because it averages out okay. He might have gotten 35 in kidneys, 90 in liver. That's why when I go to a doctor I don't want to see his degree, I want to see his report card.

Matchmaker

The Lonely Hearts Club had a big sign over the reception desk: WE ACCEPT ONLY YOUNG LADIES OF THE HIGHEST MORAL STANDARDS.

The young suitor asked politely: "Do you happen to have the names and addresses of the rejects?"

A matchmaker takes a young man to meet the girl and her family. As they're leaving, the matchmaker says, "Wonderful people, aren't they? Cultured, dignified, educated, rich. Did you see their silverware?—Pure sterling." The young man says, "Maybe they only borrowed it to make a good impression." Matchmaker says, "Ridiculous. Who would lend anything to those thieves?"

Miami

I saw a real hero during a Miami fire—he rescued fourteen mink coats and sixty-five canes.

Robert King: I was working in Florida. Everybody talks about how everyone else retires there—you know, the ambulances meet the planes, etc. I heard a conversation between an elderly man and woman. She said, "So, Irving, you want to take a walk to the corner?" He said, "Yes. That's a good idea. And while we're there we'll pick up a shower cap for Sylvia." She said, "Listen, why should we do everything in one day?"

This character from the North was in Miami enjoying the sunshine. "How do you tell the summer from the winter down here?" he asked a native. "Simple," answered the local. "In winter we get Cadillacs, Rolls-Royces and Lincolns—in the summer we get Fords, Volkswagens, and stuffed shorts."

There are three ways to travel to Miami when you get on a plane—first class—tourist, and prisoner.

Mistakes

The greatest mistake of my life is the number of temptations I've resisted successfully.

The carpenter ran up to the paymaster and said, "Hey, I'm short four dollars."

"I know," said the man with the money. "We overpaid you four dollars last week—but you didn't complain then."

"Well," said the carpenter, "I don't mind overlooking one mistake. But when it happens a second time, it would be dishonorable to keep silent."

Will Rogers told about the doctor who operated on people for gallstones who died of pneumonia. "Not my doctor," Will said. "If he operates on you for gallstones—you die of gallstones."

Mistress

My friend Herb has a perfect explanation for keeping her but not marrying her: "When she's my mistress and I buy her a mink—she is so grateful.—Once we're married—it's coming to her."

A mistress is like a wife—only you don't have to do the dishes.

She is known by the company that keeps her.

A mistress doesn't care for a man's company—unless he owns it.

A mistress is a good time that was had by one—and all.

Money

Money isn't everything—but it sure keeps you in touch with your kids.

If you saved money in the old days you were considered a miser; nowadays, you're a wonder.

I've got enough money to live the rest of my life—unless I want to buy something.

It's true that money can't buy love, but it makes shopping more fun.

Be sure and save your money—you never know when it may be valuable again someday.

The salary we used to dream of is the one we can't live on today.

Bob Melvin swears it's true: Last winter my wife was pestering me that I wasn't saving enough money, so I decided to let her handle the money. It was unbelievable. After two months she informed me that she had saved enough for us to go skiing for a week. She had made reservations at a nice resort, deluxe room.

Everything was fine but it started to bother me. As we waited to go down the slope I couldn't control myself any longer. I asked, "Where did you get this money from?" She said, "I got rid of something we never used." And off we went down the slope . . . and just as everything seemed perfect I had an accident and broke my foot.

When my wife visited me at the hospital she seemed so upset I said, "What's the matter? I'll be out of here in no time." She said, "I hope so. Do you remember when I told you I got rid of something that we never use? Well . . . it was our Blue Cross Hospital coverage!"

Money may not be able to buy love—but it will sure put you in a good bargaining position.

It's just as well that money can't buy happiness—with today's prices we couldn't afford it anyway.

A friend's son was being Bar-Mitzvahed and he asked what he could get the kid. Somebody suggested that the youngster could use the cash. "Don't be silly," he answered. "I can't get cash wholesale."

My neighbor and his wife are having money troubles—the only time they make ends meet is in bed!

Mark Twain once made an inspiring New Year's resolution: "I am going to live within my income this year even if I have to borrow money to do it."

My wife and I like the same things—only I like to save it and she likes to spend it.

George Kirby dug up an old Chinese proverb that says: "A man who squeezes a dollar seldom squeezes his wife." Well, judging by the way money is being thrown around these days, wives are getting all the squeezing they can handle.

There are more important things in life than money—but they won't go out with you when you're broke.

Making money isn't the real problem in life—the problem is passing it.

There are more things in life than money—but you need money to impress girls like that.

"You've got to admit," she said to her husband, "that spending money is my only extravagance."

Money is only important if you haven't got it.

A special curse: "You should have a lot of money—but you should be the only one in your family with it."

Harry Hershfield told of a needy man asking a friend to lend him $100. The friend was silent. The needy one said: "You owe me an answer." The friend replied: "Better I owe you an answer than that you owe me $100."

"I won't lend you the money because it's raining in Tokyo. Yes, that's a reason. If I don't want to lend it, one excuse is as good as another."

A dollar goes very fast nowadays—but not very far.

Moon

Don't misunderstand, I am a big fan of those astronauts. In fact, I was thrilled to see them take a walk in space—I've wanted to do the same thing many times when they start to show movies on the plane.

The Russians are now trying to get a man on the moon. Of course they won't be able to get him back. As a matter of fact, that's one of the inducements.

I hope they never find anybody on the moon. Think of what it would cost us in foreign aid.

Mother-in-law

For Christmas he bought his mother-in-law a lovely new chair—but his wife wouldn't let him plug it in.

Sure Adam was a happy man—he had no mother-in-law.

Adam had no mother-in-law that's why he lived in paradise.

My wife called her mother and cried that she couldn't take it any more and was coming to her house. "How will that punish *him?*" my mother-in-law asked. "*I'll* come to *your* house!"

I sent my mother-in-law to the country—they refused her.

"I hear you're taking your mother-in-law to Alaska with you. Won't the weather disagree with her?"
"It wouldn't dare."

"If your mother-in-law was drowned in that river—why are you looking for her *up*stream?"
"You know what a contrary woman my mother-in-law was."

Behind every successful man stands an astonished mother-in-law.

He sent his mother-in-law a present on Mother's Day—her daughter.

I never met a mother-in-law who was outspoken.

He sent his mother-in-law on a trip to the Thousand Islands—and told her to spend a week on each.

Movies

Cindy and I were walking around the Pigalle section of Paris when a dirty character sidled up to us and whispered: "Would madame and monsieur like to see a dirty movie?—Only twenty dollars."
"Twenty dollars?" Cindy said. "For a movie? Who's in it?"

All you hear about is dirty movies, dirty books, dirty air—we're living in the nineteen-dirties. . . .

I took a course in speed reading—just so I could read the titles on those foreign movies—before the girl puts her clothes on.

All you need to be a star in pictures today are the bare necessities.

Did you know a rabbit was technical adviser on Jacqueline Susann's *Love Machine?*

Twiggy is now in pictures—they had to take out that nude sex scene —they couldn't tell the boys from the girl.

Twiggy is the only girl I know who wears falsies—just to look flat-chested.—You gotta see what she puts in her bra—her shoulder blades.—I've seen more meat on a butcher's apron.

I can remember when if you wanted to hear cursing, you went to the poolroom. No more. Now you go to the movies.

I saw one picture that's so dirty you get yourself arrested simply for reading the marquee.

An art theater—That's a place where the theater is clean—the pictures are dirty.

"There is no such thing as a dirty theme—there are only dirty writers. . . ."   —George Jean Nathan.

In the old days actresses used to play parts—now they reveal them.

In movies today, girls who make it to the top usually wear clothes that don't.

My friend Lou Jacobi loves to tell Hollywood stories: A movie extra was becoming a problem to the director because he refused to jump from the cliff into the water. Screamed the extra, "No, I won't do it. Why, there's only two feet of water at the bottom of that cliff." "Of course," said the director, "do you think I want you to drown?"

Said the director to this same extra, "The lion will chase you for exactly 100 yards, absolutely no farther. Do you understand?" Replied the extra, "I understand—does the lion?"

Movie studios are getting so desperate for story ideas—they asked any of their starlets who got obscene phone calls to take notes.

I prefer the old movies the best where love scenes were between boys and girls—and they didn't have to take their clothes off so you could tell which was the boy and which was the girl.

They are putting things on the screen now—you wouldn't find on a French postcard.

One of these days there will be an o rating in movies—"Not suitable for anyone."

It's odd—the same movies that we slept through in the theaters are keeping us awake on TV.

Mugging

Talk about luck—The other day my neighbor got mugged at a peace demonstration.

Rodney Dangerfield was held up by a guy with a knife. "What the hell is wrong with you—holding me up with a knife?" Rodney squealed. "I'm trying to save enough money to buy a gun," the thief answered.

New Yorkers are so cold—if it weren't for the muggers—there wouldn't be any contact at all.

The man asked the stranger, "Do you know where Central Park is?" The answer was no. The guy said, "Okay, then I'll mug you right here."

Music

Jack Benny is proud of this review of his violin playing: "Jack Benny played Mendelssohn last night—Mendelssohn lost."

I admit that Jack is not too great as a violinist—in fact, I'm sure the Venus de Milo could have played better—but Jack sums it all up himself: "I might have been a fairly good violinist—maybe the second best—but who cares about the second best—This way it's fine—I'm the world's worst violinist."

Henny Youngman claims Benny has the only Stradivarius made in Japan.

Bob Hope says, "Jack Benny is very charitable. He's raised millions with his violin—just by threatening to play."

Isaac Stern: Learning music by reading about it is like making love by mail.

The kid in the rock group was asked if he could read music. "A little," the youngster said, "but not enough to hurt our playing."

"What do you have to know to play the cymbals?" someone asked Sir Malcolm Sargent. "Nothing," was the reply. "Just when."

The story goes that Caruso, at one time, took a fancy to learning to play the flute. Somebody approached him and offered to record the sound of his playing.

Asked whether he would like to buy the recording, Caruso replied: "No, thank you—but I'll sell you the flute!"

Chaliapin was generous with his talents but there were times when the demands became just a bit too much. On one occasion, when he had been invited to a dinner, he was asked by a swooping hostess to sing to the guests.

"If you ask me to dinner, you feed me," said Chaliapin. "If you ask me to sing, you pay me."

Albert Einstein, a very keen violinist, often played violin-and-piano sonatas with Artur Schnabel. After trying one passage several times, Einstein was still having difficulty in co-ordinating violin with piano.

"My dear Albert," said Schnabel. "Can't you count?"

Jascha Heifetz and Mischa Elman were sitting together at a dinner when a note was handed up. It was addressed, so the story goes, "To the Greatest Violinist in the World."

"You'd better open it, Mischa," said Heifetz.

"No, no," said Elman. "You open it, Jascha."

They agreed to open it together. It began, "Dear Fritz . . ."

She is so knock-kneed, she has to play the cello sidesaddle.

n

News

I really don't think the world is worse—it's just that the news coverage is better.

I saw three muggers, a murder, a raping, and four bombings on TV last night—and that was just the news.

There is no news in being good. You could write the goings-on of all the convents of the world on a piece of confetti.

A small town is a place where they buy a newspaper just to verify what they heard on the phone.

I used to be an old newspaperman but I found there was no money in old newspapers.

In his reporting days, Mark Twain was instructed by an editor never to state anything as a fact that he could not verify from personal knowledge. Sent out to cover an important social event some time later, he turned in his story: "A woman giving the name of Mrs. James Jones, who is reported to be one of the society leaders of the city, is said to have given what purported to be a party yesterday to a number of alleged ladies. The hostess claims to be the wife of a reputed attorney."

New York City

New York City is the most crowded city in the country—and no wonder. We are surrounded by so many toll booths and toll roads—and all of them going up in price—nobody can afford to leave.

Robert King says, "I was recently mugged and while it was happening I couldn't help but think of something that actually happened to someone else. A guy was mugged in the Bronx and he didn't have any money on him. The mugger was going to beat him up. So the guy said to the mugger, 'Can I give you a check?' But the mugger said, 'Think I'm stupid? I don't even know you.'"

This New Yorker walks to his commuter train every day, and every day he passes this little old lady selling pretzels for a dime. Each time he'd drop a dime into her cup but wouldn't take a pretzel. This went on for two years, and finally one morning when he dropped in his dime and started toward the station she said, "Wait a minute—" and he said, "Oh, don't tell me. You want to know why I don't take a pretzel." And she said, "No. Tomorrow the price is fifteen cents."

Every tourist who comes to New York says it's a cold town. Bob Orben told me, "New Yorkers are so impersonal—if it weren't for muggings there wouldn't be any contact at all."

With off-track betting and legalized abortions—no wonder Broadway is not drawing like it used to.

It's been very hot in New York. In fact, I passed Grant's Tomb—and the door was open.

Most people living in New York City come from a farm and are trying to make enough money to go back to the farm.

If you're not in New York—you're camping out.

If you live outside of New York City—it's like living in a tent.

I think I have a solution for eliminating traffic and parking problems in New York—encourage car thefts.

In New York they no longer give anyone the key to the city. Instead, they have a guy come over who tells you how to pick a lock.

They did a production of *Julius Caesar* in Shakespeare-in-the-Park in New York and when Caesar was stabbed, eight people left; they didn't want to get involved.

Nixon

Nixon is planning to open American restaurants in China so the Chinese Jews will have someplace to go Sunday nights.

If FDR's song was "Home on the Range" and Truman's favorite was "Missouri Waltz"—Nixon's song must be "Chinatown, My Chinatown."

What good is it for Nixon to go to China—one hour later he'll want to go again.

Nixon made some strong demands of Uncle Mao and his brother-in-law Chou—two from column A and three from column B.

Office

The clerk brought this letter of recommendation to the office manager: "To whom it may concern—This is to certify that Mr. Jan Franklin has worked with us for two days and we were fully satisfied with his work, except that on his last day of work he was dismissed on account of not being on time, dishonesty, vulgarity, bad temper, inefficiency, and a habit of stealing. We wish him all success in life."

Signed: J. Adams, Proprietor

Executive: Who told you, just because I kissed you, etc., a couple of times, you could neglect your work around here?
Secretary: My lawyer.

"Boss," the secretary announced one morning, "I've found a new position." "Good," said the boss, "pull down the shades."

"No," the new secretary said, "I can't type or take shorthand as fast as your former secretary—but what was her undressing speed?"

Boss: Okay now, gang, let's take a ten-minute break for work!

The young executive stopped to say good-by to the big boss. "I'm sorry to see you go," said the big shot. "I'll really miss you—In many ways you've been like a son to me—unappreciative—fresh—arrogant. . . ."

She quit because her boss drummed his fingers. She said it made runs in her stockings.

Ability is what will get you to the top—if the boss has no daughter.

Boss: You have been coming in late every single day. Now what do you have to say for yourself?
Clerk: It's true—but you must admit—I do leave early.

Employee: Boss, could I have Monday off? It's my twenty-fifth wedding anniversary.
Angry Boss: Do I have to put up with this every twenty-five years?

"What's this I hear about your going to church and praying for a raise? Don't you know I never stand for anybody going over my head?"

I'm afraid I'll have to fire my typist. She's always interrupting my dictation and asking me to spell the simplest words—and it just gets so embarrassing to have to keep saying, "I don't know."

My secretary is 42-26-35 and an expert touch typist—she has to be —she can't see the keys!

The boss caught his secretary and one of his executives in a bit of sex in one of the storerooms during a coffee break.
"Okay," the boss growled, "what's the meaning of this?"
"Well," the girl explained, "neither of us likes coffee."

"Okay," the executive said to the sexy brunette secretary, "you're hired—now would you like to try for a raise?"

"You'll like it here," the steno said to the new girl—"Lots of chances for advances."

My wife never trusts any secretary over 36-23-36.

Old Maids

Comedian Jan Murray tells of two old maids who ran a country drugstore. One afternoon, a farmer dropped in and said, "I need a pill to calm me down. Everytime I see a girl, I want to make love to her. What can you give me?" Chorused the sisters: "Seven hundred dollars and the drugstore!"

An old maid is a lady who has been good for nothing.

It's not too late—instead of giving up—give in.

Politicians know how to run other people's business and old maids know how to run other people's children.

Chinese say: "Old maid she do not have mush experience."

An old maid knows all the answers—but nobody ever asked her the questions.

Edna Ferber: Being an old maid is like death by drowning—a really delightful sensation after you cease to struggle.

Opera

A father takes his little boy for culture to the Metropolitan Opera. Out comes the conductor with his baton, and out comes the big diva, and she starts to sing an aria. As the conductor is waving his baton, the kid says, "Papa, why is that man hitting that woman?" The father says, "He isn't hitting her, that's the conductor." "Well, if he ain't hitting her, why is she hollering?"

I go to the opera—whether I need the sleep or not.

To me opera is Italian vaudeville. It's where a man gets stabbed and instead of bleeding he sings.

The trouble with opera is that there is too much singing.

They are going to do more operas in English—then you'll understand what's boring you.

Optimism

An optimist looks forward to marriage. A pessimist is a married optimist.

The greatest optimist I ever met is a guy who got married at ninety and bought a house near a school.

An optimist is somebody who hasn't been reading the paper or listening to the news lately.

An optimist is a guy who, when he attacks a girl and she files a complaint, thinks she's trying to continue the relationship.

Two good friends, one an optimist, the other a pessimist, were in an automobile accident and were lying in the street waiting for the ambulance. "I feel like my bones are broken," groaned the pessimist. "So," said the optimist, "think how lucky you are, you are not a herring."

p

Parking

New York is a city where you can get away with murder—Unless you're parked beside a fireplug.

Remember when it cost more to run a car than to park it?

Don't believe all the rumors that it's hard to find a parking space in New York. They're not hard to find if you don't mind having your car towed away by the police.

I bought a raffle from a charity group in New York—they were selling chances on a 1972 parking space.

The trouble with towns where you can park as long as you want to is you don't want to.

The Russians will never land in New York, they'll never get a parking place.

They installed parking meters on Park Avenue. "Look at that," the French poodle said to the cocker spaniel, "pay toilets."

Parking Lots

Did you see that racing car picture about the guys who drive 200 miles an hour or more—they were all parking lot attendants.

The owner of the parking lot was lecturing his boys: "You aren't getting enough cars in here. You must be doing something wrong —We haven't had a crushed fender in three days."

Parking lot attendants are often sixteen-year-old kids you pay three dollars to drive the car you wouldn't let your sixteen-year-old touch.

One parking lot attendant I know replaced the girl in the check room at the restaurant—in two hours he dented six overcoats.

Patience

When the elevator came down to the ground floor after three or four minutes' delay, the impatient tenant yelled, "Where the hell have you been?"

The elevator man answered, "Where can you go in an elevator?"

Patience is the art of concealing your impatience.

Peace

Maybe we haven't achieved a permanent peace—but we sure have a permanent peace conference.

Wouldn't it be nice if the world is in such shape next year that Bob Hope could spend Christmas at home?

Bishop Fulton Sheen in describing the Soviet concept of peace is reminded of the man who cornered his friend and said, "You say you are a lover of peace, Casey; then why did you throw the brick at Murphy?" Casey said, "Because he was very peaceful after I threw it."

Will Rogers said, "War is the only game everybody loses—I don't understand why we keep playin' it."

The Russians say all they want is peace—that's true—a piece of Asia, India, Africa, and Europe.

Pessimism

A pessimist says a bottle is half-empty—an optimist says it's half-full.

An optimist sees a doughnut—a pessimist sees a hole.

What's trouble to you—could be a big fee for some lawyer.

A pessimist is a guy who, when he has the choice of two evils—chooses both.

A pessimist always thinks everybody is as lousy as he is—and hates him because of it.

A pessimist stops by the fish store and has some fish sent home—before he goes fishing.

A pessimist is always building dungeons in the air.

Philanthropy

A philanthropist is a guy who gives away publicly what he stole personally.

Philosopher

Two old friends were sitting at the table quietly drinking tea. Finally, one broke the silence and said dramatically, "You know, Sam, life is like a cup of tea." Then there was silence again. A half hour later, the second man said, "Tell me, Charles, why is life like a cup of tea?"

"How should I know," his friend answered. "What am I, a philosopher?"

You can always depend on a philosopher—to contradict what other philosophers say.

Any nut who can analyze his delusions is called a philosopher.

A philosopher is like a diplomat—he can talk authoritatively on any subject and be convincing without knowing what the hell he's talking about. The more his weak spots—the more he speaks with that final authority.

Pills

He takes dozens of vitamin pills daily. "This blue one," he explained, "is for before dinner. The red one is for after dinner. And the yellow one—that *is* dinner."

Forget the pill—they got a better and more subtle approach to birth control—sticky zippers.

I saw a sign at union headquarters: SUPPORT AMERICAN LABOR— BAN THE PILL.

I hope the ads for that new birth-control pill that you only have to take once every thirty days aren't done by the same guy who thought of "for people who can't brush after every meal."

Quoting Phyllis Diller: "Ten million people in the world use birth-control pills. They are called progressive. One billion women don't use birth-control pills. They are called 'Mamma.'"

There is a new birth-control pill on the market—It's made from LSD. You fly so high—your husband can't reach you.

Plastic Surgery

She has had her face lifted so many times—there's nothing left in her shoes.

She couldn't afford to have her face lifted—so she had her body lowered.

Playboy

If he was living in a harem, he'd still have a girl on the outside with whom he'd be cheating.

The fastest worker I ever knew was a man who rushed up to a girl and said, "I'm a stranger in town. Direct me to your flat."

He has a good head on his shoulders—but it's a different one every night.

Playboy to playgirl at party: "You look like the outdoor type—let's go out in the bushes."

When a girl says no to his proposal—he holds her for further questioning.

This playboy was six and he was playing with the girl next door who was five. "Want to wrestle?" he asked. She said, "I can't wrestle—I'm a girl." He continued, "Want to play ball?" She replied, "I can't play ball—I'm a girl."—Finally he said, "Okay—wanna play house?" She said, "All right—I'll be the father."

Playgirl

She's crossed more state lines than Greyhound.

She only looks for one thing in a man—a rich father.

Will Rogers once said, "I never met a man I didn't like."—I got a girl feels the same way.

Her motto is, "If at first you don't succeed—marry the boss's son."

Everybody has her number—if not, they can get it on the wall of every phone booth and men's room in town.

When she reached seventeen her voice started changing—from NO to YES.

1st Girl: How can you tell me that you're marrying a man with 10 million and still insist it's a love match?
2nd Girl: It is—I love money.

She's put more guys in the driver's seat than Hertz.

She doesn't care if a man loves her and leaves her—provided he leaves her enough.

Playgirl: I don't want to marry a go-getter—I want one who already has it.

The slogan of the playgirls: "Girls who go right—get left."

She doesn't care for a man's company—unless he owns it.

Charlie was complaining about his date last night: "The minute we got to her apartment, the phone started ringing and we didn't have a moment's peace." "Come on now," said the friend, "you expect a beautiful young girl to have her phone listed in the phone book."
"Yeah—but not in the Yellow Pages."

He: Your chest sounds all congested. Have you ever tried sleeping with a vaporizer?
She: No—but I'll get around to everyone.

The girls with the least principle draw the most interest.

Belle Baden—the original good time that was had by all.

"Why do you have so many boyfriends?"
"I give up!"

Man: What do you give to a man who has everything?
Playgirl: My phone number.

Plumber

A lady I know called a plumber to fix a small leak in her kitchen sink. It took him about ten minutes to put it in shape and then he handed her a bill for forty dollars for the call. "Forty dollars," she screamed. "My *doctor* only charges twenty dollars!"

"I know, lady," the plumber said. "I used to be a doctor."

My friend Juddy Traum called in a plumber the other day to fix a couple of leaks in his apartment. When the repairs were effected, Juddy asked for the bill and the plumber told him he'd send it.

"Why not give it to me now?" my friend asked.

"Because I hate to see a grown man cry," said the plumber.

Poems

Irish Limericks:

> Sweet Janey a girl of Kilkenny
> Would do such a lot for a penny.
> Her mother was poor
> And this, I am sure,
> Made Janey so useful for many.

> A sharp wicked lady from Ennis
> Seduced a young lad playing tennis.
> "Love one and love all!"
> Was her amorous call,
> And her bribe was an orgy in Venice.

> A happy young colleen from Derry,
> On ale was loving and merry.
> She dallied with sin,
> On vodka and gin,
> But was rigid and frigid on sherry.

There was a bold girl of Kildare,
Who cuddled and hugged on a stair.
At her fifty-fourth squeeze,
She had boys on her knees,
And they shrieked out for mother and air.

> If your wife keeps pleading, please,
> For furs and pearls and so on,
> Take her out to see the trees
> Your money doesn't grow on.

A forgetful actor called Strauss
His wife called a terrible louse.
He was frequently found
In bed, sleeping sound,
But the bed wasn't in the right house.

A secretary, Lil, once late at night,
Switched off the glowing parlour light.
Her boss, beside her, whispered things
Of wedding bells and diamond rings.
In tones of passion, clear and terse
He promised her the universe,
And acted rashly, as men will,
Which quite amused dear little Lil.
Then when he'd gone, her smile grew broader
As she switched off the tape recorder.

A pretty young maiden of France
Decided she'd just "take a chance."
She let herself go
For an hour or so,
And now all her sisters are aunts.

A serious thought for today
Is one that may cause you dismay:
Just what are the forces
That bring little horses,
If all the big horses say "Nay?"

In winter when the pipes all freeze,
The plumber just ignores your pleas,
Your pipes will burst unheeded.
The only time to get the plumber
Is in the middle of the summer,
When the big jerk isn't needed.

He drinks quite a lot,
But he's always in the groove.
He doesn't stagger a single bit,
The bum can't even move.

An oversexed lady called White
Insists on twelve times a night.
A man they call Chedder
Had the big nerve to wed her,
His chance of survival is slight.

Jack be nimble—Jack be quick,
Jack jumped over the candlestick.
Alas he didn't clear the flame,
And now he's known as Auntie Mame.

A man is not old because he's gray,
Or when his teeth decay;
But you know he's ready for the garbage heap,
When his mind makes appointments
His body can't keep.

Show me a man who smiles all the time
Even though his life's in a rut.
Show me a man who smiles all the time,
And I'll show you a Gahdam nut.

Although you gave your heart to me
I still feel I'm on the shelf.
What's the good of just your lips,
Your arms—your heart—your charms—
You keep the best part for yourself.

Bend down and place your little head
Between your great big feet;
These days, that is the only way
You have to make ends meet.

Once, when I was very ill,
I called in famous Doctor Hill.
He cured me, true; I saw his bill
And found myself a sick man still.

A certain young lady called Snookie,
At betting was quite a smart cookie,
Before every race,
She went home to her place,
And curled up with a very good bookie.

Dick Cavett says: I took a look with a microscope at some still-remaining snow on the window sill of my New York apartment and made a discovery. No two particles of soot are alike.

It was a really foggy night in New York and the lady motorist asked the pedestrian, "Can you tell me where I'm going?"
"The East River," he answered. "I just came out."

If the pollution continues, walking on water will no longer be a miracle—anybody will be able to do it.

Mayor Lindsay is doing something about our air pollution. He's putting our street signs up in braille—Now the tourists can feel the sights and go home.

Air pollution is much different than the famous weather cliché: Everybody talks about it, but here everybody does something about it—they contribute to it.

Detroit is one city that knows how to deal with air pollution. It pumps its air into the tires of the cars it manufactures and quietly ships them out of town.

The smog was so bad in Central Park the other night—it's the first time I ever saw a seeing-eye mugger.

Worst pun of any year: I don't know why everybody is suddenly hollering about the air pollution and smog in New York. We had it back in the 1600s. Remember when Henry Hudson sailed into New York Bay—he peered through the smog and asked, "Is Staten Island?"

I have a friend in Philadelphia who says, "We have always had a water problem. When our water is polluted, which is always, we first filter it—then boil it—then add chemicals to it—then we drink beer."

It's great to live in California—You can open the windows and hear the birds coughing.

New York is the only city in the world where mothers call their children *in* for fresh air.

Popularity

I was so unpopular as a child. I once threw a boomerang and it never came back.

I went to a charm school that promised to make me able to charm the birds off the trees, but when I graduated a flock of blue jays attacked me.

Post Office

Postal rates are getting so high—some kids at college are complaining they can't afford to write home for money.

One bank wrote a letter to my wife: "We just cannot afford to spend eight cents to let you know you have five cents."

First-class postage was increased about 50 per cent in the last few years. Now when you begin a letter with "Dear"—you mean it.

Who am I to complain about the mail service? I'm not saying they are slow—but if Paul Revere were a letter carrier, we'd all be singing "God Save the Queen" instead of the "Star-Spangled Banner."

I wrote a letter telling the President how to improve the service at the post office—but the letter got lost.

When the post office employees went on strike it didn't affect us too much—you couldn't tell the difference.

And now it's eleven cents to mail an airmail letter—and I thought those skies were friendly? Now, eleven cents is a little ridiculous— I'd like to write the postmaster—just fly it—don't show it movies.

Eleven cents to mail a letter? I could make a fortune if I opened a discount post office.

There are those who say the mails are improving since they raised the rates. If you put on a new special-delivery stamp and the new airmail stamp you can get mail faster. The truth is, I got one letter from Chicago to New York in twenty-three hours—the fact that it was addressed to a guy in Los Angeles had nothing to do with it.

The clerk said to the customer, "The package is too heavy—you'll have to put more stamps on it."

"And if I put more stamps on it—that will make it lighter?"

Poverty

There is one thing money can't buy—poverty. The stock market can do it for you.

Don Cooper says, "When my brother heard that the government was going to 'declare war on poverty,' he wanted to know where to go to surrender. But not my dad. 'Shucks,' he said, 'if they take away our poverty, we won't have nothin'.'"

Barbra Streisand talks about her beginning days in Brooklyn: "We were very poor—but we had a lot of things that money can't buy—like unpaid bills."

The bachelor showed up in church with a hole in the elbow of his jacket. "I'll be glad to sew a patch on for you," one of the ladies of the congregation offered. "No, thanks," said the bachelor. "A patch is a sign of poverty—a hole might only mean an accident."

The biggest beef from husbands is that they are losing the war on poverty because their wives fraternize with the enemy.

Poverty is no disgrace—but neither is it an honor.

"What the hell are you so happy about? Don't you know we have nothing to eat in the house?"

"I know we have nothing to eat—but thank God I have a good appetite."

The only thing good about being poor is it's inexpensive.

Louis Armstrong's great line: "The Lord will help the poor but not the poor and the lazy—so get in there and wail, daddy!"

Milt Kamen recalls that his family was very poor: "In fact, when I was a kid, I thought knives and forks were jewelry."

Stu Gilliam talks about his "poor" days: "I come from a very poor family. We were so poor my older brother got married just for the rice. I grew up in the ghetto. I was twelve years old before I found out that concrete doesn't grow."

Anytime you think things are getting tough, and you want to feel that your problems are really insignificant, just think of the problems of a Ubangi with chapped lips or an alligator with pyorrhea.

Prayers

Yankee baseball star Bobby Richardson offered the shortest but the strongest prayer of all: "Dear God, your will, nothing more—nothing less—nothing else—Amen."

"I'm not going to pray for you," Bishop Fulton Sheen addressed the New York State legislature. "There are certain things a man has to do for himself. He has to blow his own nose—make his own love—and say his own prayers."

"Please," the little man prayed. "You know me. I'm always praying to you and yet I have had nothing but bad luck, misery, sickness, and despair all my life—and look at the butcher next door—he's never prayed in his life—and yet he has nothing but prosperity, health, and joy—How come a believer like me is always in trouble and he is always doing good?"

Suddenly a big booming voice sounded in his ear: "Because the butcher isn't always bugging me—That's why!"

Minister: Tell me, little man, do you say your prayers every night? Youngster: No—not every night—some nights I don't want anything.

Visitor: I see you have a lot of churches in your little town. There must be a lot of praying going on here. The folks here must love the Lord.
Local: Well, they may love the Lord—but they sure as hell hate each other.

Pregnancy

The sixteen-year-old girl found herself suddenly pregnant. She said it happened at home. "Where were your parents?" she was asked. "At the movies." "Why didn't you go to the movie?" "It was for adults only."

The college girl went to see the doctor when she was in her ninth month. He asked all kinds of questions and then the topper: "Do you have a husband?" "No," she answered, "I'm carrying this for a friend."

When she told her father she was pregnant and the man was the rich Charlie Brown—the old man rushed out gun in hand.

The playboy calmed him down: "Don't get upset—if it's a boy, I'll settle $50,000—if it's a girl, $100,000."

The old man thought a bit. "And if it's a miscarriage," he asked, "does she get another chance?"

The sixty-year-old woman was told by her doctor that she was pregnant. She immediately called her husband and yelled into the phone, "Max, guess what? I'm pregnant." And Max answered, "Who's talking?"

Press Agent

Heard about a new press agent who is having trouble publicizing his clients—he can't tell a lie.

I don't want to knock my publicity man—but I think his last client was the Unknown Soldier.

Proposal

He asked her to marry him, and before she accepted she inquired, "Just one thing, Harry. Are you the sort of man who would expect a wife to go out to work?" Harry said, "Look, Sybil, no wife of mine is ever going to have to go out and take a job. Unless of course she wants food and clothes and luxuries like that."

This somewhat old-fashioned young man went to his sweetheart's father, a big Wall Street broker, to ask for her hand in marriage.

"Can you support a family?" glowered the broker, across the top of the *Wall Street Journal*.

"I th-think so," the young man stammered.

"Make sure!" snapped the broker. "Remember—there are seven of us!"

He: Let's get married—I love you.
She: No, let's just be friends.
He: I don't love you that much.

They were alone in her apartment. She never looked better. She felt now was the time or never. Finally she said, "Let's get married, George, and let's do it now. I don't want to have to wait until I'm forty and have wrinkles, bags under my eyes, and a potbelly."

So George said, "Well, if that's the way you're going to look at forty, let's forget the whole thing."

The girl said to her boyfriend, "I'm sorry, Harry, I can never learn to love you." "That's too bad," he said, "I've saved $50,000." She said, "Maybe I'll take one more lesson."

Sylvia wouldn't marry Charles because of the difference in their ages. She was twenty-one and he was poor.

Prostitution

Mayor Lindsay and the New York City Police Department are having a big problem with ladies of the evening. If you're wondering why they are called ladies of the evening—you should see them in the daylight.

One of them was so old, I didn't know whether to call the cops or Social Security. In fact, I was a little embarrassed to talk to her—Boy Scouts kept helping her across the street.

Earl Wilson says three of them followed him down the street. They're a different type call girl. You don't call them—they call you —and if the answer is "No"—you should hear what they call you.

One girl came up to me and whispered, "You wanna have some fun?" Well, in the cause of research and being in show business, I'm always looking for new ways to have fun—I went up to her apartment. The room was so small you had to lie down, but being a comedian I was there strictly for laughs and fun. I finally found out what they keep in those big handbags they swing around—*Monopoly!* And just to make sure you play on the level—a kitchen knife and a gun.

The man walking along Broadway was confronted by the business gal whispering, "Love for sale." He said, "Sure—if you could do it the Jewish way." She said, "If you teach me to do it the Jewish way—I'll give it to you for half price." He said, "That's the Jewish way."

She met him at the bar—He said, "I'm ninety years old." She said, "Pop, you've had it!"—He said, "How much do I owe you?"

Did you hear about the woman of ill repute who was feeling sick? She went to her doctor and he advised her to stay out of bed for a week.

Why is everybody knocking the Broadway prostitutes? That's the only industry that isn't leaving New York.

Doctor to prostitute: Take this medicine and no drinking and I'll have you back in bed in three days.

Eighty-six-year-old Harry Hershfield was accosted by a prostitute outside the Lambs Club. Harry told her, "There are three reasons why I can't go with you. First, I have no money—" The lady interrupted, "Then the other two reasons don't matter."

I have a friend who once lived in a house of ill repute for about three months. It wasn't too fancy a place but what room service.

Did you ever get mixed up with a German call girl?—when they call, you better listen.

New York City is having a rash of prostitutes—and that's what you get if you buy one.

I know one girl in the Times Square area has been in business so long—they named a doorway after her.

A Pimpmobile is one of those big expensive limousines pimps drive.

Psychiatrists

The patient said to the doctor, "I've been listening to the news and I'm worried—I haven't been feeling nearly as depressed as I should."

Conversation when two psychiatrists meet: "You're fine—How am I?"

The delicious blonde was telling her psychiatrist the problem: "Whenever I have a drink, Doctor, I want to make violent love to the first man I see."

"Don't worry," said the psychiatrist, "as soon as I've mixed this cocktail we can sit down and discuss it."

I went to a head doctor for a ringing noise in my head and he cured me—now I got an unlisted head.

"Do you specialize in nervous people?" the lady asked the doctor.

"Well, yes, you can call it that. I do serve nervous people—Can I help you?"

"First"—she hesitated—"how much do you charge?"

"Fifty dollars for the first visit," he explained.

"Good-by, doctor—so nervous I'm not."

Wife: My husband thinks he's a refrigerator.
Doctor: If that's his only hang-up—I wouldn't worry too much.
Wife: But, Doc, he sleeps with his mouth open and the light keeps me awake.

The patient was complaining to friends: "After one year and $3,000 with that psychiatrist, he tells me I'm cured. Some cure. A year ago I was Abraham Lincoln—Now I'm a nobody."

Doctor (correcting patient on his couch): "Nobody who can afford my fees can be a total failure."

One Beverly Hills psychiatrist is so expensive that for $25 all he does is send you a get-well card.

The beautiful young girl walked into the psychiatrist's room and stood there while the doctor studied her closely. Then he said, "Come here, please." When she did, he grabbed her and kissed her passionately. Then, releasing her, he said in a professional tone, "Well, that takes care of my problem. What's yours?"

Doctor to nurse: "*Please*—just say we are very busy—not 'It's a madhouse!'"

Psychiatrist to patient on couch: "There *is* a man following you— He's trying to collect my bill."

Doctor: Are you troubled by sexual fantasies?
Patient: No—I enjoy them.

Sign in doctor's office: A CURE GUARANTEED OR YOUR MANIA BACK.

A woman complained to her psychiatrist that her brother was convinced he was a parking meter. "Bring him round and I'll talk to him," the doc offered. "Oh, I can't do that," the woman replied. "With all those quarters and dimes in his mouth he won't be able to talk till after he's been emptied."

There is one psychiatrist who specializes—he uses the back seat of a car.

Another psychiatrist I know winds up giving every patient his own special shock treatment—it's called a bill.

Puns

The pun is the lowest sense of humor—unless you think of it first. You can always tell if your pun is a hit when you're the one they want to hit. Any reaction like, "That's horrible," or "Throw the bum out" is a sure sign of success.

Here is some pun-ishment meted out by some of my favorite pun-pals that is sure to elicit an "Oh, no!" from any of your victims:

"How do you make a hormone?"
"Don't pay her." (Do this at your own risk.)

The wolf said to the girl at the party, "Bare with me."

Producer Joe Kipness laughs about some of his flops: "Some of my shows pan out—others peter out."

Dinner was served—Soviet.

He has a will of his own—and she's trying to get it made out to her.

"It's raining cats and dogs outside."
"You're telling me—I just stepped in a poodle." (Oh, no!)

I'm leafing you now (and I better go quietly).

Would you call an arrogant insect a cocky roach? (Walk quietly to the nearest exit.)

Would you call a gigolo a Fee-Male? (Run like hell after that one.)

Does a prostitute pay a Syntax?

The governess quit her job because "The child is backward and the master is forward."

"Can't you take a joke?"
"Are you proposing?"

"Let's elope."
"I cantalope."

"Oh, honeydew."
(How dare you?)

Jim Backus invested in some oil wells in Texas. After six months he sent cards to all the engineers and drillers: "Get Well Soon."

Absinthe makes the heart grow fonder.

Would you say adultery is the state of being grown up?

I'm afraid to put this one down here:
If the definition of a lass is a girl—is a little lass a small *derrière?*

HAVE SOME DAFFYNITIONS

Lovable: What a cow does for her sex life.
Diarrhoea: A dreadful posterior.
Dogma: A bitch with a litter.
Blackmail: The African postal system.
Demonstrators: Sour groups.
Spaceman: A smart astronaut.
Procurer: Fornicaterer.

r

Rabbis

"Help me," the man demanded of the rabbi. "I have a wife and twelve children and I cannot support them. Every year my wife gives me a new child—what should I do?"

"Do?" screamed the rabbi. "Haven't you done enough?"

An Orthodox rabbi awoke very early one Saturday morning. It was a beautiful morning, and being a golf nut, he decided to have a round before anybody was up, and he would still be in time for his synagogue service.

Alone on the course, he teed up and drove off. He played the first hole, which was par four, in three. In heaven there was a turmoil. The angel Gabriel pleaded with the Almighty to punish the rabbi, but the Almighty just smiled.

The second hole was accomplished in two.

Again the angel Gabriel pleaded unsuccessfully for the rabbi to be punished for breaking the Sabbath. The rabbi played the third hole in one, and followed this by playing the fourth in one.

"Please, Almighty, punish this sinner," pleaded Gabriel.

"Isn't he punished enough?" murmured the Almighty. "He will never be able to tell this to anybody."

The Canadian rabbi was bragging to the New York visitor, "We got 80,000 Jews in Toronto and not one Jew is in jail."

"Why," asked the guest, "is it restricted?"

The rabbi was defending his cause to his Christian friend. "Your entire religion is based on ours—You even took the Ten Commandments from us."

"True," said the Christian, "but you sure can't say we kept them."

"You've got to admit," the priest said to the rabbi, "we priests know more than you rabbis."

"Why not?" the rabbi answered. "Your people tell you everything."

The rabbi climaxed his sermon with "Life is like a glass of tea." Later, one of his congregants asked, "Rabbi, why is life like a glass of tea?"

"Why not?" answered the rabbi.

The young student was telling the rabbi what he had learned after reading from the Book of Leviticus. "It forbids abnormal sex practices—the only thing is—I don't understand about the abnormal sex practices."

The rabbi gave him a backhanded slap. "And about normal sex you understand?"

All members of the clergy must be dedicated because they are certainly underpaid. Which leads to a favorite story. Mrs. Abramowitz was bragging about her sons: "Jack is a lawyer and makes a fortune—sends me the whole winter in Florida—My other son, Frank—a doctor—gives me like that $200 a week spending money."

"And your son Aaron?" asked the listener. "What about him?"

"He's a rabbi."

"How is he doing?"

"Believe me—that's not a business for a Jew."

Morty Gunty tells the story: A rabbi addressed his congregation. They were very much moved by his sermon and one man stood up and said, "I'm Joe Smith. I came to this land without a cent. Now I'm worth five million. But when I hear your words I am nothing." Another man stood and said, "I started out without a cent, too. Now I'm worth ten million. But when I hear your words I am nothing." Then another man rose and said, "I work for the post office. I make eighty dollars a week. But when I hear your words I am nothing." And the first millionaire said to the second, "Look who wants to be nothing!"

Racetrack

Definition of a race track: A place where windows clean people.

Boss: I thought you were ill yesterday, Jones?

Jones: I was, sir.

Boss: You didn't look very sick when I saw you at the track yesterday afternoon.

Jones: You should have seen me after the fifth race, sir.

The cop stopped Max on his way to the race track. "All right," he snarled. "What's your hurry? Now where do you think you're going?"

"I'm sick," Max grunted.

The cop noticed the racing form in the seat next to him. "Sick, eh?" he growled. "From here it looks like you're going to the race track."

"Oy, is that a sickness!" Max moaned.

Max says he likes to take his wife with him to the track because, "When I go there, I always lose everything I have with me."

A tout is a guy who has nothing to lose and makes sure you do.

A race horse is an animal that can take several thousand people for a ride at the same time.

Real Estate

Marty Ingels reminds us of the show business real estate broker who called the actor with "some good news and some bad news."

"What's the good news?" the actor wanted to know.

"We can get that beautiful mansion you're so crazy about for only $210,000."

"Wonderful," screamed the actor. "Now what's the bad news?"

"They want $200 down."

For Rent: Four-story house on Bracken Beach—Five stories when the tide is out.

Guide: This castle is six hundred years old—Nothing has been altered, replaced, or repaired.

Tourist: You must have the same landlord we have.

"Say, that lot you sold me in Florida is covered with sea water."

"What do you want for a hundred dollars—seltzer?"

"I'm putting a mortgage on my house."

"For how long?"

"Till they foreclose."

Recession

A rich man is one who has money enough to pay his taxes.

The conservative says, "There is no recession in the United States— It's just a rumor spread by a lot of people out of work."

There is a recession in the garment industry—the bosses are laying off their sons-in-law.

A lot of people are now going out to learn a trade—so they can find out what kind of work they're out of.

I won't say we have a recession—but even the people who don't intend to pay aren't buying.

Everybody's cutting down on expenses. They just laid off my building's doorman and replaced hin with an owl who just sits there and says, "Who?—Who?"

Because of the economy—show business is suffering. Radio City is laying off the Rockettes and replacing them with a centipede.

We're a non-profit organization. We don't mean to be—but we are.

Reincarnation

"What kind of reincarnation?" asked the wife. "My husband doesn't even believe in life after dinner."

Husband: You mean if I die I could come back as something else—that's reincarnation?
Wife: Yes, dear.
Husband: Do I have a choice?—I mean, is it possible for a big man like me to come back as a worm?
Wife: Don't worry, dear, you're never the same thing twice.

I hope in your next life you're a centipede and have ingrown toenails.

Religion

When the Vatican scratched St. Christopher from the liturgical calendar, Bob Orben said, "You should drive carefully anyway—there's always St. Peter."

Father Bob, the show business priest, says he sees no reason why priests shouldn't marry. "Not that I'm so much for it," he says, "but there are a couple of monsignors I'd like to see with mothers-in-law."

Four men of the cloth were having a confidential talk and discussing their vices. "I like pork," the rabbi admitted. "I drink a bottle of scotch a day," said the Protestant minister. "I have a girlfriend on the side," confessed the priest. They all turned to the baptist minister who shrugged. "Me?—I like to gossip."

A Jew and a Christian were having a friendly argument. "Anyway," said the Jewish man, "your whole entire religion was started by us— You even took the Ten Commandments from us."

"Maybe we took them," said the Christian, "but you sure can't say we kept them."

Bishop Fulton J. Sheen tells this story: The woman heard the preacher go through the Commandments and after every Commandment she joined the rest of the audience in shouting "Amen." When he came to the Commandment, "Thou shall not commit adultery," she said, "Now he is beginning to meddle."

Pope John: When the body gets worn out—the soul gets in shape.

Billy Kelly tells the story about an order of Monks that were only allowed to speak once a year, one at a time, which had gathered for dinner. One monk said, "I don't like the mashed potatoes, they are too lumpy." The next year another monk got up and said, "I rather like the mashed potatoes here, I find them rather tasty." The third year a third monk got up and said, "I want to be transferred to another monastery, I can't stand the constant bickering."

Tim was coming out of the tavern and he ran into the father. The father said to him, "Don't you know that when you go in there the devil goes with you?" Tim said, "Well, if he does, he is going to pay for his own drinks."

Another Billy Kelly special: The rabbi went to the race track for the first time. He saw a priest there and the rabbi, not knowing anything about racing decided to watch the priest. Before the first race the priest went over to the horses, made a few signs over number three, and the horse came in second paying twenty-seven dollars. The rabbi again watched the priest and before the second race the priest went over to horse number seven and made a few signs over him. The horse came in first and paid forty-eight dollars. Before the third race the priest went over to the horses again and made some signs over number nine. So the rabbi went and put all of his money on number nine. Well number nine never came in, in fact he may be still running. So the rabbi went over to the priest and told him what had happened.

The priest looked at the rabbi and said, "It is a shame that you didn't know the difference between a blessing and the last rites."

Bob Hope says his wife, Dolores, is very religious. His grocery bill last month was $3,000. Fifty dollars was for food—the rest was for candles.

Pope John liked to reminisce about his peasant origin. "In Italy there are three ways of losing money," he enjoyed saying, "women, gambling, and farming—My father chose the most boring of the three."

I agree that so many are going back to religion—Dial-A-Prayer just added three more numbers.

He is so religious he has stained-glass spectacles.

My favorite priest story is of the father who was stopped by a cop for speeding and announced, "I'm Father Fox." The officer wasn't too impressed and growled, "I don't care if you're Mother Goose—you're getting a ticket."

The three priests dressed in slacks and T-shirts were about to tee off when the golf hustler interrupted and asked if he could make up the foursome. "Okay," said the oldest priest, "but we must tell you—we are not good golfers." Of course, the hustler swore he was a poor player, too, and how about a bet to make it more interesting. One of the priests protested they never bet but to please him they made a rather steep wager.

Naturally, the golf hustler won and the priests paid off. When they all returned to the locker rooms the hustler was shocked to see their habits and offered to return the money.

"No—we made a bet and we stick to it; it will teach us a lesson," said the eldest priest.

"Well," said the man, "I still feel funny hustling priests. Is there anything I can do?"

"Do you have parents?" asked the priest.

"Yes—I do!"

"Well, bring them to me and I'll marry them!"

Father Bob Perella, the show business priest, is a good pal and a great storyteller. Here are some of his favorites:

An Irish soldier went to confession. "I've committed a venial and mortal sin, Father," he confessed. "What is the venial sin?" "I've shot and killed a British soldier." "And the mortal sin?" "I missed the sergeant!"

Same Irish soldier also confessed he ripped up a mile of British railroad track. "What is my penance?"

"Do the stations!" "Do the stations!!!"

Someone suggested having a drive-in confessional with a huge red-and-green neon sign reading: STOP AND TELL OR GO TO HELL.

In Chinatown there is a Catholic church named Church of the Transfiguration. Someone rang the doorbell of our rectory, practically a part of Chinatown, asking for the location of the Church of the Transfusion.

Seated in a restaurant, a priest was scrutinizing the beauty of a young lady escorted by her male companion. A layman kidded him about his female interest. "Just because I'm on a perpetual diet, it doesn't mean I can't study the menu once in a while," said the priest.

During a preaching tour I stopped at one of our seminaries in Troy, New York. While in bull session I remarked how most priests own automobiles, many of them in the higher price brackets. How most priests would rather drive than walk a few blocks to pick up a newspaper. In fact, I continued, if the Almighty created a most beautiful, voluptuous woman and placed her in one corner, and placed a Continental in the other corner, most of us would choose the car.

"Which would you pick?" I asked Father Philbert. He answered, "Bob, I don't drive."

A drunk fell into an open grave and was unconscious for several hours. When he finally came to, he opened his eyes, looked around, and yelled out, "It's the Resurrection and I'm the first one up!"

Milton Berle was opposite Bishop Fulton J. Sheen on TV and felt his ratings dropping. "What the hell," alibi'd Uncle Miltie. "He's got better writers than I have."

Another time Bob Hope was a big hit at one Catholic benefit and after three encores he thanked his staff of writers. When Bishop Sheen followed him he said, "I also want to pay tribute to my writers —Matthew, Mark, Luke, and John."

A reporter asked the beloved Pope John XXIII how many people worked in the Vatican. "About half," said his holiness.

The priest asked the little boy if he said his prayers every night. "Not every night," the kid answered. "Some nights I don't want anything."

The two nuns were enjoying the baseball game when one of the shrimps in back of them growled to his friend, "You can't see a thing, these nuns' hats are blocking the whole game. Remind me to move to Cleveland where only 10 per cent of the people are Catholics."

"Better still—let's go to Omaha," his friend answered, "where only 5 per cent are Catholic."

"I got a better idea," one of the nuns said. "Why don't you both go to hell where you will find *no* Catholics?"

Father Bob was having dinner at Danny's with Rabbi Halpern. "Come on," said Father Bob, "when are you gonna let yourself go and have some bacon or ham?"

"At your wedding," said the rabbi.

TV pastor Rex Humbard says he gets some direct questions that are embarrassing. "Like one fellow," he says, "who told his minister, 'One of the first things I'm going to ask the Lord when I get to heaven is why he gave us all these sex gadgets and then told us not to use them.'"

Respect

Rodney Dangerfield says, "I don't get no respect. Prominent people hang out in fancy places, they get invited to yacht clubs—I gotta swim in.

"I got no respect even in my childhood. I remember the time my kid brother got lost and my parents sent me out to look for him. They gave me a piece of his clothing to smell."

Restaurants

The lady told the waiter, "Put the rest of my steak in a bag for my dog—and put in some bread, too, in case he wants to make a sandwich."

The man waited in the restaurant for a long time to be served. Finally, he called the owner and asked, "Did the waiter who took my order leave a large family?"

My friend just opened a restaurant with only two tables. When people ask him why only two tables, he says, "I get nervous if nobody's waiting."

Mickey Freeman complains that the Times Square area in New York is getting tougher and tougher. "I walked into a cafeteria, got coffee, and sat down. I said to the guy at my table, 'Pardon me, but your elbow's in my coffee.' He said, 'I'm stirring it, ain't I?'"

One restaurant has a midget waiter for the diners who have drunk themselves under the table.

An Italian restaurateur had a customer the other night who told him, "Your veal parmesan is better than any I had in Italy on my vacation." Said the host, modestly enough, "Of course it is. Over there they use domestic cheese and here we use imported."

The waiter took the order but it seemed an interminable time before he returned with the soup. "Are you the same waiter who took my order?" the starving man asked.
"I am. Why?" answered the waiter.
"Funny—you don't look a day older."

For $1.25 you can eat like a horse. If you want to eat like a human being it costs $8.00.

I went to one restaurant that was so bad, the other side of the menu was a prescription blank.

I saw this sign in back of the counter in a New York restaurant:
OUR CUSTOMERS ARE ALWAYS RIGHT
Misinformed—impatient—grouchy—
stubborn—even stupid—*But never wrong.*

The health inspector for the city told the owner that he examined his restaurant and that he had too many roaches. The owner asked, "How many am I allowed?"

This is a warning about those restaurants that offer all you can eat for $1.85. I went into one, took one bite—and that's all I could eat.

The lady ordered caviar and warned the waiter, "Be sure it's imported—because I can't tell the difference."

When one restaurant had a big fire some wag wired the owner:
CONGRATULATIONS—THE FIRST TIME YOUR FOOD HAS BEEN HOT IN YOUR PLACE IN TWENTY YEARS.

"Waiter," the patron shouted, "get me another cup of coffee, please."

"Very well, but you certainly are a lover of coffee. This is your seventh cup."

"I am. I am. Or I wouldn't be drinking so much water in order to get a little coffee."

"Hey!" the diner asked the waiter, "what the hell kind of pie did you bring me. Are you sure this is apple pie?"

"What does it taste like?" the waiter asked.

"I don't know," the customer growled.

"Then what difference does it make?" the waiter replied.

Dean Martin heckled a customer who didn't look up from his dinner while he was singing. "Look, Buster," said the man, "I've seen singers before—but this is the first time I've seen a twelve-dollar steak."

The lady at the Stage Delicatessen complained that her main dish didn't have a green vegetable on it. The waiter pointed to a dill pickle on the plate and belched, "That maybe by you is purple?"

I suspect a new midtown restaurant isn't very good: They honor cards from Diners' Club, American Express, and Blue Cross.

A waiter confided to a customer that the coffee he was serving was blended: "It's yesterday's and today's."

Danny Stradella of Danny's Hide-a-way told one of his waiters, "I'd certainly like to compliment you on your work—so when are you gonna do some?"

Revolt

You can't shake hands with a clenched fist.

If there is so much hate in the world—how do you account for the population explosion?

I don't want to be pessimistic about the future, but the way things are going—Benedict Arnold may wind up with a good conduct medal.

Riches

The Rockefellers really know how to live. They had a picnic—and even the paper plates were sterling silver.

It doesn't matter if you're born poor and you die poor—as long as you're rich in between.

It is better to live rich—than die rich.

Joe E. Lewis: I've been rich and I've been poor—believe me—rich is better.

He's so rich he has an unlisted zip code.

He is so rich he sends CARE packages to Rockefeller.

He is so rich he sends gift certificates to Howard Hughes.

Fred Allen: I never want to get used to anything I may someday have to do without.

Why was everybody so stunned when Jackie married Onassis? He's as handsome as Croesus.

Believe me, money isn't everything—a man with three million can be just as happy as a man with five million.

Money doesn't buy everything—but it puts you in a better bargaining position.

"Do you think she married him because he had that kind of money?" "No, she would have married anybody with that kind of money."

You can't see his hidden charms—his money is in Swiss banks.

This guy is so rich he has an unlisted wife.

He is so rich he has an unlisted number at Sing Sing.

When Howard Hughes wanted to see the Bahamas—he sent for it.

"How come we never see a picture of you, Mr. Hughes?"
   "I don't understand it," Howard answered over the phone. "My picture is on every million-dollar bill."

A rich man is an alcoholic—a poor man is a drunk.

Now that he's rich enough to afford to lose golf balls—he can't hit them far enough to lose them.

He is so rich—he cashed a check and the bank bounced.

The late Billy Rose once was teased by Abe Burrows for having abandoned Broadway. "Sure you're making millions, Billy, but we get laughs."

Billy replied: "Abe you'd be surprised at what laughs I get when my AT&T goes up three points."

Liberace has a big problem with his jeweled suits. How do you find a tailor who is also a diamond cutter?

Don Rickles

Upon seeing Frank Sinatra at the entrance of the night club: "Come right in, Frankie. Make yourself at home. Hit somebody." And, as Sinatra is seated at his table: "Remember the good old days, Frank, when you had a voice? How's everything at the Will Rogers Home? Do they give you enough blankets?"

To Ernest Borgnine: "Oh, my gosh, look at you! Was anyone else hurt in the accident?"

To Burt Lancaster: "Your career's in trouble—your curls aren't lying right any more."

To Eddie Fisher: "For gosh sakes, Eddie, next time marry someone famous and keep your name alive." Then to the audience, "You know, folks, Eddie was once married to Elizabeth Taylor. Eddie Fisher married to Elizabeth Taylor is like trying to flag down the Super Chief with a Zippo lighter."

To Anthony Quinn: "Hi, Tony, who's crushing the grapes?"

To Lee Marvin: "Hello, old-timer. Come in and watch a big star in action."

Spotting eligible bachelor Hugh O'Brian in the audience: "I understand that Hugh's visiting the White House next week. His publicity has fallen off, and he wants to find out if the President has a single daughter."

To Maury Wills: "I've watched you play shortstop. Take my advice: Improve on the banjo—fast—and a couple of voice lessons wouldn't hurt."

Spotting Perry Como in his audience: "Let's give him a hand, folks, so he doesn't doze off."

Asking his mother to stand up and take a bow: "When I was a kid she used to visit my teacher so often the other kids elected her class president."

To George Murphy: "Senator, I'd go into politics, too, but I'm already working."

Spotting Jack Benny in his audience: "Before Jack made his reservation to come in this room he called the maitre de to make sure the tips were included in the cover charge."

To Bob Hope: "You have no right to be in this city. The government hasn't got any troops stationed here."

To Michael Caine: "Hey, let's you and me sneak outside and play spy, and we'll see if you can figure out what I'm doing."

To the mayor of Lake Tahoe: "You've got a great city here—for bears and seals."

To Sandy Koufax: "What the heck are you doing, applauding or oiling your glove? Go home and pack your hand in ice."

To Jim Arness: "You've got me worried, Jim. Lately when you kiss your horse I'm beginning to think you mean it."

Spotting Liberace in his audience: "There's Liberace, folks. He's trying his best to look inconspicuous. He's the fellow with the sequined jacket and a candelabra in his mouth."

To George Burns: "There's a guy who came to California for arthritis thirty years ago, and he's finally got it."

To his audience, while taking bows at the end of his act: "My maid gets better applause when she runs a rag over the piano keys."

Riddles

Q: Which is the cleanest chemical in the lab?
A: Washing soda.

Q: Which insect is the most religious?
A: A praying mantis.

Q: What game do judges play?
A: Tennis—because it's played in court.

Q: What is a female drug addict called when she saves somebody?
A: A heroine.

Q: Which trees do hands grow in?
A: Palm trees.

Q: In which ball can your carry your shopping?
A: Basket ball.

Q: How do you make a peach cordial?
A: Buy her a few drinks.

Q: Do you stir your coffee with your right hand or your left hand?
A: Neither—I use a spoon.

Q: Who was the last man to box John L. Sullivan?
A: The undertaker.

Q: Where do bad girls go?
A: Most everywhere.

Q: What month has twenty-eight days?
A: All of them.

Q: In what country do they let prisoners go?
A: Con go.

Q: What pigeon is always expecting?
A: A carrier pigeon.

Q: Why does everybody want to be Franco's secretary?
A: Because he was a great dictator.

Q: What occupation suits everybody?
A: A tailor.

Q: Which birds are religious?
A: Birds of pray.

Q: Why are fish always well balanced?
A: Because they have scales.

Q: Why did the hippie take a bath?
A: So he could hock it!

Q: What looks like a hippie boy, acts like a hippie boy, and talks like a hippie boy?
A: A hippie girl!

Q: What happened when the hippie fell off a horse and broke his leg?

A: The horse shot him!

Q: Where is the elephant found?
A: Why, it's so big—it's hardly ever lost.

Q: What is heavier than an elephant who has just eaten a peanut?
A: An elephant who has just eaten two peanuts.

Q: Why does Snoopy want to quit the comic strip?
A: Because he's tired of working for Peanuts.

Q: What lies at the bottom of the ocean and shakes?
A: A nervous wreck.

Q: Why did the man keep his money in the refrigerator?
A: Because he wanted to have cold cash.

Q: Do you know a word that starts with E and has only one letter in it?
A: An envelope.

Q: How's the boy who swallowed the quarter?
A: No change yet.

Q: Why did you throw away your new Beatle bubble-bath powder?
A: Because it left a Ringo around my bathtub.

Q: "Do you know why they didn't bury the Duke of Wellington with full military honors in 1850?"
A: "Because he didn't die until 1852."

Q: "What does a soldier have to be, to be buried with full military honors?"
A: "Dead."

Q: Why did the hippie get out of a sick bed with 104?
A: It was too crowded!

Q: Where do hippies hide their valuables?
A: Under the soap!

Q: What do you give a hippie who has everything?
A: DDT.

Joan Rivers

I started my career in a town so small the local clinic was called Fred's Hospital and Grill.

I wear the midi because I feel if you're going to look ugly, you may as well look this year's ugly.

I told my husband I can't do everything—cook, keep house, clean, work, perform, take care of the baby—so he told me to hire a lady to be his wife!

I try to look good—I wear so much make-up I have to talk through a straw.

My husband doesn't really notice me that much. I dyed my hair from brown to blond and he said, "Hmmmm, finally washed your hair."

I wasn't very popular in school. I went to the same school for twelve years and was always referred to as the "new girl."

I buy my clothes at a store that sells irregulars. I got a beautiful coat that fit like a glove—It had five sleeves.

We moved recently and the movers were really dumb. I marked one carton "China," and that's where they sent it.

The movers also lost my bed. I wouldn't have minded so much if they'd admitted it, but they tried to convince me I didn't have one.

With the pollution of our rivers today they are changing the signs from "No Fishing" to "No Fish."

My cousin is a worse cook than I am. I caught her defrosting the stove.

My husband, Edgar, and I resolved not to go to sleep mad—as of now we've been awake for three weeks.

Sometimes I worry that our daughter doesn't get enough vitamins. The other day her first tooth came in and it had a cavity.

I have a friend who is so dumb she thinks toothpaste is for people with loose teeth.

I cleaned my closet. I found things I haven't seen in years—my vacuum cleaner, my iron.

S

Salesmen

A man comes into a store to buy a suit. The salesman tries one jacket on him after another. He says to the customer, "Turn around, let's see it in this light, now let's look at it in the rearview mirror, now from this angle, now this angle." Still the man asks to try on other jackets. Finally the boss comes up to them and picks out a jacket. The customer puts it on and buys it immediately. Says the boss: "See how easy it is to make a sale?" "Okay," says the salesman, "you made the sale, but who made him dizzy?"

A salesman kept ringing my bell at the unheard of hour of 8 A.M. at least twice a week. He sold mops, guns, paintings, watches—everything. One day I lost my patience and told him to scram or I'd call a cop. You know, the guy tried to sell me a whistle.

He couldn't sell a glass of water in the Sahara Desert.

The most successful door-to-door salesman in the country finally revealed the secret of his success and I pass it on to you. His opening line is "Miss—is your mother home?"

He's such a great salesman, you can't use that stale line about him that he would sell refrigerators to Eskimos—Actually, he could sell bathtubs to hippies.

This traveling salesman was stuck in a small town and went to the only available farmhouse for a place to sleep. "Can you put me up for the night?" he asked the farmer.

"I reckon I can," he answered, "if you don't mind sharing a room with my young son."

"My God," said the salesman, "I'm in the wrong joke!"

Sayings

Shalom Aleichem: The luckiest man was Adam—he had no mother-in-law.

Shalom Aleichem: The more poverty—the more hope.

Shalom Aleichem: Barking dogs don't bite—but they themselves don't know it.

An ass is known by his big ears—a fool by his big tongue.

Chaim Weizmann: Miracles sometimes occur—but one has to work terribly hard for them.

It's easier to fight for principles than to live up to them.

The only man who never steps on anybody else's toes—is standing still.

"It's a woman's duty to provide for the inner man and a man's duty to provide for the outer woman." —Earl Wilson.

An ounce of apology is worth a pound of loneliness.

"The only way to get rid of temptation is to yield to it." Or to put it in another Wilde way: "I can resist everything except temptation."

People who never do any work—never have a holiday.

You can't get ulcers from what you eat—you get ulcers from what's eating you.

When we are young our parents run our lives—When we get older—our children do.

Texas Guinan said it first: "Success has killed more men than bullets."

School

The teacher wrote on the blackboard, "I ain't had no fun all summer." Then she asked her students, "What's wrong with that sentence and what do I do to correct it?"

One kid in the back hollered, "Get a boyfriend."

When I was a kid I went to a really tough school. Every day after school there was a fight. Sometimes we used to bet on the fight, and if the guy we bet on lost, then we beat him up.

I think my nephew is serious about a girl in school—he carried home her picket sign.

The teacher was explaining to the principal about one of the kids in her class: "He's from a good home—has a good IQ—no emotional problems—he's just a nasty little bastard."

"I'm so happy," the confectioner said. "Where shall we send it, sir?"

"Never mind," said the customer. "I'll eat it here."

The man was out of work and nobody in the small town would give him a job. Finally the mayor of the town felt pity and gave him the job of polishing the cannon in front of the library. He stayed in the job for twenty years. One day he returned home and told his wife he was quitting. "Why?" she asked. "I can't see any future in it," he said. "I've got a little money saved up—I'm gonna take it and buy me another cannon—and go in business for myself."

Ships

A tourist aboard a transatlantic liner was curious about the bells that rang at frequent intervals. As the bells rang again, the deck steward passed the passenger.

"Pardon me, steward," the man said, "will you tell me what those bells are?"

"Of course, sir," the steward said. "They are used to tell the time."

"Thank you," said the man. "Oh, by the way, can you tell me what time it is now?"

"I'm sorry," the steward replied, "but my watch is out of order."

The man crossed the ocean by ship but was on the rail most of the trip. The captain passed and touched his shoulder as he was bent over the side like a hoop: "I'm sorry—but remember, nobody ever died of seasickness."

"Don't say that," the green man mumbled. "The thought of dying is the only thing that's keeping me alive."

Shopping

I actually saw this sign in a window on the West Side: SIX LANGUAGES SPOKEN HERE.

"Not by me," the owner of the store explains. "By my customers."

The lady in the supermarket said to the man behind the counter, "I don't like the looks of this codfish."

"Lady, for looks you don't buy codfish, you buy goldfish."

When she returned home after a day's shopping with everything but cash, she explained to her husband: "After reading those stories about crime in the streets—I decided not to walk around with all that cash on me."

If I had all the money my wife saves me with the bargains she picks up—I'd make Howard Hughes look like a bum.

"All right," my wife admitted, "so I spend money on shopping— Can you name one other extravagance I have?"

When my wife goes shopping she comes home with everything but money.

Husband: What the hell do you need with six new dresses?
Wife: Six new hats.

There was a long line waiting in the early morning in front of a clothing store that advertised a special sale. A man walked to the front of the line. The people grabbed him and pushed him back to the end of the line. Once more he headed for the front of the line and they kicked him and pushed him into the gutter. Finally he got up, brushed himself off, and said to a man at the end of the line, "If they do that once more—I'm not opening the store."

Shortness

She was so short that when she wore a miniskirt the hem got dirty.

When he sits down and stands up he's the same size.

He was so small and she was so tall—when he wanted to make love to her somebody had to put him up to it.

He was so short when he stood up he looked like he was standing in a foxhole.

Show Business

One of the late Fred Allen's favorite stories about vaudeville (and mine, too) concerns the comedian's appearance before a very unreceptive audience.

When Fred returned to his dressing room, a fellow performer asked, "How did it go, Fred? Did you kill them?"

"No," said Allen. "I didn't have to. They were dead when I got there."

Leland Hayward was a big-time talent agent in Hollywood. When he married his client Margaret Sullavan he got this wire from one of his pals: CONGRATULATIONS ON GETTING THE OTHER 90 PER CENT.

Eddie Cantor was always rich and Georgie Jessel broke—Georgie was always annoyed at this arrangement. One day coming out of the backstage door he saw a big sign with the legend JESUS SAVES. Underneath he scrawled BUT NOT LIKE CANTOR.

Irving Mansfield likes to tell about the time he was company manager for a vaudeville unit with Eddie Cantor and Georgie Jessel. When they arrived in one town, Jessel went around to the front of the theater to take a look at the billing and was annoyed with the marquee sign which read "Eddie Cantor *with* Georgie Jessel."

"What kind of conjunction is that?" he berated Irving.

Irving promised to fix it, and the next day the marquee sign read "Eddie Cantor *but* Georgie Jessel."

My theatrical godfather, Harry Hershfield, always has an inside story for me. The producer came home to his wife and gleefully announced, "I think I got a hit."

"How do you know?"

"I met three of the critics and they each told me that if I change one of the acts I'll have a hit."

"That's wonderful," she said.

"Yeah, but each picked a different act."

The manager of a touring theatrical company wired the proprietor of a small-town theater where the troupe was due to appear. HOLDING REHEARSAL NEXT MONDAY AT TWO. PLEASE HAVE YOUR STAGE MANAGER, CARPENTER, PROPERTY MAN, ELECTRICIANS, AND STAGEHANDS PRESENT AT THAT TIME, read the telegram. Later that day came the reply: ALL RIGHT. HE'LL BE THERE.

Actor Jack Albertson tells about the time he asked for a part in a dramatic show that producers Lindsay and Crouse were casting. Crouse thought very seriously for a moment. "Yes, there is an American in it," he said. "Tell me, Jack, what kind of salary do you get these days?"

"Well, my last salary was $250 per week."

"Jack," Crouse replied sadly, "you are too tall."

Joey Bishop looked out at the sparse audience and said: "You're my favorite audience—a small audience—with a small audience—if you don't do good—not too many people know about it."

The magician did his act for the agent and kept pulling dozens of cigars out of his ears, his nose, his belly button. "Great," said the agent. "I never saw anything like it—How do you manage it?"

"Simple," said the magician. "I have a friend who gets them for me wholesale."

Joe Frisco, the stuttering comic, once bought a painting of "The Last Supper" at an actors' charity function. Later, after a few bad days at the track, he took the painting to a pawnshop. The broker looked at it and said he didn't know too much about "Last Supper" paintings. "What do you think it's worth?"

"Well," said Joe, "at least t-t-ten dollars a p-p-plate."

She was the wife of a third-rate comic. When she announced she was going to have a baby, her agent said, "I hope you have a better delivery than your husband."

Shyness

He is so shy that he wouldn't open an oyster without knocking on the shell.

She is so shy she blushes when she hears the word intersection.

She blushes when the preacher says "Dearly beloved—"

She blindfolds herself when she takes a bath.

She insisted that the doctor put out the lights before he examined her. After ten minutes in the dark she said to the doctor, "Where will I put my clothes?"

"Right here, next to mine," he answered.

The shy young man was looking out the window, fully dressed, when his bride brought her nude body out of the bathroom steady and ready. "What's wrong, dear?" she asked.

"Nothing, darling," he answered, still staring out the window. "My mother said this would be the greatest night of my life and I don't want to miss a moment of it."

Small Town

Herb Shriner was the champion of the small towns. His lines are
still classics:

"I was born in Ohio but moved to Indiana as soon as I heard about
it," he said. "We used to have a pretty lively bunch in my town. Saturday nights, 'twasn't nuthin' for us to drop in to the barbershop and
watch a few haircuts . . ."

A farmer friend of his from Terre Haute went to look at the Big
City—Indianapolis. "How'd you like it?" they asked him when he
came back. "'Tain't for me, I'll still take the good old U.S.A.," he
said.

"Back home, I knew a fellow who called himself a Doctor of Laws,
and if anybody ever doctored the laws, he did.

"We had a beauty contest in my town and nobody won. . . . We
had a doctor that's different. Some doctors treat you for pneumonia
and you die of measles. When this doctor treats you for pneumonia,
you die of pneumonia.

"Heredity's the comin' science. For instance, on account of
heredity, if your parents never had any children, there's a good
chance you won't have any."

Shriner's Indiana humor was brilliant: "My town was so small it
was between the first and second line of a Burma Shave sign. I had
to leave town to learn how the poem came out."

In his town there never was a get-out-the-vote campaign: "The
problem was not in getting a fella to vote, but getting him to stop."

Shriner said in the Army there were two types of shoes, "Officers' "
and "Uncomfortable."

A home-town neighbor made a fortune selling luminous sun dials.
"Nobody found out because everybody went to bed early."

One couple married three times "because my town's so small they
just kept getting introduced."

My wife came from a very small town. One exciting evening she and the gang got all dressed up and ran down to the hotel to see who rented the room.

He comes from a town in Connecticut so small that the mayor is an elk—a *real* elk.

The town was so small that during a boxing match, both fighters had to sit in the same corner.

A small town is where the real news comes over the fence—not over the radio.

Dave Barry says he lived in a town so small the Howard Johnson's only had one flavor.

The town is so dull—the other day the tide went out—and never came back.

The airline is so small—you have to have the exact change to get on the plane.

The only town in the world with dead-end one way streets.

A small town is a place where everyone knows who's check is good and who's husband isn't.

Don Cooper says: Deborgia, Montana, where I live, is what they call an "outlying community"—people here can outlie anybody. It's so small we have only one Yellow Page. Tried to call home once and the area code was busy. Plugged in my electric razor and blew out the powerhouse. Trouble is, we never get any bigger—every time a baby is born some guy leaves town.

We're starting a big campaign to attract tourists. First thing we did was put up a sign on the road. It says ENTERING DEBORGIA—it says the same thing on the other side. Also, we are putting in a traffic light. Haven't bought the light yet but we have already picked the colors.

My town was so small we didn't even have one professional call girl—we had to get along with volunteers.

Smile

A smile is the shortest distance between people.

Phyllis Diller explained why she smiles a lot: "My teeth are the only things I have that aren't wrinkled."

Snobs

Lady Herring was an extreme snob. Being interviewed by a society reporter, the journalist happened to admire the huge bloodhound that lay at her ladyship's feet. "It's a blue bloodhound," said her ladyship. The interviewer asked, "Does he always stay indoors?" "No," was the answer. "He has a very large custom-built kennel on the grounds." "And how do you keep the kennel clean?" asked the journalist. "Ah," said her ladyship, "he has a French poodle who comes in twice a week."

She lives in a neighborhood that is so exclusive—that Chicken Delight has an unlisted number.

She always walks with her nose in the air—that's to avoid smelling herself.

She's such a snob—she won't eat a hot dog unless it's registered in the Kennel Club.

She won't even eat ladyfingers unless they're manicured.

Sports

The only wrestling matches that aren't fixed are those in back of a car.

Bowling is the second most popular indoor sport.

The wrestler couldn't understand why he lost the bout—he won the rehearsal.

He broke the underwater record by staying under for three hours and twenty-five minutes. Funeral services will be held tomorrow.

The Attorney General's office was after him as a monopoly. He was operating six ski lodges and two hospitals.

Clerk at ski lodge to registering guest: "Just your name, address, and Blue Cross number."

The son says to his father who is watching television: "What are you watching, Dad?"

"Basketball game."

"What's the score?"

"It's 103 to 101."

"Who's winning?"

"The 103."

Yogi Berra was trying to console his teammates: "We could still win the pennant—all we have to do is win ten out of our last five remaining games."

One fan wrote to the Mets office and complained about all the night games and weekend double-headers. "I prefer midweek afternoon games—it's much easier to get away from the office than from the wife."

Did you hear about the football player who got married? Getting into bed on the first night of his honeymoon—he slipped and injured his back—so he sent in a substitute.

Two Greek visitors to England were taken to see their first football match. They watched for a while but couldn't understand what the hell was going on. Finally one turned to the other and said, "I don't know about you, but this is all English to me."

Joe Namath is so rich now—next season his football jersey will have an unlisted number.

Football coach: We got a great team this year—no losses—no draws —no goals scored against them.

Reporter: How many games have you played?

Football coach: The first one is next Saturday.

Two football nuts were discussing the game. "My wife put her foot down last night—she said she will leave me if I don't give up following football."

"I'm so sorry," said his pal.

"Me too—I'm going to miss her."

The famous sports announcer was "on" at Teddy's Bar. "Do you know," he was telling his listeners, "it took me twenty years to realize that I know nothing about football."

"Well," interjected Sal who owns Teddy's, "why don't you give up commentating, then?"

"I can't—It's too late—I've become an authority on the game," he replied.

The lady approached the perfume counter and asked the clerk: "What do you have that will compete with four hours of football on TV?"

I went to a ski resort that had three slopes: Beginners—intermediate —and call-an-ambulance.

The basketball coach of a well-known college team had to alibi to a disappointed alumni for an unexpected trouncing. "What can I do?" he burbled. "All of my college boys played like a bunch of amateurs."

Famed basketball coach Frank McGuire was always calm under fire. During one game when his team was being murdered, his assistant screamed, "Frank, they're killing us—What are we gonna do?"

"Get better players," Frank said softly.

The basketball player from the University of Texas came to New York to be interviewed by the coach of a professional ball club. "I got good news and bad news," he told the coach. "First the good news— I'm the fastest runner and best dribbler in basketball—I scored more than anybody in the history of Texas U.—and can shoot a goal at eighty feet."

"And what's the bad news?" the coach asked.

"Well," he answered, "I'm from Texas—I exaggerate a lot."

Bobo Newsom was pitching for the St. Louis Browns and really taking a beating. They were hitting everything he threw all over the lot and out of it. By the sixth inning he was losing 15 to 0. When he came back to the dugout—he snarled: "Look at that score 15 to 0— How can a guy win ball games with this lousy club if they don't give him any runs?"

Baseball's Babe Herman was the wackiest Dodger of them all. And his malaprops were as famous on the field as well as off. Once when he was wearing a white suit after a win, some lady approached him in a restaurant and gushed, "My—how cool you look."

Babe blushed and looked at the low-cut dress she was wearing and blurted out: "Thanks, lady, you don't look so hot yourself."

Yogi Berra is the unconscious wit of baseball. "I think Little League baseball is good," he said seriously. "It keeps the kids out of the house."

One of the great headlines in sports after the fabulous Dizzy Dean was hit by a pitched ball: DIZZY DEAN'S HEAD X-RAYED—REVEALS NOTHING.

Squelches

"Why, ya crum-bum," Toots Shor said to Jackie Gleason, "I'll put you in my back pocket."

"Then," the Fat One answered, "you'll have more brains in your pocket than you have in your head."

Oscar Wilde said: "Bernard Shaw hasn't an enemy in the world—and none of his friends like him."

The noisy diner was banging on the table with his cutlery. "The service here is lousy," he bellowed. "Look at my glass, it's empty. What've I got to do to get some water?"

The quiet waiter leaned over and whispered, "Why don't you set fire to yourself?"

George Bernard Shaw received an invitation from a celebrity-hunter with this legend, "Lady Martin will be at home between 7 and 10 P.M." The vitriolic author returned the card with his own notation: "Mr. Bernard Shaw likewise."

President John F. Kennedy used his great wit on all—including family, friends, foes, press, and himself. Barry Goldwater is an excellent photographer. The former presidential candidate took a good picture of Kennedy and sent it to him for an autograph. Then Kennedy inscribed it: "For Barry Goldwater, whom I urge to follow the career for which he has shown so much talent—photography. From his friend, John Kennedy."

At one point when Kennedy was asked to comment on the press treatment of his Administration, he replied: "Well, I'm reading more and enjoying it less."

Like the true wit he was, nobody escaped his bite—not even his family: "I see nothing wrong with giving Bobby some legal experience as Attorney General before he goes out to practice law."

A pompous senator once sounded off to Dorothy Parker. "It's one of the disadvantages of statesmanship," he said, "to realize, as Heraclitus did, that there'll always be a majority of fools. I simply can't bear fools."

"How paradoxical," observed Mrs. Parker. "Your mother could."

The politician was raving and so was the audience. He tried to hold the unruly mob by exclaiming: "We seem to have a bunch of fools here tonight. Wouldn't it be easier if we hear them one at a time?" Came the proverbial voice from the rear, "You're right, sir—get on with your speech."

The great Bert Lahr was putting Monty Woolley on. "I'm just as good as any actor," said the comic. "In fact, who's got my good looks and my sparkling teeth?"

"I don't know," squelched Woolley, "but you'd better get them back!"

Sam Goldwyn was having an argument with John Barrymore and the producer was getting pretty excited. "Don't you point your finger at me," shouted Barrymore. "I knew it when there was a thimble on it."

At one party for Elizabeth Taylor, the toastmaster opened the ceremonies by toasting, "Tonight we present the lives and loves of Elizabeth Taylor." Jack E. Leonard interrupted, "Relax folks—we're going to be here a long time."

When Winston Churchill was a young man he was growing a mustache. The young lady who was to be his dinner companion didn't seem to appreciate the future Prime Minister. "Mr. Churchill," she remarked, "I care for neither your politics nor your mustache."

"Don't distress yourself," Churchill replied. "You are not likely to come in contact with either."

The picture was so bad—they had to do retakes before they put it on the shelf.

She: You don't love me any more. I'm going back to Mother.
He: Don't bother—I'll go back to my wife.

The great John Barrymore made one picture in which a monkey

played a small part. The Great Profile took a liking to the monkey and he called the animal's trainer to his dressing room to buy the monkey: "I like her and I'd like to keep her as a pet." . . . "That's swell of you," said the trainer, "How much do you make a week?" . . . Barrymore said, "Three thousand dollars." . . . "Well," said the trainer, "she seems to like you, *too*—and she makes $5,000 a week— she'd like to buy *you!*"

"How do you like our salad?" the waiter asked the bitchy customer.
"It's fit for pigs."
"Here, then let me help you to some more of it."

The old actor was boring his youthful listeners at the Friars Club: "Why," he exclaimed, "when I walked on stage the audience sat there open-mouthed."
"You mean," heckled a renegade, "they all yawned at once?"

Jack Benny is the only fiddler who makes you feel that the strings would sound better back in the cat.

Henny Youngman to a pal: "I think the world of you—and you know what I think of the world."

A: Kiss my ass.
B: Okay, but better mark the spot—you look all ass to me.

Lady Astor to Winston Churchill: "If you were my husband I would poison your coffee."
Winston to the lady: "If I were your husband I would drink it."

Suburbs

Suburbia—where the houses are farther apart—and the payments are closer together.

An American city is a place where by the time you've finished paying for your home in the suburbs, the suburbs have moved twenty miles farther out . . .

A suburban husband is a gardener with sex privileges.

Little did Bing Crosby know when he recorded "Love Thy Neighbor" that it meant all those suburban couples would start playing musical beds.

I don't know who said it, but it sounds good: "Suburbs are affluent slums."

Suburbs are where you consolidate all your little bills into one big impossible payment.

You work all your life to buy a house with four bathrooms and once you get there, you find you can't go.

He believes in life, liberty, and the pursuit of his neighbor's wife.

Success

A guy I know started out at the bottom. He struggled, sweated, worked, climbing the ladder of life hand over hand, rung by rung. He's not exactly a fantastic success, but you should see him climb a ladder.

Larry Gore lectures on success:
"Behind every successful man is a private detective his wife hired to follow him.
"Behind every successful man is a secretary who wants to marry his son.
"Behind every successful man is his golf pro.
"Behind every successful man stands his mother-in-law who couldn't be more surprised.
"Behind every successful man is a woman who takes all the credit.
"Behind every successful man is a guy who'll settle to be No. 2."

If at first you don't succeed—marry the boss's daughter.

Mark Twain said it: "There's always something about your success that displeases even your best friends.

t

Taxes

The government must really need money—I heard the Internal Revenue is now selling gift certificates.

Motto in filing your income tax: "It's better to give than to receive —and it's safer too."

There are no atheists in the waiting room of the Internal Revenue.

One more deduction in my take-home pay—and I won't have a home to take my pay to.

The novelist when asked what was his greatest work of fiction: *My Income Tax Return.*

There was a time when a fool and his money were soon parted. Now it happens to everybody.

Income tax tale: A partner listed a $500 bad-debt deduction, claiming his partner hadn't paid back a loan. IRS agents said, "Your partner had five witnesses testify he paid you back."—"To show you what a liar my partner is," was the reply, "I never lent him the money."

The owner of a small delicatessen was summoned by the Internal Revenue Service and questioned about his $6,000 income. "Why are you bothering me?" demanded the incensed owner. "I work like a slave to make a living. My wife and two sons work alongside me. And you question my measly $6,000?"

"It's not your income," the IRS agent said. "It's these deductions you took for trips you made to Spain. Six times last year you and your family went to Majorca."

"Oh, that!" exclaimed the owner. "I forgot to tell you—we also deliver."

The overnight star, suddenly in the big money, was complaining about the high taxes: "I never knew what it meant to be poor— until I got rich."

One tax consultant has a sign in his window that advises, TELL IT LIKE IT IS.

The tax boys are getting tougher all the time—"He wouldn't even let me deduct the cost of my wife's stolen mink coat unless I listed the name of the thieves."

The husband came home excited and announced to his wife, "I got a promotion that gives me a raise—That puts me in a higher tax bracket—That means we have to economize."

Groucho says that actors should never complain about the money they pay as income tax. These actors should remember no matter how much they pay—they never pay as much as they think they're worth.

Tax forms are now computerized. How do you like having it done to you by a machine?

In some states they tear down buildings to save taxes—they ought to tear down taxes to save buildings.

If taxes go much higher a guy will have to work like a dog to live like one.

April 15—that's the rainy day we've been saving for.

April 15—that's the day you count your blessings—before sending them to the Internal Revenue boys.

April 15—Instant Poverty.

Those government boys are pretty clever. They figured out a way, with that withholding tax, to get to my salary before my wife does.

I'm putting all my money in taxes—it's the only thing sure to go up.

In America we have about seventy million taxpayers who are alive —and kicking.

The Internal Revenue boys are the ones who know what to give the man who has everything—an audit!

Income tax time—when millions of Americans test their powers of deduction.

April is when the government spring-cleans your bank books.

Lady: Could I pay my income tax with Green Stamps? Her luck— that year they were only taking Plaid.

Have a switch: "Build a better mousetrap and the Internal Revenue boys will beat a path to your door."

Remember the good old days when money went to your head instead of the Internal Revenue?

I put all my relatives down under contributions. If anything is an organized charity—they are.

Would you say your income tax return was a Grim Fairy Tale?

I'd like to see income taxes get back down where we can afford to make a living.

This is Lyndon B. Johnson's story about a Baptist minister in Texas who got a call from an Internal Revenue Service agent who was checking up on a member of his congregation.

"He says he gave $1,000 to your church," the agent told the pastor. "Did he give $1,000 to your church?"

There was a slight pause. "Well," the minister said, "he did—or he will."

The woman said to the Internal Revenue agent, "And what did you do with all the money I gave you last year?"

If you're looking for a good way to beat income tax—quit your job.

The bachelor sent in his income tax return and deducted $600 for the up-bringing of a baby. The IRS sent him a letter saying, "It obviously must be a stenographic error."—The return letter said, "You're telling me!"

It's the men of untold wealth who scare the most when they see that letter from the Internal Revenue Service.

I saw Mayor John Lindsay of New York glancing through the Yellow Pages—to see if he'd skipped anything to tax.

"I wanted my son to share in the business—but the government beat him to it."

Nothing is certain but death and taxes—and each get you in a hole.

Congress puts a big tax on liquor and then raises other taxes that drive you to drink.

The businessman looked over a simplified tax form and sighed, "Every year they make them easier to fill out—and harder to pay."

Taxis

Have you noticed that every year it costs less to fly to Europe—and more to get to the airport?

A half hour after the taxi strike ended I saw a driver with an off-duty sign. Then I knew they were back to work.

The cab was crawling in New York traffic and the lady passenger pleaded, "Please, mister, can't you go any faster?" "Sure, lady," said the cabby. "But I ain't allowed to leave the taxi."

I know a guy who is so rich he takes taxicabs to go to a drive-in theater.

The woman passenger was complaining that the cab was filthy. "You don't even have an ashtray back here," she squealed. "'At's okay, lady," he said. "Just throw it on the floor—I got a woman who comes in once a week."

The cab driver was recklessly running in and out of traffic. The scared little lady in the back seat was frantic. "Please," she pleaded, "be a little more careful—I have twelve children at home."

"Lady," the driver answered, "you're telling *me* to be careful?"

There is still some risk in aviation—the taxi ride from the airport to the city.

Teen-agers

Most kids are going steady these days—before their voices do.

Jay Marr says: "They say teen-agers bring sunshine into a house. And it must be true. By the time they come home it's morning."

"I'm looking for excitement, beautiful women, sex, adventure," the teen-ager said to his father. "I'm leaving home—don't try to stop me."

"Why try to stop you?—Take me along," said the old man.

Teen-age girl to mother: "Don't yell at me—I'm not your husband."

During the prom season, a teen-ager sitting in a cafe told his young date: "Remember—we have to leave promptly at ten dollars."

Bob Orben: No question about it. Teen-agers today live the perfect life. They have an inexhaustible supply of money—father. They have a built-in maid service—mother. They have something to take their hostilities out on—everybody. They have the final word on everything—and if you should ever prove them wrong, they look at you and say, "What do you expect? I'm only a kid!"

Boy: Can I take you home?
Girl: Sure—where do you live?

Children grow up so quickly. One day you look at the phone bill and realize they're teen-agers.

"Mother," the hippie daughter announced, "I'm pregnant."
  "My God!" screamed the mother. "Who is the father?"
  "How should I know? You never would let me go steady."

Father: Son, do you know when Abraham Lincoln was your age—he was earning his own living?
Son: Well, father, do you know when he was your age he was President of the United States?

The latest report on marijuana says that mostly teen-agers use it. That's one of the big reasons they are against it. Smoking marijuana makes fools of the kids—and since they are fools to begin with—then it's actually compounding a felony.

One father doubts that his teen-age daughter's tour of Europe impressed her much. "All she remembers is that Mona Lisa needed more eye shadow. . . ."

This businessman announced to his family that he had to go out of town for a week and was taking the family car and chauffeur. "But Dad," cried his son, "how will I get to school?"
  "You'll go to school like every other real kid in America—take a cab!"

Those teen-age marriages are sometimes a little late. By the time he pops the question, she's popping a little too.

College girls all over the country are graduating magna cum pregnant.

Father to mother: "At least this report card proves our son is not taking any mind-expanding drugs."

Thelma Lee talks about her teen-agers: Teen-agers do everything with a telephone except hang it up. My son was always on the phone talking to his girlfriend. So I got him his own phone. One day I came home and he's talking on my phone. I asked him, "What are you talking on my phone for?" He said: "I can't tie up my line."

When he turned seventeen, we had to find my son a college, which was not easy. There were none that had courses in which he excelled —advanced eating, intermediate sleeping. You know how you send away money with each application? I'd shove in an extra ten. You never know who's on the other side opening envelopes—it works! He went away to a university in Africa. And he belongs to a marvelous fraternity, called the AA—Academics Anonymous. I'll tell you how it works. If he gets a desire to study, he calls up another dumb kid and they both stay on the phone till they lose the desire.

My daughter is twenty-four and I was always worried about what kind of boy she'd bring home. One day she came home with one and I knew this was going to be my future son-in-law—because as I helped him off with his coat, his mittens were pinned to the inside.

When we were planning my daughter's wedding, somebody said, "You know, when you send invitations you're not supposed to send respond cards—so I put in pledge cards!"

The teen kids are getting all the things their parents never got when they were young—pregnant, ulcers, disease—neuroses. . . .

Telephones

Did you ever stop to think that wrong numbers are never busy?

The presidency is now the second hardest job in the country. The first is public relations man for the phone company.

I'm sure there is something wrong with my phone. I picked it up and got a dial tone.

"These street phone booths are like people employed by the government—only one out of three works. . . ."

I know a guy who swears his phone company is much more friendly than ours. In his town when a nut makes an obscene phone call and gets cut off, the company sends him dirty pictures instead of stamps.

The telephone situation is so bad lately that when they arrest people nowadays they give them one phone call or thirty days—whichever comes first.

The telephone service is now bringing us all different kinds of things —like Dial-A-Prayer. That's for when you're feeling despondent and want someone to talk to, to make you feel better. But I think, to be fair, they should also have a phone number for the atheists. When they're feeling bad, they should be able to dial a number and hear the phone ring—ring—ring—ring.

One politician complained there were so many people listening in on his phone—every time he dials he gets stage fright.

We had wiretapping in our home a long time ago—only then they called it a party line.

I've had my phone bugged so many times—three FBI agents are doing my act in Vegas.

With two teen-age daughters and a wife in the house, my neighbor says opportunity has to knock—if it phoned it would get a busy signal.

Bob Melvin wasn't surprised at the boost in phone rates: "After all, they have to pay for all those OUT OF ORDER signs."

Ken Friedman: Last week local burglars ransacked the telephone company. They got everything but a dial tone! That's not surprising . . . even the people who work there don't know where that's hidden.

Phone service is getting worse every day. It now takes twice as long just to get a wrong number.

Television

It's a family show—more families started during the show.

I'm enjoying TV more than ever. I have a six-foot screen—it's Chinese and I have it in front of my TV set.

He'd be the most popular man on TV if he were as well known as his jokes.

Television is really getting to be murder. You turn on the set and you see the worst kind of violence, crime, degeneracy, murder, and rape—and that's only the news.

TV is a wonderful thing. You meet so many new people—mostly repairmen.

Pay TV is here—I just got the bill from the repairman.

David Ben-Gurion explained why they don't have TV in Israel: "A nation surrounded by Arabs has no need of cowboys and Indians."

We owe a lot to daytime television. If it weren't for game shows and soap operas, millions of women would be out driving.

Mickey Marvin says, "We already have pay TV. The other day I gave my son a dollar to shut it off."

Mickey says, "What really got me mad was when my TV repairman sent me a card from a resort hotel that even I couldn't afford."

TV is still in it's infancy—which explains why you have to get up to change it so often.

I'm having trouble with my TV set. Since they stopped cigarette commercials, it's gained forty pounds.

One of the new TV medical dramas was about a disease so rare— they haven't even decided on a fee for it yet.

The TV repairman knocked at the door. "Is this the house with the burnt-out picture tube?" he inquired.
"So you finally decided to show up," replied the irate housewife. "I called you sometime last May."
"Sorry, wrong house. The party I was looking for called sometime in April," said the repairman, turning away.

Job titles get fancier all the time. For instance, a "TV archaeologist" is a guy who digs up movies for the Late Show.

When I was a kid you could see two pictures for a dime in any theater—Now with TV it costs you $400 for a TV set and what do you get?—The same two pictures.

Television is becoming educational—it's driving people to reading books.

If TV programs don't improve, husbands may go back to listening to their wives.

You think TV is bad now—go to the movies and see what it's going to be like ten years from now.

That TV set you gave me brought me a lot of entertainment—I sold it and bought booze.

Texas

"The biggest baby ever born," the Texan was bragging to the guys at Danny's. "I just got word—drinks are on me. Why, the nurse just told me that they have to use sheets 81 inches wide and 108 inches long!"

"Hey," one New Yorker interrupted, "what's the big deal?—I happen to know that 81 by 108 is standard size. That's no longer than anybody else uses."

"For diapers?" he squelched.

One Texas oilman I know has a bankroll so big he has to have it put on microfilm before he can stuff it in his pocket.

A Texan was dictating his will to his lawyer: "To my son I leave three million dollars—and he's lucky I didn't cut him off entirely."

Another oilman from Houston is dickering to buy Hollywood because his kid would like to study the stars.

The oilionaire drove his special Cadillac to his car dealer and announced modestly: "I don't want to show off by buying a new car this month—Just do over the inside—Take out the swimming pool and put in a badminton court."

A Houston playgirl walked into a bar and seated herself next to a prosperous-looking chap in his early millions. Before you knew it they were talking business. In the middle of it all, the girl asked pleasantly, "Pardon me, how much did you say your name was?"

I just heard the impossible. There is a psychiatrist in Austin, Texas, who really is confronted with a major problem. One of the native sons was found to have an inferiority complex.

It's easy to spot a Texan at a football game—he's the one with the electric blanket.

A Texan died and went to heaven. St. Peter greeted him at the gate and asked, in a friendly kind of way, where the man was from.

"Texas," he replied.

"Well," said St. Peter, "come on in, but you aren't going to be satisfied."

This Texan has so much money—they had their kid's nursery bronzed.

Talk about rich. This Texan bought a Volkswagen to get around in his limousine.

This Texan has four Cadillacs—one for each direction.

Thin

She is so thin, she put on an ermine coat and went to the masquerade ball as a pipe cleaner.

I don't want to say she is thin—but I've seen more meat on a ten-cent hamburger.

My girl is so skinny—she swallowed an olive and four men left town.

This girl was so thin—I have seen more meat on a busboy's vest.

She was so flat-chested—she wore Band-Aids instead of a bra.

She's so thin—she got a run in her body stocking and fell out of it.

She's so thin—when she went swimming a dog brought her back three times.

She's so thin—if she had one eye, she'd look like a needle.

She's so skinny—when I took her to dinner, the captain insisted I check my cane.

She's so thin—if she drank a bowl of borscht, she'd be mistaken for a thermometer.

If she didn't have an Adam's apple—she'd have no shape at all.

Toast

A toast for the New Year: "May all your troubles last as long as your New Year's resolutions."

My favorite toast: "May you live as long as you want—and may you never want as long as you live."

He drank a toast to so many people's health—he ruined his own.

Toilet

Ethel Merman swears it's a true story. Tallulah Bankhead was in a booth at the Plaza Hotel ladies' lounge and found there was no tissue. She noticed a pair of feet with patent leather high heels on them in the next booth. She knocked on the wall and asked: "Do you have any tissue?"—"No," was the answer. Then she asked: "Do you have any Kleenex?" After a moment her next door neighbor replied, "Sorry—I don't have any Kleenex." A couple of moments of silence and Tallulah boomed, "Do you have two fives for a ten?"

Tolerance

Be tolerant of someone who disagrees with you—after all, they have a right to their stupid opinions.

Topless

The boss said to the topless barmaid, "Put something on—you're driving the customers away."

"You don't have heartburn," he explained to the topless waitress. "Your bosom is in my soup."

What's the big deal—once you've seen two, you've seen them all.

She's so dull she'd have to be topless just to be a wallflower.

This topless craze has proved one thing—how many underprivileged there are.

One thing about a topless ventriloquist—they'll never notice her lips moving.

I worked with a topless girl orchestra and the first night the cymbal player had an accident. The accordion player was always in trouble.

Tough

They grew them tough in my old neighborhood in Brooklyn. One kid came home with a black eye and a bloody nose and told his father that some other kid hit him.

"Would you recognize him if you saw him again?"

"Sure," the kid replied, "I'd know him anywhere—I got his ear in my pocket."

I came from a neighborhood so tough—they sold Bibles under the counter.

He lived in a neighborhood so tough—anybody with both ears was a sissy.

If you wore a clean shirt they hissed you.

He lived in a house that was a short run to the subway.

Where I came from the flies are so tough they use flit for perfume.

This kid is so tough—his parents have to play strip poker with him to get him into bed.

Traffic

The only way to get around in city traffic is to follow a demonstration.

The main reason for traffic congestion in New York City is—automobiles. There are more cars in New York than in all of Germany. There are more cars in California than in England and France put together. There is only one solution—we will have to park overseas.

While driving crosstown—I got a ticket for parking.

Alleviate traffic in one way: make every two-way street—a dead end.

I love those helicopters that give traffic statistics. They say, "Traffic on the highway is moderate." Well, up there it's moderate. Down here it's jammed.

New York's midtown traffic is getting worse every day—I just saw a fire engine going to last week's fire.

You can always tell who isn't a native New Yorker. When the DON'T WALK sign blinks—they don't walk.

More companies want to move out of the city—but they can't get through the traffic.

Remember the old saying "You can't go home again"? Well, it's true today with our one-way streets.

Crosstown traffic in New York is getting better. I drove clear across town the other day and only had to shave twice.

Travel

Sign in the window of American Airlines: WHY DON'T YOU GO AWAY?

Once I was on a cruise ship, just out of Africa. I was in the ship doctor's office and I met a woman who was on crutches, couldn't move, and had her arm in a sling. I asked what happened. She said, "I was mauled by a lion—and my husband didn't even get a picture!"

I took my wife to Las Vegas with me. You know how it is when you take a trip—you always pack something you don't need.

A guy in a travel agency offered me a twenty-one-day tour. He said they'd fly me to London and then fly me home from Tokyo. I said to him, "How do I get from London to Tokyo?" He said, "That's why we give you twenty-one days."

First woman: This year I went to Majorca.
Second woman: Where's Majorca?
First woman: I don't know—we flew.

The Eiffel Tower looks like an erector set that made good.

The Colosseum is nice, but I think they ought to fix it up a little—it could use a good paint job.

Travel is educational—it teaches you how to get rid of money in a hurry.

I had such a bad cold last week—my nose ran more than a tourist in Mexico.

When my wife goes on a trip she packs by the "Noah method"—she takes two of everything.

There's a book in the stores describing how to enjoy traveling on five dollars a day. The book costs ten dollars.

A travel agent described the lovely girls of Tahiti, and a man asked,

"What's the best time to go there?" "Anytime," said the agent, "between twenty-one and forty-five."

I've seen more strange places than a Swedish cameraman.

When you begin to look like your passport photo—you really need the trip.

ILGWU operator who was looking to do some part-time work and applied for a job at Mike Levine's. "How long you worked as an operator?" Mike wanted to know. "Sixty years," he said proudly. "And how old are you?"—"Fifty-nine."—"Okay," Mike said. "How could you work as an operator in cloaks and suits for sixty years when you are only fifty-nine?"—

"Easy," he answered. "I did a lot of overtime."

The union boss was asked by his kid to tell him a bedtime story. He started, "Once upon a time-and-a-half . . ."

Did you hear about: The Schenley Distillery that pays their employees time and a fifth for overtime?

The Union of Telephone employees that pays you time and charges for overtime.

The four-day week is winning a lot of backers. In fact, many places of business already have it—only it's spread over five days.

Every child born in America has two strikes against it—at least.

There was a postal strike—and nobody could tell the difference.

V

Vacations

It's amazing how well things work out at resort hotels. Half the girls there are looking for husbands and half the husbands there are looking for girls.

Frank's doctor gave him three months to live—He's sent his wife away on a twelve-week holiday.

There's nothing as dull as going on the kind of vacation you can afford.

The secretary was complaining about her weekend at the Concord Hotel, "Those singles weekends are a phony—instead of meeting a lot of single guys who want to get married, I met a lot of married guys who want to be single."

The only book that really tells you where to go on your vacation is your checkbook.

A girl met a boy on a European holiday, but they've agreed not to marry until they both finish paying for their trips.

Vacations are easy to plan. The boss tells you when and the wife tells you where.

Vacation time: That's when the highway departments close up all the regular roads and open up all the detours.

It's very easy to spot the man who has everything—it's usually in his car when he takes a vacation.

I'm going to the same place I went last year—to the bank for a loan.

Husband: Some place we haven't been for a long time? How about home?

Postcard to psychiatrist: "Having a wonderful time. Why?"

Virgin

Discovering a virgin these days is like finding a parking space in

New York City. There are very few left—and just when you think you've found one—some guy moves in ahead of you.

Clare Boothe Luce: Nature abhors a virgin—a frozen asset.

A twenty-five-year-old virgin is like the man who was set upon by thieves—everyone passed her by.

Groucho Marx: I've been around so long—I knew Doris Day before she was a virgin.

Wall Street

It's Myron Cohen's story about a little tailor. You know, you've seen him many times, cleaning, dyeing, pressing, repairing, alterations. He's going along making a living for many years. One day the butcher comes in, gives him a red-hot tip on a stock. He makes himself $50. The following week in comes another guy with a tip. He makes himself another $40. So now he closes the tailor's shop and he's sitting in the broker's office. In the brokerage business he's doing extremely well. Unfortunately in recent years you know what's happened to the stock market. Well, it took a tremendous dive, and he was wiped out. He goes home, he's ready to kill himself. His wife says, "Don't worry, sweetheart, all the years you gave me an allowance I saved a few dollars each week. Here's that money. Open another tailor shop." So he opens a tailor shop. On the window it reads: SAM COHEN, CLEANING, DYEING, PRESSING, REPAIRING, AND ALTERATIONS. FORMERLY: MERRILL, LYNCH, PIERCE, FENNER AND SMITH!

He bought some Canadian Uranium at ten cents a share on a can't-lose tip. When it went to twenty he called his broker and ordered another 5,000 shares. When it went to fifty cents he called again and said to his broker anxiously, "Get me another 10,000 shares." When it went to a dollar he called again for 20,000 more. When it finally hit five dollars he called his broker gleefully. "Sell," he shouted, "it's time to take my profit—sell everything."

"To who?" asked the broker.

I wasn't affected by the stock market crash in 1968—I went broke in 1967.

Talk about hard luck. My broker told me my stock went down twelve points—and I bought it at six.

The famous businessman was received at the White House by Nixon who said, to be sociable, "If I weren't President, I'd be buying stocks now."

"If you weren't President," said the tycoon, "I'd be buying them too."

What we need is a little encouragement in the market. Not people calling it the "Down-Jones" averages.

I know one broker who is really in trouble. He has a wife, a girlfriend, and a ticker—and they're all late.

This stock market is creating a whole new class of people in the United States—the *nouveau* poor.

Phyllis Diller says, "I am so unlucky that if I invested in a mouthwash stock—bad breath would suddenly become popular."

There is a teen-age investment group. They trust no stocks over thirty.

The big thing on Wall Street today are these investment clubs. Do you know what an investment club is? It's a way to lose money legally by a board of bookmakers.

I won't say it's been a bad year on Wall Street—but they *are* beginning to call it the Damn-Jones averages.

Two brokers were talking at lunch about the dip in the Dow-Jones. "Does the market bother you?"
   "No. I sleep like a baby."
   "Really?"
   "Yes—I sleep an hour—then I get up and cry for an hour."

The Camelot's Mark Singer phoned his Wall Street broker, said he felt lucky, and asked the stock expert if he had any good buys.
   "Sure, plenty of 'em," the broker retorted, "good-by house, good-by car, good-by summer vacation."

They say the institutions are buying—directors or inmates?

At a recent party on the East Side the talk was about nothing but the sagging stock market. Only one guest did not join in, he just kept at the martinis. Finally he was asked if he was in the market and he admitted he was and rather heavily, too. "Aren't you worried about your stocks dropping?" was the next query.
   "Not with the price of wallpaper today," he said cheerfully.

Maxwell, a seventy-five-year-old stockbroker, lay dying in the hospital. His friends came to pay their last respects. One of them tried to re-assure him by saying, "Maxwell, you'll live to be ninety." To which Maxwell replied, "You're talking to me, Maxwell, the stockbroker. If He can get me at seventy-five, He'll wait till ninety?"

I made a killing in the market today—I shot my broker.

I had a bad day in the market—my shopping bag broke.

You've heard of stocks splitting?—Well, mine just crumble.

Bob Orben says he doesn't believe in that silly saying, "You can't take it with you"—His broker just opened an office at Forest Lawn.

War

The girlie show was touring the army camps in Vietnam. At one outpost, arrangements were being made to feed them before leaving.
"I say," said the officer in charge, "would you like to mess with the officers?"
"Don't mind if we do, dear," said the leading lady, "but can't we have something to eat first?"

One young soldier wrote home to his family: "I think the public should be told just how good things are here in Saigon. Nobody does any work—bribery and corruption are everywhere. Most of the day seems to be spent in drinking, gambling, and sex. Now, as to the natives . . ."

The Egyptian regiment was in full retreat. A private chose this moment to ask for a leave.
"Are you nuts?" his commanding officer barked. "Don't you know there's a war on? Absolutely impossible. But I'll tell you what, Achmed—I'll try to retreat through your home town."

Private: Say, sergeant, remember my coming to the Army recruiting station and asking about life in the Army? And remember you told me what a great life it is—travel—sports—opportunities to learn a trade—fun—games—and a great future.
Sergeant: Yes, I do!
Private: Well, would you mind telling me again? I'm getting a little discouraged.

The new recruit just out of the quartermaster's store walked past his CO without saluting.
The officer called him back and said, "I'm sure you didn't recognize me, son, but just take a look at this uniform I'm wearing, do you mind?"
The new soldier looked him up and down and said, "Cripes. You done all right, pal. Look at the load of garbage they palmed off on me!"

"We're out of ammunition," the private cried hysterically to his CO during one of those fierce battles.

"We mustn't let the enemy know," said the officer. "Whatever you do—keep firing."

One soldier was regaling his comrades about the girl who passed herself off as a man and joined his infantry regiment during the Six-Day War. "She was just one of the boys. Ate with us—marched with us—slept with us—took showers with us—Everything! And she was beautiful, too."

"But how did she get away with it?" he was asked.

"Who was going to tell?"

Two young WACs were discussing the handsome young captain for whom they both worked.

"He sure is good-looking," said the blonde. "Have you ever seen him out of uniform?"

"You bet," said the redhead.

"I mean, he dresses so well."

"Yeah—and so quickly, too."

The medic was examining the new recruit: "Do you have any physical disabilities?"

"Yes—definitely—one of my legs is shorter than the other."

"That's nothing to worry about—we'll make sure you're stationed in hilly country."

The recruit was told to bring a sample of his water. To fool the doctor, he got his dog to provide the sample. The medic made a thorough analysis and faced the young soldier with a puzzled frown: "I think you're in trouble—not only do you have rabies—but I think you're pregnant as well!"

The soldier was explaining why he joined up: "I wanted to serve my country. I wanted to fight Communism. I wanted to build a free world—and furthermore, I was drafted."

My brother-in-law had a very impressive military record. He blew up two ammunition dumps, destroyed six tanks, knocked out an antiaircraft gun singlehanded. And that was *before* they sent him overseas!

A private and a WAC were court-martialed for running across the parade grounds in the nude. The defense counsel got them acquitted when he quoted the Army manual which states, "Wearing of uniform by other ranks when off-duty is not compulsory, so long as they are appropriately dressed for whatever sport or activity they are engaged in."

"When did you decide to become a parachute jumper?"
"The day my plane caught fire."

I can't wait till the war in Vietnam is over so our boys can come home from Canada and Sweden.

War does not determine who is right—only who is left.

The newly inducted soldier was unhappy. "Cheer up," said his friend. "It's Christmas—Santa Claus and all that." "What Santa Claus?" cried the GI. "Twenty years ago I asked Santa for a soldier suit—now I get it!"

War is like a fight with your wife—it's practically impossible to win it or end it.

Sign on the wall of a Saigon Army Post: IF GOD WANTED US TO BE IN THE ARMY—HE WOULD HAVE GIVEN US GREEN, BAGGY SKIN.

The soldier was proudly showing off his new medal: "I got it for saving two women from attack."
   "How?" asked the civilian.
   "I changed my mind."

The soldier returned home unexpectedly on a fast leave. A few minutes later he was in bed with his wife when the janitor knocked on the door. "My God," he screamed, jumping out of bed, "it's your husband!"
   "Don't be silly," said his wife. "My husband is in Germany."

Washington, D.C.

A political reporter was sent to cover a Washington rally. When he returned, the editor of the paper asked, "Well, what did the speaker have to say?" "Nothing," the reporter replied. "In that case," the editor said wryly, "hold your story to one column!"

Somebody called the Senate "The Schenley Building" because everybody who goes there for an investigation "takes the Fifth."

After JFK was nominated for President, all the hecklers started their campaign against him. The biggest target was his father's money. JFK beat them to the punch. At one dinner he read a wire from his father: DEAR JACK, PLEASE DON'T BUY A SINGLE VOTE MORE THAN NECESSARY—I'LL BE DAMNED IF I'M GOING TO PAY FOR A LANDSLIDE.

Bob Hope was playing golf with President Nixon. One reporter asked him what the President's handicap was and Bob answered without hesitation, "Senator Fulbright."

Congress: Where a man gets up to speak, says nothing, and nobody listens, then everybody disagrees.

Will Rogers turned his wit on the entire government: "We are a nation that runs in spite of and not on account of our government —yep, the United States never lost a war or won a conference."

Congress is anxious to adjourn—I'd imagine they'd be scared to go home.

The tourist asked the Capitol guide about the man with the collar who seemed to be in a hurry. "He's the chaplain of the Senate"— "Really?—Does he pray for the Democrats or the Republicans?" the man asked. "Well," the guide explained, "he stands before the senators—and prays for the country."

There is only one way to balance the budget—tilt the country.

The most important thing to come out of the Pentagon Papers affair—is that men can't keep secrets, either.

Mae West

I used to be Snow White—but I drifted.

The best way to hold a man—is in your arms.

It's not the men in my life—it's the life in my men.

It takes two to get one in trouble.

I like only two kinds of men—domestic and foreign.

When I'm good, I'm very, very good—but when I'm bad I'm better.

John Chapman reviewed a Mae West show: "Miss West has one more bust than she needs."

Widows

Two middle-aged widows were talking about how tough it is to find a man—any man. One said, "Finding a husband at our age is like trying to find a parking space in New York—you have to be right behind someone who's moving out."

With all the liberal judges around, one of them takes the prize. She was found guilty of killing her husband, but the judge suspended the sentence—He had compassion for her because she was a widow.

Biography of a four-time widow: She first married a millionaire, then an actor, then a preacher, and then an undertaker. One for the money—two for the show, three to make ready, and four to go.

The widow was left $100,000 in his will. But suddenly she was lonely and cried, "I'd give $25,000 to have him back."

Wills

Then there was a man who was married to a shrew. She kept saying, "I can't wait until you die so I can walk on your grave." Finally, he died and they opened his will. And there in his will was the specification: "Bury me at sea."

Where there is no will—there are no lawyers.

She got rid of him because he had a will of his own—that wasn't made out to her.

The widow sold her husband's Rolls-Royce for fifty dollars when it was worth twenty thousand. "Why?" his friend cried. "In my husband's will," she explained, "he asked me to sell his car and give the proceeds to his secretary—I am following his wishes to the letter."

All the relatives sat around as the lawyer read the will, "Having been of sound mind—I spent all my money."

I leave to my beloved brother-in-law—all the money he owes me.

Wolf

Sylvia has found the perfect way to keep the wolf from the door. She goes to *his* house.

He never gives a girl a second thought—he's too busy with the first one.

"The difference between American wolves and European wolves is 3000 miles."
—Marlene Dietrich.

"I didn't say I don't fool around with women—I said when it comes to women, I don't fool around."

If at first you don't succeed, try another girl.

Women

A patron at the theater was annoyed because two garrulous women in seats directly in front of him kept up a running discussion about their families all through the first act of the play. He tapped one of the women on the shoulder and said angrily, "Do you mind? I can't hear a damn word!" The woman turned round and snapped, "I wasn't talking to you."

Even the wisest men make fools of themselves about women, and even the most foolish women are wise about men.

Sir James Barrie: It is not true that woman was made from a man's rib. She was really made from his funny bone.

If women dressed to please men, they'd dress a heck of a lot faster.

Hurricanes cause a lot of trouble. They make a lot of noise, do a lot of damage, and nobody can control them—no wonder they named them after women.

Women's Lib

A career woman is one who'd rather go out and be an employee than stay home and be a boss.

She: I'm for Women's Lib because I'm tired of dancing backward.

Thelma Lee says, "It's not easy to be just a housewife. I want to tell you something. When my husband picked me up and carried me across the threshold it was not an act of love—he was taking me to work!"

Women's Lib and Gay Lib demonstrations around town prompted

one singer to announce, "I'd like to sing some love songs about boys and girls—while that combination is still allowed."

Women were meant to be loved—not to be understood.

Jack Wakefield says, "Personally, I think this Women's Liberation movement is getting out of hand. Women should realize their place and keep out of men's affairs. In fact, I'm currently in the process of producing an album on male liberation. It will be recorded as soon as my wife clears the material."

How much can these girls know about politics? One Women's Lib gal thought a press conference was a discussion about their ironing.

My uncle says his wife demanded the same responsibilities as he has—Now *she* takes out the garbage.

Jackie Kannon says, "Forget that campaign to keep women out of bars. Let's keep 'em out of department stores."

My secretary joined Women's Lib to find her real identity—which is ridiculous. She wears a wig, false eyelashes, and a padded bra.

What's so new about Women's Lib? They want women to go out and earn a man's salary. Most of them do it anyway—They stay home and take it away.

I'm for a woman for President. At least a woman wouldn't spend billions for atomic weapons and stuff. She'd shop around until she found them on sale.

One Women's Libber was demonstrating in front of a department store in New York City and screaming, "Free women—free women."

A drunk just coming out of the store belched, "Great! Do you deliver?"

Man: Isn't that great about the Swiss women?
Lib Gal: What about the Swiss women?
Man: They've got the vote—isn't that great?
Lib Gal: What's so great about it? They had to be given it by men!

The first edition of the new Women's Lib magazine will carry Hugh Hefner in the centerfold.

A neighbor explained he is doing all he can to help the Women's Liberation Movement: "The first thing I did was divorce my wife."

The only thing I like about the Women's Liberation Front is the no-bra trend.

My sixteen-year-old niece has the logical answer. She says, "I don't want to be liberated—at least not until I know how it feels to be captured."

Marty Allen says that Bernadette Devlin, the Irish Leftist leader who won't name the father of the baby she had, is letting Women's Lib take her too far.

"There are still some things," he says, "that even Women's Lib must give a man credit for."

You can never please these broads. If they are in business with you and you treat them like men they get mad. If you treat them like women—your wife gets mad.

Astronaut Michael Collins says he did a little research and found that the average man speaks 25,000 words a day and the average woman 30,000. "Unfortunately," our hero says, "when I come home each day I have spoken my 25,000 and my wife hasn't started her 30,000."

Am I glad my wife joined Women's Lib. Now she complains about *all* men—not just me.

The only comment ballerina Dame Margot Fonteyn had about Women's Lib was, "Not if it means I have to carry the male dancers instead of them carrying me."

She believed in women's rights and worked for it. She even ran for office and campaigned day and night. After six weeks away from home she returned and announced to her husband, "It's been a great campaign—it looks like I'll sweep the state"—"Why don't you start with the kitchen?" he growled.

At the Women's Lib meeting in New York, Mildred said to Marilyn, "Between you and me—this is a lousy place to meet men."

Z

Zsa Zsa

I've known Zsa Zsa Gabor when she only had one Zsa.

Zsa Zsa does social work for the rich.

Everybody is always worrying about the poor and the lonely. Zsa Zsa Gabor worries about the overdog. Here's some of the advice she has given as the prophet of the prosperous:

"The best years of your life are figured in man hours."

"Girls who do right—get left."

"I think a girl should get married for love—and keep on getting married until she finds it."

"If a girl breaks her engagement, she should return the ring—but she should keep the stone, of course."

"The only way to cure a man in love is marriage—and if that doesn't cure him, nothing will."

"A smart female is one who quits playing ball when she makes a good catch."

"Husbands are like fires—they go out when unattended."

"Sometimes a woman gets a mink coat the hard way—by being nice to her husband."

"I think Henry Kissinger is a great diplomat. Anybody who can date all those girls and still stay single must be a great diplomat."

"You don't need money to be glamorous. A chic lady is always chic, even if she's in a five-dollar dress—with the right jewelry to match, of course."

"Fellows don't whistle at a girl's brains."

"They say baseball is our national pastime—You'll never convince me."

"I love America. I love everything about America; the people of America, the songs of America—and the Bank of America."

"I believe in large families. I believe each woman should have at least three husbands."

"I think the right time for a girl to marry is—whenever she's single."

"My mother taught me I should always sleep in a king-size bed—with a real king in it."

"I have come to the conclusion that all men between the ages of fifteen and ninety-five have the same attitudes about sex—they like it."

I love Zsa Zsa. I predict that Zsa will marry again and again and again, but then I predicted Zsa Zsa Gabor would become a nun.

The aged billionaire said to Zsa, "Tell me, would you still love me if I were penniless?" She said, "Certainly, darling, and I'd miss you, too."

Zsa Zsa says: "When a wife wears the pants—some other woman wears the fur coat."

"A smart lady never lets a fool kiss her or a kiss fool her."

"They say sex is overrated—Can you imagine where everything else stands?"

"Look for an older man with a strong will—made out to you."

"Diamonds are a girl's best friend and dogs are a man's best friend —Now you know which sex has more sense."

Zoo

The oversized elephants were picketing the zoo. A lion happened to be strolling by and asked, "Why are you picketing?" and one of the elephants answered, "We're tired of working for peanuts."

The zoo keeper crossed a parrot with an orangutan. They're not sure what they got, but when it talks they certainly listen.

The mother rabbit at the zoo told her small child, "A magician pulled you out of a hat—now stop asking questions."

Two drunks staggered into the zoo and stopped in front of the lion's cage. They stood watching for a few minutes and suddenly the lion let out a roar. "Let's get out of here," slobbered one souse. "Not me," said the other, "I'm gonna stay for the movie."

The Central Park Zoo has a donkey with an IQ of 180. In spite of that he doesn't have one friend in the whole zoo—"Nobody likes a smart ass."

The leopard complained to the keeper at the zoo about his eyes. "Every time I look at my wife I see spots in front of my eyes." "What do you expect," the zookeeper asked, "you're a leopard aren't you?" "Yes, but my wife is a zebra."

The zoo keeper was sobbing because the elephant lay dead at his feet. "You must have loved that elephant very much," said a visitor. "It's not that," he answered. "I'm the guy that has to dig the grave."

The beautiful girl was one candidate for the job at the zoo as a lion tamer. The other was an eager young man. The manager said he would give them both a chance, and told the girl to go into the cage. The girl, wearing a big fur coat, did so. The huge lion was let in with her and he immediately started to charge at her. Suddenly she stood upright, opened her fur coat and stood there, completely naked. The lion stopped dead, spun around, and went meekly back to the corner. The manager was properly amazed. He turned toward the young man. "Well, pal, do you think you can top that?" "I'd like to try," said the guy. "Just get that crazy lion out of there."

Index